HEALING

Through

STRESS

MANAGEMENT

Darrell Franken

WELLNESS PUBLICATIONS

Holland, Michigan 49423

LIBRARY OF CONGRESS CATALOGING

FRANKEN, Darrell   1930

HEALING THROUGH STRESS MANAGEMENT

    Bibliography p.
    1. Stress
    2. Values
    3. Nutrition
    4. Meditation
    5. Prayer
    6. Faith
BF 575.S75
ISBN 0-934957-02-9

Published by WELLNESS PUBLICATIONS
        Box 3021
        Holland, Michigan
        49423

DEDICATED

TO MY

PARENTS

Rev. and Mrs. Henry E. Franken

DISCLAIMER

The ideas in this book are not meant to take the place of medical treatment from authorized medical doctors. Practices advocated in this book are supplemental and adjunctive. Confer with your physician. Share your treatment ideas with him. Start all treatment programs by seeing your physician first.

Healing through Stress Management puts its focus on degenerative disease processes. It does not become relevant for healing from accidental wounds, genetic disorders, contagious diseases, viral disorders, bacterial disorders, etc.

Concepts set forth in this book are composite and distilled refinements of practices and wisdom held by persons from a wide theological spectrum. Every attempt has been made to be evangelical and Biblically based.

TABLE OF CONTENTS

SECTION 3

Healing from Mind-over-matter Coping Skills and Divine Healing

INTRODUCTION

There is a healing movement going on outside of the medical world, which incorporates nearly every concept in this book. People are finding healing through a multiple number of mind-over-matter and stress-reduction skills. Many of these skills have been used by religious and secular persons for centuries. Some have only recently been scientifically validated.

I want to show you these life-saving skills. The skills are available through both secular and religious sources, but I want to show you these healing skills from a Christian perspective. These skills are not replacement for medicine or other treatment. These skills are adjunctive skills, to be used along side of medical treatment.

The Wellness movement in industry, and the wholistic movement of current treatment practices, have brought forth powerful tools to reduce stress and foster health. These tools are largely unknown to the general public. There are literally hundreds and hundreds of published research studies on how to reduce stress and prevent certain illnesses. Books on healing are now incorporating stress-reduction theories.

Jesus was the Great Physician. The church has promoted the healing power of faith in Jesus. For centuries, the church has built healing institutions and carried out healing ministries. Today, the church has another opportunity to have a healing ministry. It is a ministry of helping persons reduce stress and learn coping skills to enhance health. It is no small task, but the material of this book should be helpful.

You can conduct a healing ministry in your personal life or in the lives of your friends through your church. This book can give you some of the skills which you can use personally to enhance healing in your life. It can launch a healing ministry in your church.

Chapter 1

HEALING

AFTER STRESS REDUCTION

"Fear the Lord, turn away from evil. It will be healing to your flesh."   (Proverbs 3:7-8)

You hold the key to your health. Pains are stress signals, telling you to change some stressful behavior, like eating less to curb indigestion pains. If you do not listen to the signal, and do not make some changes, medical treatment or hospitalization will probably be needed. Therfore, to encourage healing, eliminate stressful behavior. Trace early pains back to their cause. Change what you are doing, and stop those pains from becoming illnesses. You hold the key to your health.

Answer the questions on the next page. Evaluate the effect of what is happening in your life. How close are you to an overload of stress which could produce illness?

STRESS DUE TO CHANGES IN LIFE STYLE

By Thomas Holmes and Richard Rahe

Circle the values (points) for the following Life Changes which have happened to you in the past year.

1. Death of a spouse.. 100
2. Divorce.. 73
3. Marital separation from mate.................................... 65
4. Detention in jail or other institution........................ 63
5. Death of a close family member............................... 63
6. Major personal injury or illness............................... 53
7. Marriage.. 50
8. Being fired from a job.. 47
9. Marital reconciliation with mate........ 45
10. Retirement from work.. 45
11. Major change in the health or behavior of a
          family member... 44
12. Pregnancy... 40
13. Sexual difficulties... 39
14. Gaining a new family member (e.g. through
          birth, adoption, oldster moving in, etc.)......... 39
15. Major business readjustment (e.g., merger,
          reorganization, bankruptcy, etc.).................... 39
16. Major change in financial state (e.g., a lot
          worse off or a lot better off than usual)........ 38
17. Death of a close friend.. 37
18. Changing to a different line of work....................... 36
19. Major change in the number of arguments
          with spouse (e.g., more than usual
          or a lot less than usual.)................................. 35
20. Taking out a mortgage or loan for a major
          purchase (e.g., for a home or a business) .... 31.
21. Foreclosure on a mortgage or loan.......................... 30
22. Major change in responsibilities at work (e.g.,
          promotion, demotion, lateral transfer)............ 29
23. Son or daughter leaving home (e.g., marriage,
          attending college, etc.)................................... 29
24. In-law troubles.. 29
25. Outstanding personal achievement........................... 28

26. Wife beginning or ceasing work outside the home..... 26
27. Beginning or ceasing formal schooling..................... 26
28. Major change in living conditions (e.g., building
         a new home, remodeling, deterioration
         of home or neighborhood)................................. 25
29. Revision of personal habits (e.g.,dress, manners,
         associations, etc.)... 24
30. Troubles with the boss..................................... 23
31. Major change in working hours or conditions............. 20
32. Change in residence....................................... 20
33. Changing to a new school.................................. 20
34. Major change in usual type and/or amount
         of recreation... 19
35. Major change in church activities (e.g., a lot
         more or a lot less than usual)......................... 19
36. Major change in social activities (e.g., clubs,
         dancing, movies, visiting, etc.)....................... 18
37. Taking out a morgage or loan for a lesser
         purchase (e.g., car,TV,freezer, etc.).............. 17
38. Major change in sleeping habits (a lot more or
         a lot less sleep, or a change in
         the part of day when asleep)......................... 16
39. Major change in the number of family (a lot
         more or a lot less than usual)......................... 15
40. Major change in eating habits (a lot more or
         a lot less food intake, or very different
         meal hours or surroundings)............................. 15
41. Vacation.. 13
42. Christmas... 12
43. Minor violation of the law (e.g., traffic
         ticket, jaywalking, disturbing the peace) 11

TOTAL________

(Enter this score in the summary SCORING on Page 358)

(Reprinted with permission from the Journal of Psychosomatic Research 11, 213-218, 1967)

INTERPRETATION

Less than 150	The stress you have from CHANGES IN LIFE STYLE is MILD. Your likelihood of illness in the near future is 30%. That is the conclusion of Dr. Thomas Holmes and Dr. Richard Rahe of the Unversity of Washington. Their research has been helpful to show that the human body can only withstand a certain degree of stress before it begins to suffer.
150 to 299	The stress you have from CHANGES IN LIFE STYLE is MODERATE. Your likelihood of illness in the near future is 50%. Dr. Thomas Holmes and Dr. Richard Rahe have substantiated the research of Dr. Hans Selye, pointing out that the human body cannot tolerate an overload of stress. Some part of the body (the weak link in the chain) will begin to become diseased under excess stress. You can forestall or possibly prevent an illness by increasing your coping skills: exercise, relaxation, better nutrition, socialization, meditation, faith and assertiveness.
Above 300	The stress you have from CHANGES IN LIFE STYLE is SERIOUS. Your likelihood of illness in the near future is 80%. The Holmes and Rahe Stress Test has been used to identify stress factors in a person's LIFE STYLE. The body cannot tolerate excessive changes, whether those changes are positive or negative. Many points in this test represent loss of a loved one, loss of a job, loss of a home, loss of a business or loss of money. In many cases a person may have no control over these stress factors. Many points in this test represent conflictual human relations. In many cases you do have some responsibility over how you handle interpersonal conflict on the job, at home, with relatives, with neighbors, with friends. Try to resolve as many interpersonal problems as you can to reduce the likelihood of illness.

HEALING FOR DEGENERATIVE DISEASES

Jesus could heal you instantly with a touch. Perhaps you have prayed for such instantaneous healing, and have been disappointed. Do not give up. Add some human effort to the healing process. If you are ill, and there has been a lot of "changes" recently, to bring that illness on you, do not fret. Do not give up. Correct every illness-inducing life-style behavior you can find.

Most Christians have believed that illness happens because God allows it to happen. Research in the field of "stress" is now saying that you may be responsible for some of your own illnesses, not God or the devil, when you stress yourself through overindulging in some things and depriving yourself of other things. Germs, bacteria and contagious microbes are not the only cause of disease. "Stress" on various mental, emotional and physical parts of our lives can bring on a group of diseases which are called "degenerative" diseases. They are different from the "contagious" diseases, which are largely preventable through vaccinations. Some "virus" illness is communicable while other virus problems are endemic, peculiar to and restricted to their place in the body.

The heart will "degenerate" under the stress from many things including lack of exercise, excess consumption of animal fat, excessive smoking, excessive alcohol consumption, anger, etc. The digestive system will "degenerate" under stress from inadequate nutritional requirements, emotional pressures which convert anxiety into illness, etc. The musculo-skeletal system can be stressed, weakened, and "degenerate" into back pains when people carry grudges, don't exercise, don't resolve problems, etc. In a great many instances its us, not God or the devil, that allows "degenerative" processes.

Healing, in part, through Stress Management is geared to be helpful for such "degenerative" diseases as cancer, lupus, multiple sclerosis, mental illness, gout, arthritis, neurological problems, and possibly more than we dare to imagine. Medicine has almost conquered the contagious diseases. Medicine does fairly well with bacterial and viral ailments. It has met its match, so far, with "degenerative" diseases. A wholistic treatment plan, with patient, doctor and God, needs to be devised.

HEALING RESULTS FROM STRESS MANAGEMENT

Mrs. S. was a client of mine after being told her throat problems were a result of stress in her life. She had had nodules removed from her vocal cords two years prior to this, and now they were reappearing. She was extremely shy and embarrassed about it. After a year of counseling she had worked through some negative feelings about her past. I even spent an evening in the home of her father, while she and her father discussed things about the past that had bothered my friend Mrs. S. This dialogue was an attempt to follow the commands of Jesus in Matthew 18:15-17 about "take a witness along", and it was believingly beautiful to see the recovery in somewhat short order. The nodules disappeared.

A brilliant computer analyst came to be my client. He was psychotic. He saw images of people and animals coming out of the walls. He heard voices. He had the clicking tongue and the occasional puckered-protruding lip of a psychotic. I don't normally accept these severely disturbed persons but he had no money, and preferred to "die rather than go to a mental hospital". I used every wholistic idea in this book, and after time my client's mind was clear and brilliant as it was before the illness. He saved thousands of dollars, and likely prevented a permanent booth in a psychotic ward. I was not the only person helping. He experienced whole person health care. I am particularly grateful for the wisdom I have gleaned from the orthomolecular physicians who have written about treatment programs other than drug-oriented programs.

A local college student was seeing images of persons, and hearing voices. He was envisioning his roommate as "Werewolf". He had a pulse rate of 110. He was hallucinating. He wasn't suicidal, but getting closer. He had enough unhappiness in his life to keep a psychoanalytically oriented psychiatrist busy for months. I heard he was hooked on about 10 Pepsi Colas a day.

That is roughly 500 milligrams of caffeine and 2 cups of sugar. I read some reports to him about mental illness from the caffeine-sugar combination. He quit Pepsi Cola cold turkey. He had a splitting headache for 12 hours, but 48 hours later he was back to normal. He had slept two 12 hour nights, the first in weeks. He had been stressing his system this way for about 4 years. It finally overwhelmed him and nearly destroyed him. Before he quit cola, in consultation, a physican chided me for not committing him to a mental institution.

This healing can be yours. The method is a combination of stress reduction, stress management (coping skills), and solid Christian faith, hope, love and prayer.

DEFINITION OF A STRESSOR

Any excess or deficiency of supply for the working of the body, mind and spirit constitutes a stressor. When people suffer from heart disease it is now becoming clear that such persons have excessively overloaded their heart. They either have high cholesterol, are overweight, smoke too much, consume too much alcohol, failed to exercise, or some of each. Stress was from excesses. Stress also comes from deficiencies. For example, 200 years ago, when sailors were at sea for long periods, many became ill and died from scurvy, a vitamin C deficiency disease.

Excesses and deficiencies set people up for illness. This is true for body, mind and spirit. Excesses and deficiencies in a human life reduces its capacity to run smoothly. Out of balance, it wears out more quickly. In part, the body has a healing power all its own if the degenerating stress factors can be slowed or halted.

Stress is not simply "overload". Stress is also low level functioning or not rising to meet the average challenges. You see this in a variety of ways when you read the HANDBOOK OF STRESS, edited by Leo Goldberger and Shlomo Breznitz (Macmillan, 1982). This magnificent work brings together nearly all the research on stress up to this point. In this exceptionally documented compilation you feel a sense of "truth" about stress and coping that validates all a Christian might say about "truth" in the religious sense.

A stressor is not necessarily bad. Distress is the harmful effect of stress. Eustress is the good effect of stress. Stress, in fact, can make persons productive. I doubt that it was "love" of cutting grain with a scythe that made Cyrus McCormick invent the reaper. I doubt that Eli Whitney "loved" picking seeds out of cotton. I'd say "stress" drove him to invent the cotton gin. There are even some stress factors which have prompted me to go to the cutting edge of health enhancing techniques and write this book. I consider my personal stressors "distressful", but by God's grace and strength I will turn them into "Eustresses".

SINGLE STRESSORS CAN CAUSE ILLNESS

Intense, unending bombardment from a single source has been shown to produce illness and death in animals. Dr. Hans Selye, former professor at the University of Montreal spent nearly 35 years in stress research. This "grandfather" of stress research has received more acclaim than almost any other person in the field. Dr. Selye placed animals under cold, heat, electrical stimuli, siren noise, and many other external and internal stressors. After varying amounts of time the animals got sick and died. Postmortem analysis always identified diseased tissue. The animals became ill and their death could be traced to the stress factors. Identical "control" animals from similar genetic strains, living in non-stressed conditions continued to live.

Dr. Hans Selye promoted the idea of a General Adaptation Syndrome (G.A.S.). The animal's capacity for adaptation was "finite". Animals could not cope indefinitely. There were three stages to the G.A.S.

> 1. ALARM REACTION. The body senses
> a danger and the body is aroused.

> 2. STATE OF RESISTANCE. When the
> body is subjected to continued exposure
> to stress, it attempts to resist the stress
> but fixates in a highly aroused position.

3. STAGE OF EXHAUSTION. With long term exposure to stress, the adaptation energy is exhausted. The animal dies.

Selye went on to document his findings and conducted intensive searches to isolate pathological findings in the deceased animals. Organ by organ, tests were made to find alterations. Selye came up with three conclusions.

1. The ADRENAL CORTEX becomes enlarged. Under stress, the brain tells the adrenal glands to turn stored glycogen into glucose for energy. The Adrenal Cortex is the outer layer of the adrenal glands. Under stress the brain tells it to shut down the immune system, so there is plenty of energy for fight or fight. Excessively long and intense stress overworks the Adrenal Cortex and it enlarges to compensate for becoming less effective.

2. The THYMUS AND LYMPH GLANDS shrink in size. This is because the messages (corticosteroids) sent by the Adrenal Cortex suppresses the thymus gland and lymph nodes. These glands have to be shut down during stress to conserve energy. With the immune system shut down or at least slowed down, people can get sick very easily.

3. There were STOMACH ULCERS.

Symptoms of stress reactions include -- dry mouth, urinary frequency, irritability, sweating, inability to concentrate, heart palpitations, hyperkinesia, diarrhea, migraines, upset stomach, nightmares, menstrual disorders, emotional upset, proneness to accident, etc.

Under stress disease fighting lymphatic cells (called T lymphocytes) in the thymus, in the lymph nodes, and in the blood, disintegrate. Other cells which are important to the immune system disintegrate. The body becomes far more subject to disease at this point. Stress works on the lymphatic tissue, suppressing it, so that the body is able to defend itself against disease, infection, and foreign substances. The body can become allergic to many invading substances at this time of weakness. (Hans Selye, The Stress of Life, N.Y.: McGraw--Hill, 1976, p.22,149) Exhausted adrenal glands, and overly suppressed immune defense systems account for a variety of illnesses.

MULTIPLE STRESSORS CAN CAUSE ILLNESS

While a single long-term stressor can cause illness, several mild stress factors can have just as powerful an effect. Probably more persons are victims of a multi-blitz overload than the single-irritant, long-term killer. The leading authorities behind the multiple-stressor approach to illness are Dr. Thomas Holmes and Dr. Richard Rahe from the Department of Psychiatry, University of Washington School of Medicine, Seattle. In 1967 they published THE SOCIAL READJUSTMENT RATING SCALE which has since become a Stress Test used in research, clinical counseling and in industry. A group of 394 persons originally rated the degree of stress they believed existed. The questions in the inventory at the beginning of the chapter are the questions used to develop their conclusions.

You probably noticed that both the supposedly "good" experiences, like "marriage", and the understandably "bad" experiences, are able to produce stress. The major finding of the inventory by Holmes and Rahe, is that multiple stress factors can have as powerful an effect on health as any single one long-term factor.

INTERNAL -- EXTERNAL FACTORS

The formula for stress-induced illness must acknowledge interaction between internal and external factors. Whatever may blast us from the outside by single-long-term stress, or whatever may be the multiple-short-term stressors, there are internal coping mechanisms at work, and they may be weak or strong. Therefore, stress-induced illness must be understood to come from weak coping systems inside the person, as well as strong substressors from the outside.

TREATMENT FOR STRESS INDUCED ILLNESS

Healing in degenerative diseases comes, partly from some life-style changes. You need to eliminate the stressors, as much as possible, and build up the coping mechanisms. Body, mind, and spirit are charged with this responsibility.

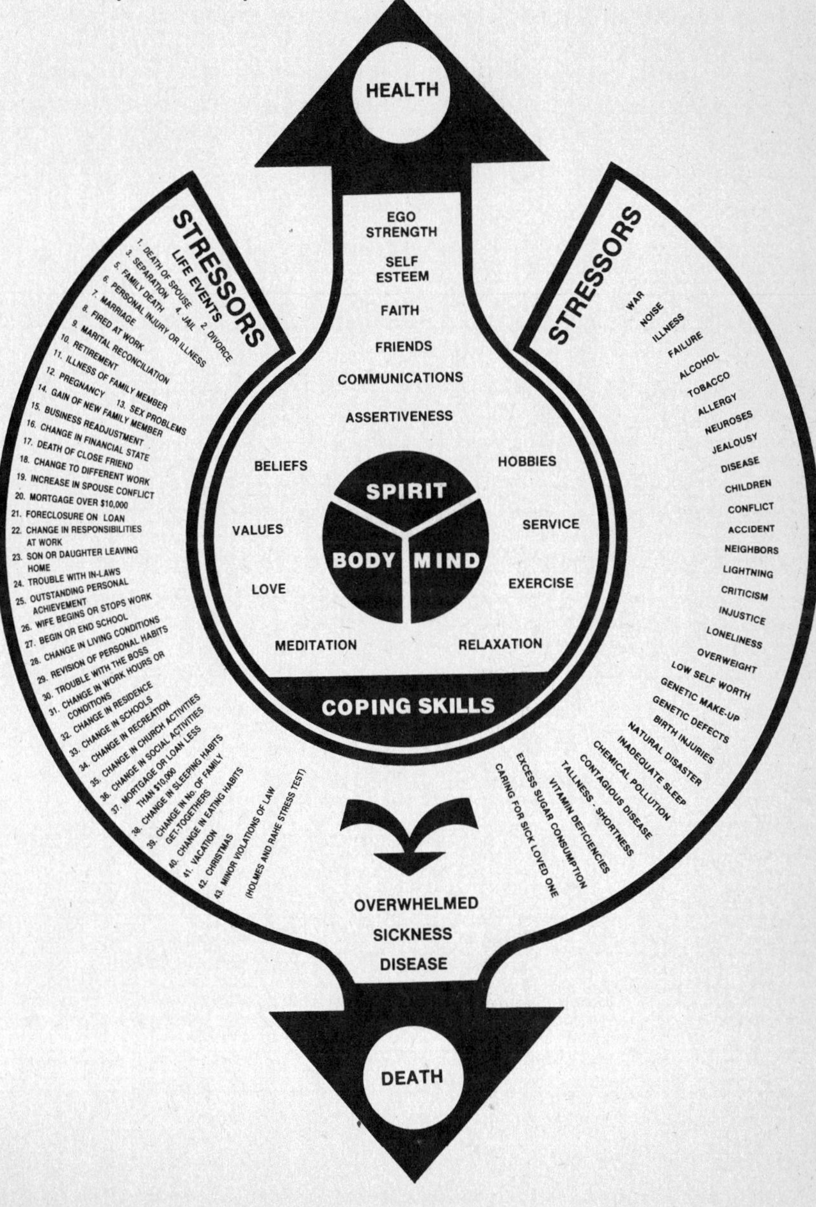

A STORY OF HEALING   A fictitional Jim Smith

Jim Smith was very ill. Jim prayed very hard to be healed. His pastor and friends gathered for prayer. They knelt beside his bed. They laid their hands on his head. They formed a human-touching chain and prayed. First the pastor prayed. Then Jim prayed with the pastor, repeating the pastor's words. Jim's wife prayed. His children prayed. Then a neighbor prayed. An elder in the church prayed. Then they all went into their own prayers. It sounded like pentecost, although they all spoke the same language.

Meanwhile, God is looking down from heaven. He is concerned too. Jim Smith is Mr. Average Christian. His soul is precious to God. His life has been of service to God. Now God has a problem. Should He listen to these prayers and grant healing or not? God could get some good points with these people if He reached down from heaven and touched Jim. Those dear Christians would spread the good news of this healing. They could write up the story for Guidepillar magazine, and it would be a blessing for many praying persons. Seriously, the world needs to hear of God's healing power.

God knows something about Mr. Smith that those praying persons do not know. God knows that Mr. Smith's arteries are coated on the inside with "plaque" so that the blood flow is restricted. Jim's arteries are about three-fourths clogged with a buildup from excessive cholesterol. God knows that. God knows that Mr. Smith has been eating high fat food for years. Centuries ago God told His chosen people to burn all fat on the sacrificial altar. It was an act to provide atonement for sin, but it was also a good health law. Jim didn't know for years that excess cholesterol was in his system, and now his health is poor. God said to Himself, "Am I going to restore his health? I can't really do that. Jim will just go back to eating high fat food. He will continue to indulge himself. Jim will have another illness in a couple of years, if I heal him tonight, and then, two years from now we'll have another prayer meeting like this for him because he hasn't learned anything.

There is another thing that God knows about Jim Smith. Jim has been nipping at the alcohol bottle more than anyone knows. He is really addicted to alcohol, and the sugars of the alcohol are making him fatter by the week. Jim's overweight condition has been overworking his heart for years. Jim has been abusing himself, but only God really knows. Now God looks down from heaven and shakes his head. God says to Himself, "Jim really puts me in a bind. He has been putting on such a good front that he is a Christian. I hate to let those praying friends down, but Jim really deserves this illness." Said God to Himself, "Jim actually set himself up for this illness. He did it to himself. Now, I'm supposed to rescue him, or else my Name is mud."

There is a third thing which God knows. Jim has been under other stress. At work, Jim has been getting upset with his boss. He keeps letting the "sun go down on his wrath." (Ephesians 4:26) and all those bottled negative feelings are sitting inside of him. He went too far with the concept of "turning the other cheek". The suppressed anger is overloading his heart.

So what is God going to do? If God decides to heal Jim, will he change any of his behavior to prevent the same thing from happening all over again? Or will God have to go through the same process all over again in a couple of years?

Who is going to tell Jim about the problems of over-weight, excess cholesterol, excess alcohol consumption, and suppressed anger? Ah Ha!!!! God's sees a traveling evangelist coming to town in 10 days. God planned this months ago, but sort of forgot. "There's my solution." said God to Himself.

The Local Civic center was jammed for the evangelistic healing services. Jim's friends brought him. That night Jim heard God speak to him about his self-indulgent style of living. That night Jim was converted from self-indulgence to a life of service.

That night God healed Jim.

NEW INSIGHTS INTO LONGEVITY

Jim Smith didn't know the full effect of a combination of stresses like cholesterol, alcohol and suppressed anger. It was putting stress on his life and illness was the result. Early death is just down the road for persons who overstress their lives. Research data is pouring in from many sources to validate the concept that many illnesses in Jim Smith everywhere, are a result of a variety of stress factors. There is evidence that persons who stress their bodies with a serum cholesterol of over 300, do not exercise, smoke 40 cigarettes a day, and have high pressures on their jobs, have a 96 percent chance of having Coronary Heart Disease, and a 75% risk of a fatal heart attack. Lower your cholesterol below 180, exercise, don't smoke, resolve overload stress, and you reduce your chances of Coronary Heart Disease to 3 percent and your risk of heart attack to 1.5 percent. This information comes out of a very extensive study by Forrest Blanding and Associates, of 200 research projects. The data is published in The Pulse Point Plan by Random House in 1982. You cannot escape the conclusion that persons are largely responsible for some of their own illnesses.

ABANDON "RESCUE ME" NOTIONS

There is some Jim Smith in all of us. We see modern medical technology and believe we can be rescued. Many of us have learned to live by the model of **Rescue-Me-From-All-the-Abuse-I-Give-My-Body.** People fail to realize they may have to pay a price for over-indulgence. We need to be thankful that God still does rescue persons from illness and death. God does hear and answer prayers of the faithful. Yet it is time to accept our responsibility.

A local professional died of alcoholism. The insurance company paid over $100,000.00 for the last weeks of his life in the hospital. Many of us who hardly ever see a doctor helped pay for that man's self-destructive behavior.

TAKING PERSONAL REPONSIBILITY FOR HEALTH

How easy it is to adopt the attitude, "The devil made me do it." Children are quick to point the finger of blame. How childish we often are. We are blinded by our pride, ignorance and capacity for self-deception. We hate to face the fact that some self-indulgence produces health problems.

Wholistic thinking on health suggests persons become more responsible. Too often preaching puts the blame for illness on the devil or on God. Baptists, Calvinists, Lutherans, Catholics shift from one foot to the other on whether to lay the responsibility for illness on the devil or God. There are enough biblical references on both sides of the issue to stress you to become ill. I believe God is soverign and he lets the devil undermine health. That is another fine paradox, of which there are many in the Word. I cannot be driven into pushing either side into a logical conclusion. Somewhere in the middle of this paradox is human responsibility. The Devil is actively undermining. God is actively laying the principles of healing. I need to be responsible in the middle. A fundamental principle of the "wholistic" or "wellness" movement today, is the emphasis on taking more personal responsibility for one's health.

CATCHING THE VISION

Was Jesus ever sick? We know he was human and subject to illness. Yet, Jesus was always putting himself in tune with God, his father in heaven. Chances are he was ill less than most. From volumes of research we learn that lonely people die earlier, self-indulgent people die earlier, and people who suppress hostility have more problems (just to name a few). I cannot imagine that Jesus would set himself up for illness by violating divinely ordained principles for good health and happiness.

Persons who allow the spirit of Jesus into their lives and discipline themselves to be like Jesus are simply going to be statistically healthier and happier. God engineered us to function according to principles and laws, which, when violated, automatically produce excessive wear, resulting in illness. When anyone focuses his or her value system on those divinely ordained principles, health has to be a natural consequence.

A survey of 65,000 women, answering 97 questions in Redbook in September, 1976 (Pub. April, 1977), reported, "The more religious a woman is, according to our survey, the happier she is.....Health is another blessing for the very religious woman. She suffers less from headaches and stomach upsets than do women who are less sure of their beliefs.....and is least likely to report loss of sexual feelings in the past year." That doesn't surprise me. It validates the blessings of a life committed to Christ. I hope you can catch the vision that your health and happiness will be enriched through Christian commitment and discipline.

FINDING THE BEST LONGEVITY FORMULA

Living for 70 years or "even by reason of strength fourscore (80)" years, has been a biblical guideline ever since the Psalmist spoke of this in Psalm 90:10. We don't know why Adam, Seth, Enosh, Kenan, Mahalelel, Jared, Enoch and Methusalah all lived about 900 or more years. Living 70 - 80 years is being accomplished by high numbers of persons. Age 100 is not unusual either.

The exact formula isn't available, if you are looking for how much exercise, how much caffeine to avoid, or how many friends to have, etc. Man has looked endlessly for the fountain of youth. He has spend fortunes experimenting with remedies and cures. Man's finiteness has limits, preventing man from usurping God's position. Nevertheless, we continue to look.

The best available approach to longevity is loving God and synchronizing one's life style with Divine principles. That fosters health. The human emotional system is capable of forming an attachment to ideas, processes, goals, people, God. Above all, people influence people. Some of them are our "heroes". I have "heroes". You have "heroes". They influence us. God is our supra-human hero. The emotional attachment and allegiance to God shapes the individual's destiny. There is an integration of the person's unique qualities with those of the "hero", that allows for growth and creativity.

Worshipping God and all that He stands for, puts a person in touch with the greatest creative and transcending force there is. God's longevity of existence can never be equaled by humans but to live with God's image set before us as the "hero", gives the highest standard for our own longevity.

LONGEVITY FROM RESPECTING AUTHORITY

"Honor your father and your mother that your days may be long in the land which the Lord your God gives you." (Exodus 20:12, Deuteronomy 5:16, Ephesians 6:3).

Respect for authority is a Divine guideline for longevity. Persons who carry a basic antagonism to authority and rules are constantly in trouble. Rebellious teens, defiant lawbreakers, hostile juveniles, non-complying employees, non-submissive soldiers, insolent jail occupants, unruly college students, insubordinant officers, etc. make life miserable for others. Don't worry about them. They generally do not live as long. They manage their life style and finances in self-destructive ways. They will find some behavior that is contrary to the norm, get hooked on it and become dissipated by it.

To respect authority means to encounter it, test its validity, understand the perspective, and dialogue over the difficulties. Respect does not mean knuckle under.

When you and your father do not agree, ask to sit down and negotiate a contract. Write down the reasons for your desires in a left column, and ask him to write down his reasons in the right column. Negotiate, trade, exchange something you will do for what you want. Do the same with a marital disagreement. Remember, "Do not let the sun go down on your wrath, lest you give opportunity to the devil." (Ephesians 4:26)

LONGEVITY FROM TRUST IN GOD

"He who abides in the shelter of the most high, who abides in the shadow of the almighty, (who) will say

to the Lord, My refuge and my fortress, My God in whom
I trust....with long life I will satisfy him."
Psalm 91:1,16

The element of TRUST and faith in someone or
something highter than oneself is health-giving. Such
trust or faith enables persons to transcend self-defeating
attitudes and self-destructive behaviors.

I cannot produce a research study showing that persons
who place their trust in God, live longer. The Redbook
article, cited previously, said that very religious women
considered themselves to be healthier. By simple logic
we can conclude that if illness is less, people should
statistically live longer. That may not satisfy the critics.

I can argue that "trust" is beneficial to our health
and eventually to the length of our lives. Electrical
shock has been used on dogs who tried to get to their
food, until the dogs simply became so freightened they
refused to move for fear of shock. The dogs were going
to die as a result of their fear. When the electrical current
was turned off, the dogs feared crossing over to their
food until they were physically dragged across a few
times to assure them of safe passage. People become
equally fearful. Fears are powerful. Anorexics die
from fear of eating too much food. Fear creates a
fairly strong depression, which cuts into appetite, and
can eventually cause death.

You need to be able to trust. Without trust, anxiety
can build up and drain or burn out the emotional system.
It is good to have friends we can trust. It is good to
be able to have some degree of trust in ourselves. Yet,
there are times in life when neither we, nor our friends
have the answers that are needed. In times like that
TRUST in God's providential workings comes to the rescue
and saves us a great deal of anxiety. Its nice to have
a back-up system working for us. We'll live longer with
it.

LONGEVITY FROM KEEPING GOD'S COMMANDMENTS

"My son, do not forget my teachings, but let your
heart keep my commandments, for <u>length of days</u> and

18

<u>years of life,</u> and <u>abundant welfare</u> will they give you."
(Proverbs 3:2)

We have been so "Pasteurized" that we think every illness comes from germs and bacteria. It is difficult for us to consider that complete dedication to the Word of God might keep us healthier and thus, enable us to live longer. We all acknowledge that we are sinful human beings and prone to fail, but that doesn't give us the right to dump all our troubles on God and avoid many of His mind-over-matter principles.

In a literal way, the vigor of the Israelites and their length of rise and fall in power, was directly related to their obedience to God's commands. Frequently, sin among the Israelites brought weakness and invited invasion by the Syrians, Assyrians, and Babylonians. When they returned to keeping the commandments, God allowed them to revive. When we fail to follow divinely ordained principles, we can expect problems of a mental, physical and spiritual nature. When we return to obedience to fundamental devine laws we can expect some degree of recovery, unless we have crossed over the point of no return.

LONGEVITY FROM REVERENCE

"Be not wise in your own eyes: fear (reverence) the Lord, and turn from evil. It will be <u>healing</u> to your flesh and refreshment to your bones." (Proverbs 3:7-8)

"The fear (reverence) of the Lord <u>prolongs life,</u> but the years of the wicked will be short." (Proverbs 10:27)

People who worship God are constantly attempting to look outside or beyond themselves. That is extroversion. Introversion is basically looking inward most of the time. All the literature I trust sees the extrovert more healthy than the introvert. To focus attention on higher values, more noble principles and service to others, counteracts narcissistic preoccupations with self and selfish pursuits. Not all extroverts have noble principles or have a healthier life style, so extraversion must be coupled with higher values to sustain health.

Turning from "evil" and "wicked" pursuits is scarcely possible without some focus on a system of transcending values. That focusing is "reverence" with your heart committed to something much bigger and more rewarding.

"Fear" or reverence promises "healing". It sounds like it is a direct result. We have, however, generally felt that there must be some intermediate step or steps, like prayer, anointing, or laying on of hands. I accept all that to be a part of the process, but I see another step which I call either stress--reduction or stress-management. This is a step between "reverence" and "healing". You need to make sure that every stress factor which pressed you into illness, is worked on, dealt with, or counteracted by a coping skill, many of which are described in this book. Change your life-style to be like God wants and you increase the chances of healing or staying healthy.

LONGEVITY FROM WISDOM

"Wisdom has built her house......The fear of the lord is the beginning of wisdom, and the knowledge of the Holy One is insight. For by me (wisdom) your days will be multiplied and years will be added to your life." **(Proverbs 9:1,10-11)**

We are told here that if we avoid or violate the acquisition and use of <u>wisdom</u> we can expect to have a shorter life. To think that illness can come upon us when we don't listen to good health ideas, is rather foreign. We've bought the germ theory of illness "hook, line and sinker". We need the word of God to call us back to the truth. Degenerative processes, because we fail to use "wisdom", probably create more illness than germs.

In the Judeo-Christian tradition, education has been a high priority item. Synagogues were educational as well as worshipping institutions. Churches have pursued the same high goals, and have pioneered in the establishment of most of the world's major educational institutions. "Knowledge" and "wisdom" are advocated by God with the promise of extended longevity. It is sad that many young persons become disenchanted with education and remain at status quo levels all their lives.

THE SIN-ILLNESS CONNECTION

I couldn't understand the sin-illness connection, which Jesus spoke of to the man he healed at the Pool of Bethesda, until I had read current stress-reduction literature. After Jesus had healed this person, ill for 38 years, he met him in the temple and said, **"See, you are well! Sin no more, that nothing worse befall you."** (John 5:14) Jesus obviously knew about the sin-illness connection. Sin is a violation of God's will. And God's will is not simply a set of moral laws. God is in the entire universe and the very structure and dynamics of its functioning are God. If you violate God you violate the very principles which run this world. And if you violate the very principles, which are in this world, for your own health and healing, you set yourself up for the consequences. If you sin, you violate God's fundamental being. Put yourself in tune with this Being and all its principles work for you. Go contrary to this Being, and all of its clock-work gears and fine tuned mechanisms will grind you into destruction. We are part of the flow from time into eternity. We can go with the flow or be an obstructionist and pay the price in our own bodies, minds and spirits.

Be careful with this thinking. Don't push it too far. Remember Job in the Old Testament. He was a righteous man. We know of no sin-illness connection in him. We conclude that illness cannot always be traced back to some violation of the divine order of the universe. Some illness can and some illness can't be traced back to unresolved stress factors.

The only way you can handle such thinking is to understand that religious truth is paradoxical and not always logical. There are polarities. That is O.K. Jesus was human and divine. God is three and one. We are saved by faith, and faith without works is dead. These are paradoxical. Both ingredients of the paradox are true, though logically disconnected. The same is true for illness. Sin, as a violation of God, will bring illness, but not all illness is from sin. That violates logic, but it makes good sense biblically.

DISCUSSION

1. How is stress bad for us, and how is it good for us?

2. Name some good things that come out of stress.

3. Name some of the things that prevent us from reducing stress in our lives.

4. Recall Jim Smith's illness. Does it make sense that God may not be answering our prayers because we do not change our life-styles?

5. If it is true that the Bible has some answers to enable us to be healthier and live longer, why don't we study the Bible more?

6. Do we have more stress in our lives today than a generation or more ago? Or do we not know how to cope with the stress as well as our forefathers?

7. If medicine, prayer and stress-reduction are needed to regain or maintain health, what kind of a program needs to be developed to get a doctor, clergyman, and psychologist together to treat the whole person?

8. Since Psalm 90:10 suggests that a good life span is between 70-80 years, should people work at eliminating stress so they may, perhaps, live longer?

9. Should the church get into some stress-reduction and stress-management programs in some way like the Wellness movement is in industry?

10. Sin causes illness, yet Job was a righteous man and he became ill too. Those are the brackets within which we live. Discuss what percentage of persons are ill because of sin, and what percentage of persons are ill because of a Divine order or Divine permission?

Chapter 2

ILLNESS FROM STRESS

King David — Psalm 38

King David became severely ill from guilt over his adultery with Bathsheba. Guilt, grief, and suppressed anger are deathly stressors. David just about died from guilt. If Nathan the prophet, had not confronted David, to make David confess, the array of David's illnesses described in Psalm 38, would likely have run their course, producing death.

There are quite explicit symptoms of stress related illnesses. The list of these symptoms of stress related illnesses, in the following inventory, is a composite list of known symptoms. Take the test. Evaluate your symptom level.

SYMPTOMS ASSOCIATED WITH STRESS RELATED ILLNESS

Pick out the most appropriate response. Write the number of that response in the space provided by that statement.

0. Never   1. Rarely   2. Occasionally   3. Sometimes
4. Frequently   5. Almost always

1. _____ I have headaches.
2. _____ I am irritable or anxious.
3. _____ I feel fatigued or excessively tired.
4. _____ I do not sleep well.
5. _____ I have indigestion, heartburn, hiatal hernia.
6. _____ I have shoulder, neck or back pains.
7. _____ I have constipation or diarrhea.
8. _____ I have flu or colds.
9. _____ I cry easily.
10. _____ I have high blood pressure or racing heart beat.
11. _____ I have low grade temperature or infections.
12. _____ I have irrational, impulsive behavior.
13. _____ I have nausea or stomach pain.
14. _____ I have numbness or tingling in my arms or legs.
15. _____ I have cold or sweaty hands or feet.
16. _____ I have lost my interest in sex.
17. _____ I have skin rashes, dry spots, or hives.
18. _____ I am depressed.
19. _____ I am nervous, slur my words or stutter.
20. _____ I overeat or do not have a good appetite.
21. _____ I have poor concentration, am forgetful.
22. _____ I am restless, pace, walk fast, or talk fast.
23. _____ I grind my teeth while sleeping.
24. _____ I have been smoking or drinking more than usual.
25. _____ I use tranquilizers or anti-depressant medication.
26. _____ I have skipped or irregular menstrual cycles.
27. _____ I am fearful.
28. _____ I have unexplained pain.
29. _____ I have chest pains.
30. _____ I withdraw from people more than usual.
31. _____ I do finger tapping, foot tapping, pencil tapping.
32. _____ I get dizzy or lack physical coordination.
33. _____ I have dry mouth or cough a lot.
34. _____ I have a nervous tic or twitching muscles.
35. _____ I blow up more than usual.

_____ TOTAL (Range 0-175) (Enter this on Page 358)

24

INTERPRETATION

0 – 40   Your score for SYMPTOMS OF STRESS RELATED
ILLNESS is very low. This means that you do
not have a tendency to allow personal stress
to overwhelm you. You are apparently meeting
stress with coping strength so that there is
no buildup of tension in your life.

40 – 80   Your score for SYMPTOMS OF STRESS RELATED
ILLNESS is in the moderate range. You seem
to have a moderate number of symptoms
which are stress related. The symptoms you
checked for this category could be symptoms
of medical problems and should probably be
analyzed by a physician. If you have found
no relief through this means and the symptoms
continue, it would be wise for you to consider
the fact that stress in one's life puts pressure
on the body's organs and they can become irritated, producing the symptoms you checked.
It is important for you to consider reducing
the stress factors in your life, or work on some
coping skills which might include better nutrition, exercise, relaxation-meditation, more
socialization, more assertiveness, and increasing
the level of your values for living.

ABOVE   Your score for SYMPTOMS OF STRESS RELATED
80   ILLNESS is very high. You have a very large
number of symptoms which are stress related.
You should consult your physician regarding
them, but you should also consider that excess
stress can overload the body's ability to cope.
When the body is put under excess stress, various
illnesses can take place. You need either to
reduce the stress factors in your life, or practice
the coping skills of better nutrition, exercise,
relaxation-meditation, more socialization, more
assertiveness and increasing the level of your
values for living. You may even need professional help in reducing the "symptoms" you scored.

WHEN STRESS BECOMES DISTRESS

There is growing awareness that one or many stressors can produce an overload on the body, mind and spirit. In 1945 the Minnesota Multiphasic Personality Inventory was created with approximately one-tenth of questions relating to a phenomenon called "hypochondriasis". In hypochondria there is a tendency to suppress negative feelings instead of dealing with them, and that results in physical illness. The ailments have real aches, pains and illness symptoms, but many people erroneously believed that the symptoms were "just in your head".

An excellent updated list of those symptoms or "stress indicators" is found in a book by Edward B. Diethrich, M.D., entitled The Arizona Heart Institutes HEART TEST, (1981) Here is their list of indications of unresolved or excess stress in a person's life.

    Increased smoking, or chain smoking
    Increased sweating
    Headache, dizziness
    Dry mouth or throat
    Irritability or bad temper
    Lethargy or inability to work
    Cold, clammy, or clenched hands
    Sudden bursts of energy
    Finger-tapping, foot-taping, pencil-tapping
    Fatigue
    Pacing
    Frowning; wrinkling forehead
    Restlessness
    Rapid walking
    Rapid speech
    Muscular aches (neck, shoulders, back or legs)
    Increased or decreased appetite
    Inability to sleep, or nightmares
    Desire to cry, or crying
    Fear, panic, or anxiety
    Coughing
    Excessive snacking
    Nagging
    Unnecessary hand-waving, making wild gestures
    Continuous talking
    Nervous tic

> Stuttering
> Nausea or stomach pain
> Grinding teeth
> Low-grade infections
> Rash or acne (especially on face or back)
> Constipation or diarrhea
> Frigidity or impotence
> Loss of sex drive
> High blood pressure
> Depression
> Hives
> Withdrawal

We will all have some of these "stress indicators" from time to time. We need to remember that these symptoms are the results of many factors. Do not avoid medical attention for these symptoms, just because they are "stress indicators". Nevertheless, assist the healing process by dealing with the stressors in your life.

PHYSICAL AILMENTS RESULTING FROM STRESS

Stress indicators point to deeper problems. The list of symptoms, which you have just seen, may point to problems in one or more of several systems in your body. Here is a list of the systems which medicine uses to classify illness, with some representative illnesses for each. You will see many of these illnesses spoken of in Psalm 38, the Psalm many interpreters believe David wrote during the time he suffered guilt over his affair.

CARDIOVASCULAR DISORDERS
> high blood pressure
> chest pains
> heart disease
> tachycardia, etc.

GASTROINTESTINAL DISORDERS
> hiatal hernia
> gastritis, ulcer, colitis
> diarrhea, constipation
> gall bladder problems, etc.

DERMATOLOGICAL DISORDERS
> hives, skin rashes, acne
> itching, boils
> allergies, etc.

MUSCULOSKELETAL DISORDERS
    back pains, leg pains, shoulder pains
    numbness
    rheumatoid arthritis
    bursitis, etc.

NEUROLOGICAL DISORDERS
    headache, dizziness
    epilepsy
    Multiple Sclerosis
    Myasthenia Gravis

GYNECOLOGICAL DISORDERS
    endometriosis, vaginitis
    amenorrhea, dysmenorrhea
    postpartum depression, etc.

METABOLIC DISORDERS
    diabetes, hypoglycemia
    vitamin deficiency diseases
    obesity   osteoporosis, etc.

UROGENITAL TRACT DISORDERS
    enuresis (bed wetting)
    infections, inflamations
    prostatitis, etc.

PSYCHIATRIC DISORDERS
    neurotic and psychotic
    depression, schizophrenia, etc.

All of these illnesses have been associated with stress to some degree. They require medical attention, but healing and future prevention necessitates stress-reduction and stress-management skills. Now let us look at King David's description of himself and let us diagnose his problems in Psalm 38 in light of the above disorders.

KING DAVID'S STRESS RELATED ILLNESS

Psalm 38:1-2

"O Lord, rebuke me not in thy anger, nor chasten me in thy wrath. For thy arrows have sunk into me and thy hand has come down on me."

King David feels very guilty for his involvement with Bathsheba, and the manipulated murder of her husband. Nathan the prophet, had confronted David with his sin, so the whole nation must have known about King David's sin.   Guilt is one of the prime causes of depression, along with repressed anger, loss, loneliness, low self worth, fear, worry, indecisiveness, hopelessness, and worthlessness.   King David had nearly every cause for depression.

Psalm 38:3

"There is no soundness in my flesh because of thy indignation; there is no health in my bones because of my sin."

King David does not name his illness, but something is not functioning properly in his body.   King David could be suffering in nearly all of the categories mentioned. He specifically refers to his "bones", the musculo-skeletal system.   Many depressed persons also have physical complaints.   The stress does not have to be "guilt" like King David.   The stress can be financial, social, inter-personal, etc., and the effect can be depression.

Psalm 38:4

"For my iniquities have gone over my head; they weigh like a burden too heavy for me."

The picture of depression, a psychiatric illness, is getting even stronger.   Depressed persons feel over-whelmed and hopeless.   They feel a great amount of fatigue.   The slightest task feels impossible. Guilt which starts out as real, gets blown out of proportion and the person's self-worth gets driven into the ground by personal self-depreciation.   In King David's case the depression is due to unrepented and unforgiven guilt. Without dealing with this amount of guilt a person is liable to become extremely ill and die.

Psalm 38:5

"My wounds grow foul and fester because of my foolishness."

King David sees his illness as a result of his guilt. David is becoming more specific.   It is easy to hazard the guess that David is refering to some "dermatological disorder".   Does he have hives, skin rashes, itching, allergies, boils, abscesses?   David uses the word "grow".

Could his body be suffering from a cancerous growth on the skin? This is speculation, without laboratory evidence, and may be inaccurate, but you can sense that David's illness is related to his sin and guilt.

Psalm 38:6

"I am utterly bowed down (bent, withered) and prostrate. All the day I go about mourning."

One Bible scholar by the name of Hengstenberg translates this as "I am crazy" and "I am beside myself." That is not a very literal translation, but Hengstenberg certainly caught the picture of a depressed person. "Crying" (mourning) is on the list of "Stress Indicators", as well as a behavior people display in time of depression. Notice also, that King David is spending more time in a "prostrate" or prone position, like a depressed person not wanting to get out of bed to go to work.

Psalm 38:7

"My loins are filled with burning, and there is no soundness in my flesh."

"Loins" is a term to describe the lower abdomen where your intestines are. King David seems to have an inflamation in the intestinal tract. He has some kind of "gastrointestinal problem". The fact that he talks of a "burning" sensation is a fairly good indication of some inflamation, whether it be in the gastrointestinal tract or in the liver, pancreas, prostate, or other. How one person can have this many problems, is a wonder, but David, the Psalmist is not finished describing himself.

Psalm 38:8

"I am utterly spent (benumbed or feeble) and crushed (weakened)."

These are words of hopelessness, worthlessness, and brokenness. Persons who are this depressed need the help of someone to assist them out of their depression. Without someone reaching out to such a person that person is almost doomed. Professional treatment may be the only thing that brings this kind of person out of the downward spiral into illness and death. Relief from the "stressor" and Christian love are also powerful adjunctive therapies.

Psalm 38:9
"Lord, all my longing is known to thee. My sighing is not hid from thee."

The sense of futility in a depressed person is large. King David has not lost his faith in God. That is a good sign.   He has not come to the point where he feels life is not worth living. He does not appear to be suicidal. In "sighing" one is actually drawing in a larger amount of oxygen. Stress makes the physical system work harder and use more energy. This requires more oxygen. A deep "sighing" breath stretches out the lung capacity to prevent hyperventilation under anxious conditions.

Psalm 38:10

"My heart throbs. My strength fails me."

This is quite a clear indication that, among other problems, Kind David is suffering some stress to his cardiovascular system. His heart is pounding. It may be tachycardia, a rapid heart beat that can sometimes get out of control. Stress can also create arrythmia or irregular heart beat. There are medications which restore the heart to regular activity, but elimination of a variety of stressors may have the same effect, without possible side effects.

Psalm 38:10 (Part B)

"The light of mine eyes, it also has gone from me."

There are times when depressed persons tell me that their vision is blurred. They see their eye doctor because they cannot read as well as they previously could. Most of the time lens correction is not advised until the stress subsides.   In addition, the sparkle of one's eye leaves during time of stress.

Psalm 38:11

"My friends and companions stand aloof from my plague, and my kinsman stand afar off.

King David must have had some skin rashes, body sores, abscesses, or something like that to cause his friends to be so distant. Even his "kinsman" (relatives) did not appear to want to get close to him. The "plague" must have been more than emotional depression, since people usually try to talk to a depressed person. Again, I suggest that he was afflicted with some "dermatological disorder" due to the stress of his guilt.

Psalm 38:12

"Those who seek my life lay their snares. Those who seek my hurt speak of ruin, and meditate treachery all the day long."

King David may have become paranoid, and believed that people were out to kill him or ruin him. If this is true then we see David suffering another symptom of a "psychiatric disorder". The other consideration is that David lived in the day of "eye for eye and tooth for tooth". He might have been legitimatly (and not psychiatrically) fearful of those who would take his life for the life of Bathsheba's husband.

Psalm 38:13-14

"But I am like a deaf man. I do not hear, like a dumb man who does not open his mouth. Yea, I am like a man who does not hear, and in whose mouth are no rebukes."

King David is talking like a person who was experiencing some catatonic schizophrenia. Catatonia is a state of emotional turmoil in which there is a split, a depersonalization, a spacing out. Persons deeply catatonic cannot talk, and appear not to be able to hear. These persons formerly took up much space in mental institutions, before psychotropic medication became helpful in their transition back to reality.

This is the end of the series of descriptive statements about Kind David's illness after his guilt. Somewhere in the middle of David's depression Nathan the prophet confronted David regarding his sin. David repented and hung on to God's goodness. Listen to David's strong claim on God for his healing and restoration.

Psalm 38:15-22

"But for thee, O lord, do I wait. It is thou, O lord my God, who wilt answer. For I pray only let them not rejoice over me, who boast against me when my foot slips..... I confess.... I am sorry...... Do not forsake me, O lord, O my God, be not far from me! Make haste to help me, O Lord, my salvation."

KING DAVID — STRESS MANAGEMENT PROTOTYPE

The story of Psalm 38 deals with the effect of basically one type of stress - guilt. Yet, like every stress, unless you do something about it, the body, mind and spirit continue to pay a price. I know we live in a sinful world, and there will be some types of stress we cannot avoid or change. This does not mean that we cannot do anything about the stress from them. You may not be able to change the stress of war, but you can exercise, practice faith, pray, stay assertive and maintain friendships to counteract the effect of war stress. You may not be able to bring back a loved one. The stress of grief may be intense and long. Yet, you can use counter-stress awareness or coping skills to maintain your health and welfare.

In King David's words of verses 15-22 you see a very challenging faith. You see a carbon steel will. You see assertiveness in the face of God. You see backbone reinforced with hope. You see a man talking like the apostle Paul, "In all these things we are more than conquerors through him who loved us." (Romans 8:37) You see in David, a person who believes in transcendence, getting on top of problems.

You see David as a mind-over-matter person. Much of the material written for industrial Wellness programs is built on the philosophy of using knowledge for self improvement. You have to know what is attacking you before you know how to fight back. Fighting the gremlins of ill health requires a return to more self-awareness, and more personal responsibility. Above all it requries the belief that stress-reduction and coping

33

skill education works and pays off. King David seems
to have had these qualities which enabled him to regain
his health and sanity.

DISCUSSION

1. Have you, at one time, believed that a hypochondriac
    was someone whose pain was in his head?

2. Were you surprised to discover that David's guilt
    could possibly cause all this illness?

3. What percentage of people get sick and die from
    an overload of guilt?

4. Would you be willing to guess how many years of
    life we lose because of unrepented, unconfessed,
    and unforgiven guilt?

5. Do you realize that Solomon, the wisest leader the
    Israelites ever had, was born to David and Bathsheba?
    What is the significance of that?

6. Psalm 38 illustrates the proposition that stress causes
    illness. Why haven't we, therefore, as Christians,
    talked about this more?

7. The medical world is very dedicated to treat people's
    illness. How can the church be more helpful to
    enable persons to prevent illness?

8. Confession is necessary to enable persons to live
    without the stress of guilt. How can we stimulate
    people to be more repentant? How can we get
    people to confess their sins, and change their
    behavior?

9. This chapter mainly illuminates the problem of guilt
    causing illness. What other sins might cause illness?

10. Why doesn't all sin cause illness?

Chapter 3

ANXIETY - DEPRESSION STRESS

King Saul I Samuel 7:1 - 31:13

The biblical description of King Saul is one of anxiety, depression, and severe bouts with mental illness. King Saul started out as a superior person, who became ill over a period of time, due to a number of unfortunate encounters with Samuel, the last of the Judges. In these encounters we find many of the causes for anxiety and depression. The same encounters produce the same stresses today. The causes of Saul's depression are the same causes today. If you have been troubled with anxiety and depression you may find some of the same issues in your life, as occured in the life of King Saul.

ANXIETY FROM STRESS

Pick out the most appropriate response. Write the number
of that response in the space provided by that statement.

0. Never 1. Rarely 2. Occasionally 3. Sometimes 4. Frequently
5. Almost always

1. _____ I have difficulty breathing.
2. _____ I feel tense.
3. _____ I get lightheaded and dizzy.
4. _____ I have an uncontrolled appetite.
5. _____ I have tingling in my fingers or toes.
6. _____ I am forgetful.
7. _____ I have headaches.
8. _____ I am nervous or restless.
9. _____ I have chest pains.
10. _____ I feel overwhelmed or overloaded.
11. _____ I cry easily.
12. _____ I have diarrhea.
13. _____ I blow up over little things.
14. _____ I have a nauseated stomach.
15. _____ I get disappointed easily.
16. _____ I am not able to make up my mind.
17. _____ I shake or sweat for no apparent reason.
18. _____ I have a fast heart beat or I can feel it pound.
19. _____ I have indigestion or heartburn.
20. _____ I wake up at night and cannot get back to sleep.
21. _____ I find it difficult to relax.
22. _____ I am easily bothered by noise.
23. _____ I am high strung.
24. _____ I have times when my vision is blurred.
25. _____ I find it difficult to regain composure after crises.

_______________ TOTAL (Range 0 – 125)

(Enter this score in the summary SCORING on Page 358)

INTERPRETATION

0 - 30 Your ANXIETY level is mild. People function at this level from time to time. Pressure and crises make people concerned and it shows up in the way the body responds with some degree of anxiety.

31 - 60 Your ANXIETY level is moderate. Messages from your body are telling you that anxiety levels are somewhat higher than they should be. You are at a fairly safe level, but there is not much reserve if there should be other pressures.

61 - 90 Your ANXIETY level is serious. Periodically, any person can have this level of anxiety, but if it continues for a long period of time, such anxiety can wear you out and make you ill. Do some aerobic exercising to help lower the anxiety levels. Make sure you are eating mostly fruits, vegetables, and whole grains. Cut out the refined carbohydrates such as products containing white sugar and white flour. Work at resolving all interpersonal conflicts. Practice relaxation exercises, meditation, or other rituals to reduce the tension in your life.

Above 90 Your ANXIETY level is critical. You cannot remain at this level of anxiety very long without increasing your risk of illness. According to current research it is just a matter of time before your body (or mind) will be unable to bear any more. You are a human being. You do not have an infinite capacity for stress, even if you are religious. Seek professional help if the current reasons for your anxiety are not relieved soon. Exercise, relaxation, resolution of interpersonal conflict, emphasis on fruits, vegetables and whole grains instead of products with white sugar and white flour, will all help you lower your score and improve your health.

DEPRESSION FROM STRESS

Pick out the most appropriate response. Write the number
of that response in the space provided by that statement.

0. Never 1. Rarely 2. Occasionally 3. Sometimes 4. Frequently
5. Almost always

1. _____ I have feelings of sadness.
2. _____ I feel down hearted.
3. _____ I feel fatigued.
4. _____ I distrust myself and others.
5. _____ I fear and worry more than usual.
6. _____ I have lost interest in what I used to do.
7. _____ I am constipated.
8. _____ I am restless in my sleep.
9. _____ I have a poor appetite.
10. _____ I have feelings of low self worth.
11. _____ I find myself withdrawing from groups.
12. _____ I have feelings of hopelessness.
13. _____ I have "I don't care" feelings.
14. _____ I have feelings that people and God are distant.
15. _____ I have feelings that meditation and prayer don't work.
16. _____ I have less interest in sex.
17. _____ I have less interest in talking with friends.
18. _____ I feel "Life isn't worth living".
19. _____ I experience despair and despondency.
20. _____ I am having more "sick days" off from work.
21. _____ I think or talk about death.
22. _____ I spend more and more time sleeping.
23. _____ I have had suicide thoughts cross my mind.
24. _____ I have had thoughts of guns and knives.
25. _____ I have threatened suicide.

_____ TOTAL (Range 0 – 125)

(Enter this score in the summary SCORING on Page 358)

INTERPRETATION

0 - 50   NO DEPRESSION. People have temporary disappointments which cause a feeling of depression. Sometimes an interpersonal conflict or a suppression of hurt and anger can cause a mild depression. Such mild depressions will usually disappear after a time, but if they do not go away, they can become more serious over a period of time, or if the causes of the depression are not dealt with.

51 - 70   MODERATE DEPRESSION. It would not be good for you to continue living in this state of depression too long. Conflict, loss of a loved one, poor nutritional levels, insufficient social involvement, anger, guilt, and physical illness can keep persons depressed. Do something different. Walk, run, swim, bike, take a vacation, visit old friends; anything to counteract your current routine and deal with the causes of depression.

71 - 90   SERIOUS DEPRESSION. With a score in this range of depression, it is advisable for you to seek professional help from someone. Tell your doctor, your clergyman, or even a close friend, but do not keep this situation to yourself. You need to sort through what is causing you to be depressed. There may be number of things, some of which you cannot change but others you can and should change.

Above 90   CRITICAL DEPRESSION. A medical doctor, psychologist or psychiatrist should be consulted. There are medications which will help you control your emotions while you go through counseling to discover the source of your depression and while you are being treated for the problems.

SAUL EXPERIENCES MANY CAUSES OF DEPRESSION

There are roughly 15+ causes for depression with as many or more levels to each cause. Here is a composite list of those causes.

1. Anger — (put down, embarrassment)
2. Guilt — (real and imaginary)
3. Loss — (of relationship or object)
4. Loneliness – rejection
5. Fear – worry
6. Low self worth feelings
7. Unresolved conflict
8. Indecision
9. Hopelessness — bondage
10. Lack of positive input
11. Poor nutrition
12. Weather conditions
13. Allergic reactions to food or environmental pollutants
14. Hereditary factors
15. Victorious success
16. Other

King Saul had 10+ of these factors in his life over the course of the years of his reign before he committed suicide. We don't know his nutritional or allergic factors: nor do we know the weather factor in the final phase of his life before suicide. King Saul might have, in fact, suffered from every one of the above factors.

Persons who suffer from anxiety and depression usually have at least 3 – 4 of the above factors which combine to create the depression. In counseling with depressed persons, you almost always see multiple sources of stress factors which create depression. People cannot always correct every one of the stress factors, but if they deal with 2/3rds to 3/4ths of the causes of depression, they are usually freed from depression.

THE HISTORY OF KING SAUL'S DEPRESSION

Saul was the first king of the Jewish people about 1000 years B.C. Saul ascended his throne following a long line of priestly leadership, of which Samuel was the last. The people did not like Samuel's sons and began to clamor for a king. Samuel disliked this, but Samuel's sons were considered incompetent to cope with the economic and political problems of the day. The ever present Philistines had risen to power and had occupied the central highlands of Palestine. They had destroyed Shiloh, the holy central city of the Jewish people, the place where Samuel had exercised his priestly functions, and the place which acted as a rallying point for the Jewish people.

The Philistines had succeeded in gaining a monopoly on iron and used that monopoly to gain definite military superiority over the Jewish people. We are told, "Now there was no smith to be found throughout the land of Israel; for the Philistines said, Lest the Hebrews make themselves swords or spears." (I Samuel 13:19) The priestly leadership of Samuel had not been able to give the kind of security which the people were now demanding.

STRESS FROM UNRESOLVED CONFLICT

The seeds of pathological conflict existed from the moment that Samuel realized his power and influence were waning. If someone were made king, Samuel would be only second in command. Thus, when Samuel gave in to the people and anointed Saul to be king, Samuel had to deal with a new power structure. Samuel's own anxiety is quite apparent and he becomes defensive. "Behold, I have hearkened to your voice in all that you have said to me, and have made a king over you. And now behold, the king walks before you, and I am old and gray, and behold, my sons are with you; and I have walked before the Lord and before his anointed. Whose ox have I taken? Or whose ass have I taken? Or whom have I defrauded? Or from whose hand have I taken a bribe to blind my eyes with it? Testify against me and I will restore it." (I Samuel 12:1-3) Samuel is still desirous of the affirmation of the people, but he has to begin to share some of his privileges. The question is, Can he relinquish them, some of them, many of them, or compromise?

Looking at Saul, we see a man who is apparently a gifted leader; one with a sense of identity; seeing his own charismatic, gifted leadership. Even before he is publicly invested with the title of king he has won a stunning victory over the Ammonites (I Samuel 11:5-11), the first after a long series of previous defeats. Samuel is forced to come out publicly in favor of Saul as king, and proceeds to call the people to Gilgal to make him king. Now Saul's own sense of identity, as a capable leader, is validated both by the people who were thrilled by his victory, and by Samuel, their former leader. Saul also shows himself a man of will. Samuel wanted to have all of Saul's antagonists killed (11:12) but Saul exercised his first voice of power over Samuel and said, "Not a man shall be put to death this day, for today the Lord has wrought deliverance in Israel." (I Samuel 11:13) Samuel submitted to Saul in this first of many political battles. It was their first encounter, and while Saul seems to be the winner, this appears to be about the only time.

The conflict gathers momemtum. In the face of the gathering armies of the Philistines, Saul wants to go to battle, but Samuel says Saul must wait seven days, at which time Samuel would come and offer a sacrifice before the battle was to begin. Saul waited but the members of his army became more fearful each day they had to wait, because each day more and more Philistines gathered for battle. Saul's troops began to flee, and hide in caves, rocks, tombs and cisterns. The choice was either to go ahead with the sacrifice and fight, or lose the troops and the battle. Saul waited out the seven days, but then performed the sacrifice himself, which was his right since Samuel was not there. Just as Saul finished, Samuel arrived. He chastized Saul verbally, "You have done foolishly, you have not kept the commandment of the Lord your God, which he commanded you; for now the Lord would have established your kingdom over Israel for ever. But now your kingdom shall not continue; the Lord has sought out a man after his own heart, and the Lord has appointed him to be prince over his people, because you have not kept what the Lord commanded you." (I Samuel 13:.13-14) Saul had not violated Samuel's commandment,if you read the scriptures carefully, but Samuel's insecurity reads it as defiance. This is not the first time, nor has it been the only time, that a godly man has made a poor judgement in the name of the Lord.

Saul and Samuel had apparently not worked out the lines of political, military, and religious authority. Samuel had been president, pope, and general. He wore three hats of power all in one, and probably never distinguished the one from the other. He seems to have found it hard to give up the military and the political authority, while only keeping the religious authority.

The first act of Saul in reversing Samuel's idea of killing Saul's opponents, seems to have whipped Samuel into a paranoid frenzy. The verbal tongue lashing which Saul received is reminiscent of slavery days and prisoner of war camps. Saul had committed no sin or defiance. Read again I Samuel 13:8 "He (Saul) waited seven days, the time appointed by Samuel...." Samuel is acting like a religious bully and bigot. Just because Samuel's name is found in the list of the saints in Hebrews 11:32, does not mean that this verbal face-slapping is a saintly gesture.

People get put down every day like Samuel put Saul down in public. Some of those who uncork their anger at others claim to be as religious as Samuel. Some who claim no religious feelings, do the same thing. People who wield power and speak as harshly as Samuel did, do not realize how destructive their actions are. The counseling profession continues to be busy mopping up the effects of this behavior. Countless lives are forever maimed by the venom spewed from the mouths of angry, threatened and insecure persons. When that anger is sprayed out day after day, with nothing positive to counterbalance it, people become mentally and physically ill. The body and mind cannot withstand continual humiliation. Illness will result unless there is some escape or reprieve.

SAUL SPEAKS UP TO SAMUEL

After Saul's first denunciation by Samuel, Saul went forth to win many battles. One day Samuel commanded Saul to conquer the Amalekites, and slay every person including the king. Saul didn't follow the literal command of Samuel, but kept king Agag alive and the choicest of the animals for sacrificing. Samuel "was angry". (I Samuel 15:11) Saul tried to explain, "I have performed the commandment of the Lord." Samuel became even angrier, and denounces Saul. Saul speaks up again, "I have obeyed the voice of the Lord....but the people took the spoil....to sacrifice to the Lord." (15:20) Saul is surprised at Samuel's rigid demands. Saul had tried to interpret the leading of the Lord too, but was told by Samuel he had made an irreconcilable mistake.

I know that Saul disobeyed. I believe Jesus would have forgiven. Yes, we do pay a price for errors in judgment. Yet, God's justice does not always demand that a person suffer depression and suicide like Saul did, because he disobeyed. King David was responsible for a murder and God forgave.

I have a problem liking Samuel. I'll keep him in the list of biblical "saints", but I do not have to set him up as a better person than Saul. As a counselor I hear stories of Samuel's kind of behavior by parents, bosses, landlords, abusive husbands, molesting uncles, and others, every day. Religious hypocrits and charlatans abound. They are usually as rigid as Samuel in their demands. They are literalists who crush people due to a slight variation. Religious or not, such autocratic domineering violates biblical concepts of "Love, joy, peace, patience, kindness, goodness, faithfulness, gentleness and self-control." (Galatians 5:19) People deserve better treatment than Samuel gave Saul, or those persons become ill as did King Saul.

SAUL SUFFERS MULTIPLE CAUSES FOR DEPRESSION

Over a number of years several things continued to occur which kept Saul in a constant state of insecurity. Having suffered two major public embarrassments for errors in judgment, he could not feel secure.

#1 REJECTION

"Because you have rejected the word
of the Lord, he has also rejected you
from being king." (I Samuel 15:23)

If you had been subjected to similar public denunciations and condemnations, you would be depressed. Furthermore, the loneliness and alienation after such an attack would make the heartiest person withdraw.

#2 GUILT

> **"And Saul said to Samuel, I have sinned;
> for I have transgressed the command–
> ment of the Lord and your words,
> because I feared the people and obeyed
> their voice." (I Samuel 15:24)**

Guilt is a prime cause of depression. Saul felt guilty. He had been disobedient. Saul begs for forgiveness, saying, "Now, therefore, I pray, pardon my sin, and return with me, that I may worship the Lord." And Samuel says, "I will not...." (15:25-26) It is no surprise to see that Saul becomes a depressed man. For some persons, finding forgivenss is the key to being healed of depression.

#3 LOSS

> **"Saul laid hold on the skirt of Samuel's
> robe, and it tore. And Samuel said
> to Saul, The lord has torn the kingdom
> from you this day...." (15:28)**

Loss of something precious creates depression feelings. The depth of the depression will be partly related to the degree to which we have invested our emotions in that loved person or object. Grief over loss is very natural and necessary, for us to move through the experience and come out well. Add this threatened loss of the kingdom and the loss of honor Saul experienced, and you have a good case for Saul's depression.

#4 UNRESOLVED CONFLICT

> **"Then Samuel went to Ramah; and
> Saul went up to his house in Gibeah
> of Saul. And Samuel did not see Saul
> again until the day of his death." (15:35)**

Samuel remained non-negotiable. The next thing Samuel did was anoint David secretly (Ch.16) Samuel, who wrote the book of Samuel, says he did this out of divine command. That need not be questioned. Yet, the natural effect of this was to add one more factor to the multiple factors that made Saul depressed and end up committing suicide. Don't let your unresolved conflicts depress you. Your healing may be quicker if you settle such problems.

#5   ANGER

(After David slew Goliath, and won battles, people sang) "Saul has slain his thousands, and David his ten thousands, And Saul was very angry ... And on the morrow an evil spirit from God rushed upon Saul, and he raved within his house." (I Samuel 18:7-10)

Anger that stays inside a person is another major source of depression. Where could Saul go with his anger? A good 4 mile jogging run would have done Saul a lot of good. An hour on a punching bag would have done a lot to relieve his depression. In Saul's day people believed illness came from divine permission and command. It was not unusual to think a person was afflicted because God was responsible for it. Yet, while that still holds true, there are compensating behaviors which counteract emotions of depression. Healing is dependent on the removal of stress factors, or getting involved in some stronger coping strength skills.

#6   LOW SELF WORTH FEELINGS

"And when Saul saw that David had great success, he stood in awe of him. But all Israel and Judah loved David, for he went out and came in before them." (I Samuel 18:15)

Once a person starts sliding into depression, it does not take much more to accelerate the process. Saul is not able to tolerate himself slipping lower and lower in the eyes of the people. He had had the rug pulled out from under himself so often, by now, that he was having trouble maintaining his composure. His ego strength was being undermined. People often get out when such situations arise. They will resign and go elsewhere or even return to a former job, when under such heat. If you are ill, and suffer from humiliation, you might have to get out. (Jesus says you can if you follow the rules of Matthew 18:15-18)

#7 LACK OF POSITIVE INPUT — LOVE

**"And Saul gave David his daughter Michal for a wife, But when Saul saw and knew that the Lord was with David, and that all Israel loved him, Saul was still more afraid of David."
(I Samuel 18:28-29)**

As time went on Saul seems to have had more and more difficulty in trusting persons and experiencing their love. Saul planned to allow David to marry his daughter Michal so he could exploit David, and cause his death. Saul was becoming mean, hostile, and paranoid. He was heading for a nervous breakdown. Saul needed love to be healed. There is tremendous healing power in Love. Jesus was sent as God's love in this world. Jesus was the great physician. Jesus healed people. He can heal you, but you need to let love flow through your life to make healing possible.

#8 FEAR — WORRY

**"Saul was still more afraid of David. So Saul was David's enemy continually."
(I Samuel 18:29) (Following this are several stories of Saul going on expeditions to try to kill David.)**

Fear and worry are other added factors to Saul's growing mental illness. Saul becomes obsessed with eliminating David. Saul's mental state is reaching the intensity of paranoid schizophrenia. Healing from this emotional condition will have to include the elimination of the fears and worries. That will not be easy. Saul has still not made peace with Samuel. Chances are that Saul will not be healed until he gets at the root of the problem, the repressed hostility which exists

between him and Samuel. Until then fear and worry
will lead Saul around in emotionally dizzying circles.

#9 INDECISION

**"When Saul saw the army of the
Philistines he was afraid, and his heart
trembled greatly, And when Saul
inquired of the Lord, the Lord did
not answer him. . ." (I Samuel 28:5-6)**

Saul's military judgments were no longer functional.
The instincts which lead him to victory, so often in his
younger years was gone. Not being able to trust others,
or even himself, he turned to a medium. Samuel had
died, and Saul sought the help of a "wizard" to get in
touch with Samuel's dead spirit, to obtain information
about the the upcoming battle with the Philistines. If
you ever get to the point where you need help, go to
the professionals, the persons who have their creden-
tials in order, people who deal in facts. You can find
healing when you seek out the truth from respectable
persons. Healing can be yours. Do not take advice
from the person who put you under in the first place.
Get help from outside sources.

#10 HOPELESSNESS

**"Because you did not obey the voice
of the Lord, and did not carry out
his fierce wrath against Amalek,
therefore the Lord has done this thing
to you this day." (I Samuel 28:18)**

Out of Samuel's grave he curses Saul one more time.
Fear so overwhelmed Saul that he fainted. Saul had
not been eating, another sign of deep depression, and
thus Saul was practically disfunctional. Oh, dear friend,
do not wait so long to get out of your hopeless bondage.
Break out before you breakdown. "Ye shall know the
truth and the truth shall make you free." (John 8:32)
Freedom is highest form of existence. "Truth" (Jesus)
is the means by which we transcend the curses of our
fellow human beings. With "truth" we break out of bondage
and become like God wanted us to be. God does not
intend for his creatures to deteriorate, but to surmount

obstacles. God does not intend for us to get sick early so he can take us to heaven. God wanted his chosen people to "live long in the land which the Lord thy God giveth thee", so they may be "lights" and "salt" and "leaven".

THE SUICIDE OF KING SAUL

God forbid that anyone decides to commit suicide. There is no need for such an act. I believe that almost everyone gets the feeling sometime, that life is not worth living. But we do not live by feelings alone. We live by faith. Most suicides occur at a moment of deep anger, of the kind that Saul had carried around for years about Samuel. Bottled anger is deadly. The Apostle Paul said it, "Being angry, do not sin, (by letting) the sun go down on your wrath, (lest) you give opportunity to the devil." (Ephesians 4:26) Saul was "possessed" in the later years of his life. Saul was driven and obscessed. Saul was emotionally unstable. Do not forget how it all started. Saul had to suppress his anger against a dominating, unrespected, insecure, hot-headed, and unforgiving person. He could have saved himself a lot of emotional pain by resigning, abdicating his throne, taken his lumps and gone back to farming. Sometimes you have to deal with the problem, before the problem cripples your health or drives you crazy. Stress management can preserve health and bring back healing.

COUNSELING THERAPY FOR KING SAUL

Saul could have benefited from therapy. Therapy does many things, but if the therapist does not help the client deal with suppressed and repressed anger, treatment is inferior. A good therapist would have uncoverd most of the dynamics of depression and mental illness outlined in the story of Saul. Whether Saul would have been willing to alter any of his attitudes or learn to communicate better, I do not know. He could have been helped if he would have been willing.

The will of a client is very crucial. No counselor can bend the will of a client, as such. The counselor can bring new information and data which may help the person change the will. Yet, if the will of the client is resistant, the counselor is powerless.

Seeing a professional counselor when you are depressed is not necessary if you use some of the wisdom gained in seeing the mistakes of Saul, read fine books on mental health, or spend time talking with your friends about some of the stress factors in your life. Sidney Jourard wrote one of my favorite books, entitled The Transparent Self, in which he defines the need for more "self-disclosure" as a partial solution to health, sanity and happiness. I believe that if Saul would have "disclosed" his feelings to the people, slowly, one by one, and then broadened his base, he might have been able to at least save his sanity. "Self-disclosure" is so powerful it could finally have convinced the entire nation, who believed their religious leader to be incompetent. David, Saul's successor made a fairly sizeable mistake, but with the prophet Nathan's help, David transcended the problem. Saul had no help. Saul seems to have had no confessor or counselor to be the buffer between himself and Samuel.

Make sure you have someone you consider sufficiently friendly and accepting, to help you in time of greatest stress. (See the chapter on social relations.)

HEALING — HUMAN AND DIVINE

While not doubting the miraculous healing power of God through prayer, self-healing through a process of mind-over-matter skills is also possible. The body has a powerful system of defenses against illness, and equally powerful capacity to heal itself. If we prevent the overload of invading bacteria, or remove stress from deteriorating organs of the body and mind, we can heal more readily.

Healing for Saul's mental illness could have been done instantly by God in response to prayer from the people. That did not happen. God may not have intended for it to happen, due to Saul's disobedience.

The chances of Saul being treated today and finding health are extremely good. He would have had to be treated quite early to find optimum success. He could have been treated with some medication, but that would only cover up symptoms, or at best, be temporary.

Saul needed to come to terms with Samuel. Jesus had a presciption for problem solving. It is found in Matthew 18:15-17

STEP 1 **"If your brother sins against (tresspasses, offends) you, go tell him his fault, between you and him alone. If he hears you, you have gained your brother."**

STEP 2 **"But if he (she) does not listen, take one or two others along with you, that every word may be confirmed by the evidence of two or three witnesses."**

STEP 3 **"If he (she) refuses to listen to them, tell it to the church." (a higher level of counseling)**

STEP 4 **"If he (she) refuses to listen even to the church, let him be to you as a Gentile and a tax collector."**

These four steps, when used in order, have power to process suppressed and repressed negative feelings for one to regain emotional stability. (You will see in later chapters that some depressions are result of nutritional problems, pharmaceutical drug interactions, losses, etc.) I would like to have been Saul's therapist. I would have followed Jesus steps, with some degree of flexibility, and I believe Saul could have resolved the factors which eventually pushed him over the hill into suicide.

Through stress management of this type, healing can take place. In reality, it is cleaning out the debris so that God can really function again in that body, mind and spirit.

DISCUSSION

1. We have traditionally believed that Saul became mentally ill because he was disobedient to God. Was God really speaking through Samuel, or was Samuel mentally deluded by his own pride to think that it was God who was speaking and giving orders to Saul?

2. If the conflict between Saul and Samuel became the seed of Saul's depression, why don't all unresolved conflicts lead to depression?

3. Mental and physical illness result from stress. We know that instinctually, but it is being scientifically validated. What should we do to eliminate stress in order to prevent illness?

4. Healing has been thought to be God's business. However, what could Saul have done to become healed of his mental illness?

5. Saul's mental illness seems to have become progressively more severe. Was there a point beyond which cure by human treatment was no longer possible?

6. If some mental and physical illness comes from bottling up angry feelings, shouldn't people speak up more than "turn the other cheek" and "go the second mile"?

7. If people become mentally ill today, for similar reasons, like Saul, what can they do to counteract the problem and find healing?

8. Job had a great loss, and became depressed. (Job 1:1-3:3). Elijah had a great victory over the Baal prophets and this was followed by depression. (I Kings 19). Jonah experienced astounding success from his altar call to Ninevah, and became depressed afterward. (Jonah 1-4) Thus, being depressed is not necessarily a sign of lack of spirituality. Read Galatians 5:19-21, about the "sins of the flesh, and decide which of those sins can cause depression.

SECTION 2

§§§§§§§§§§§§§§§§§§§§§§§§§§§§§§§§§§§§§§§

HEALING

RESULTING FROM

STRESS REMOVAL

§§§§§§§§§§§§§§§§§§§§§§§§§§§§§§§§§§§§§§§

INTRODUCTION

TO SECTION 2

HEALING —YOU CAN HELP YOUR DOCTOR

Since research shows there is a connection between stress and illness, if you will work at eliminating some of the stress factors in your life, you make it easier for your medical doctor to restore you health.   You need to think of yourself as a partner in the healing process. This section of the book deals with some areas of stress which set people up for illness. Each chapter is designed to help identify the problem of that stressor, and show some guidelines for resolution of that stress from both a secular and a religious point of view.

HEALING — YOUR PARTNERSHIP WITH GOD

God is able to do anything.   Sometimes he chooses not to do what we want, because he can see that we can do it for ourselves. God does not cater to childishness and irresponsibility, and therefore, some of our requests are denied. If people pray for God to discard his laws, it encourages people to do "poor me" and "help me". It does not encourage responsibility.   God has set up laws to govern the world. God can circumvent those laws, or suspend them as he wishes. Yet, if circumventing and suspending his own laws fosters more human irresponsibility, God will probably cut back, slow down, or stop answering prayers until we learn to be personally responsible.

No one of us can expect being rescued again and again, if we ignore the lessons to be learned in the first place.   In the following chapters you will be able to evaluate some areas of stress in your life and learn to begin to do something about these stress factors. Once you get your life back in line with God's laws you can expect more healing.

HEALING FOR DEGENERATIVE ILLNESSES

Degenerative disease is the kind that comes from excess stress, as opposed to contagious diseases that result from the transmission of virus, bacteria, germs, etc. Degenerative diseases are diseases of the heart, stomach, intestines, muscles, bones, nerves, glands, etc. The medical world has known that there is a connection between these illnesses and the stress of life. Until recently, the connection was not scientifically documented. Stress management for healing will not be helpful for contagious diseases. Stress management for the purpose of health and healing will probably only be effective for the degenerative types of illness and disease.

MIND OVER MATTER HEALTH AND HEALING SKILLS

We cannot go to mind-over-matter coping skills until Section 3 of this book. Just as you do not paint over chipped paint, you do not cover over what is basically unsound underneath. Stress counseling requires a thorough evaluation of what is corrupting the emotional, physical and spiritual system before teaching some coping skills.

SELF EVALUATION OF VARIOUS STRESS FACTORS

Make a personal study of the Word of God in the following chapters and evaluate yourself for stress. When you violate either the natural or the divine law you will pay some price. You cannot violate the law of gravity without paying a price, and you cannot violate the law of honesty without paying a price, etc. There are some fundamental principles for health and healing and we need to find them. In the chapters of Section 2 we will deal with

        Marriage and interpersonal relations (Ch. 4)
        Suppression of negative feelings (Ch. 5)
        Burnout from our responsibilities (Ch. 6)
        Financial Stress (Ch. 7)
        Alcohol stress (Ch. 8.)

Smoking stress (Ch. 9.)
Overweight stress (Ch. 10)
Poor nutrition (Ch. 11)
Excess sugar consumption (Ch. 12)
Allergic reaction under stress (Ch. 13)
Stress of caring (Ch. 14)

Chapter 4

HEALING AFTER CONFLICT

RESOLUTION IN A MARRIAGE

"When a person's ways please the Lord, he makes even the person's enemies to be at peace with the person."
(Proverbs 16:7)

If you are a marriage counselor, and you do not ask questions about the effects of alcohol, drugs, sugar addiction, allergic reactions to foods and chemicals, you may not solve the marriage problem. The reverse is also true. You can have an illness problem, and sometimes that illness is traceable to a poorly functioning marriage.

Take the following inventory of marital stress. Find out how much it contributes to illness.

STRESS IN THE MARRIAGE

Pick out the most appropriate response. Write the number
of that response in the space provided by that statement.

0. Never 1. Rarely 2. Occasionally 3. Sometimes 4. Frequently
5. Almost always

1. ____ I feel dissatisfied with my marriage.
2. ____ I do not feel I am No. 1 in my spouse's eyes.
3. ____ I feel I am overloaded with responsibilities.
4. ____ I feel we are not working as a team in our marriage.
5. ____ I feel like a servant to my spouse or children.
6. ____ I feel that my spouse is too critical of me.
7. ____ I feel neglected or criticized by my in-laws.
8. ____ I do not have as much to say about spending money.
9. ____ I do not have as much time to do as I please.
10. ____ I feel like I am in bondage, rather than being free.
11. ____ I do not feel I am treated equally in my marriage.
12. ____ I get upset when my spouse is harsh with the children.
13. ____ I give in to my spouse in decisions or arguments.
14. ____ I feel my needs are not getting met.
15. ____ I have problems enjoying sex.
16. ____ I dislike staying home with the children.
17. ____ I believe my spouse is too jealous.
18. ____ I feel I do not get heard.
19. ____ I work more hours in a day than my spouse.
20. ____ I feel dissatisfied with our social life.

__________ TOTAL   (Range 0 - 100)

(Enter this score in the summary SCORING on Page 358)

INTERPRETATION

0 – 25 Your score on STRESS IN MARRIAGE is very good. Your marriage seems to be a delight to you. You are to be congratulated.

25 – 50 Your score on STRESS IN MARRIAGE indicates that you have some disappointment in your marital relationship. Please try not to let unhappiness continue for more than a few weeks without getting help.

50 – 75 Your score on STRESS IN MARRIAGE indicates there is considerable stress. Such a level of stress can have serious consequences without attempting to come to some resolution. Illness is one possibility. See a marriage counselor with your spouse, before separation, divorce or illness happens.

75 – 100 Your score on STRESS IN MARRIAGE indicates almost a maximum amount of stress in your relatioship with your spouse. Do not allow conflict to continue to destroy your health and happiness. Seek professional help.

LET YOUR SPOUSE KNOW YOUR FEELINGS

Yesterday, your spouse did something minor which irritated you. Today it happened again. It was not really big enough to talk about. Tomorrow he/she will do that same minor irritating thing again. Day after tomorrow you blow up. You did not plan to blow up but the accumulation of those minor irritations created an explosion. Your psychic computer was keeping a running total.

Copy this inventory. Give one to your spouse. After your spouse has filled it out, share your results and let each question be a topic. Follow more of the rules in the remaining pages of the chapter.

MARRIAGE AND MULTIPLE STRESSORS

Suppose you are married, have sexual difficulties, have separated from your spouse, then reconciled, and finally divorced, all in one year. The Holmes and Rahe Stress Test of Chapter 1 would say that you have an 80% chance of being ill in the following year. Then, throw in some poor nutrition, conflict with the boss, getting fired, stressful financial situation, etc. You might become desparately sick, but now it is more difficult to analyze. The stress factors are more numerous. If you have been ill periodically, or chronically, you need to ask yourself the very hard question, "Do I live with unresolved conflict?". Here is a case-story of healing which took place after the person was able to work through a marital conflict, compounded by other factors. It is a case of physical healing after marital healing.

THE CASE OF M.J. (Told in her own words)

"In the fall of 1981 I contracted a strep infection. I thought it was only the flu. I didn't get it treated, and it turned into rhumatic fever. When the symptoms subsided I went back to my busy life. I was always tired, taking haps almost every day, complaining to my family and friends that I thought I had some form of arthritis."

"Everyone agreed that was probably what it was. Finally, I had to know for sure and went to the doctor. After seeing the doctor twice and being told that the tests showed no arthritis, which often happens in the early stages of my disease (lupus), I sought a specialist. This specialist was satisfied that the previous tests had been run properly, but after other tests I was diagnosed as having rhumatoid arthritis."

"A woman from my church (a physical therapist) heard I had this, and she called to come over. She told me all about what not to do with my hands and what exercises to do with my body. She told me about another specialist in another town, with whom she had worked some years previously. She said he was excellent and specialized in rhumatology. Immediately after this friend left, I called for an appointment. I had to wait two weeks."

"I grew steadily worse. My body was retaining fluids severely. I woke up one morning and my left leg was twice the size of my right. The pain was excruciating. I hurt to stay in bed. My joints would get stiff in bed, but it hurt worse out of bed. One time I dragged myself out of bed and down the hall to the kitchen, only to find my seven year old sitting at the breakfast table looking at me in horrors."

"Mom", she said, "What's the matter?"

"I hurt hon, I hurt real bad." is all I could say.

"My five year old stared at me in similar horror. I got to the phone and called my mother-in-law, who came over right away. Two days later I broke down. I had just awakened from another painful nap. I hadn't slept in months because the pain was so unbearable. My husband heard me crying in the kitchen. He didn't know what was happening to me either."

"I was so sick of being sick, so tired of it all. All I did was complain of how much I hurt. That wasn't me. My world was falling apart. I couldn't accept the fact that I was going to have this arthritis the rest of my life. I cried to Jesus, as I did before. The phone rang. It was my sister. She wanted to talk to me and she couldn't, because I couldn't get myself together to talk to her. She told my husband she was calling the arthritis foundation, and she hung up."

"My sister called me back in 10 minutes and told me there was a woman I could call who would help me. After pacing back and forth before the phone for 30 minutes, I called. She was a beautiful young woman who had rhumatoid arthritis since she was 16. When I told her I hurt, she knew. When I told her it was hard and the medication wasn't helping, she understood. She had gone through it all. The next day, she drove 50 miles to come to see me. I was comforted and thanked the Lord for some help."

"Steadily, I grew worse. People began to bring in dinners. I woke up one morning in pain and cried out to the Lord,"

"Please, send someone my way today, Lord."

"An hour later a dear sweet friend appeared at my door with a bag full of household goodies. She cleaned my house and just loved me. I was comforted again. With one week left to go to the specialist, I was still getting worse. A rash had started on my elbow, when I first started my medication a few months prior. It seemed to be getting worse, spreading over my whole body. All I could do was hope for Friday to come fast, when I could see the specialist. By Thursday the rash had spread to 75% of my body, so I went to see my local doctor. He called his associate in and both just stood there, not really knowing what to do. They knew I was seeing the specialist the next day, so they gave me heavy pain killers, and I went home. "

"I saw the specialist on Friday. He viewed the rash with equal dismay. There was so much wrong with me he didn't know where to begin. He said I had bleeding under my knees, dead tissue on my upper leg (due to lack of circulation), phlebitis of the left leg, damaged speen, damaged kidney function, liver was less than 10% functional, urinary tract infection, vasculitis, with a positive strep infection. I had Rhumatic Fever, Rhumatoid Arthritis or Lupus or all three."

"They hospitalized me immediately. I was glad to go in. It took me three days to come out of the danger zone. I was in isolation for 10 days."

A HEALING CHURCH TO THE RESCUE

"Here is where the real story begins, of a church, town and people who serve and love the Lord. I had been warned by the doctor that I had to be away from stress for 6 weeks, else a relapse could occur and I'd be sick for another 3 months. Knowing this, the women of my church organized a list for someone to come in every day to help me. Someone else brought dinner in every night for 6 weeks. They turned people away; so many persons wanted to help. Cards came from all over the area. I didn't know so many people could care."

"Money came in anonymously. I'll never know who sent it. Only my Lord will know. The church helped with medical bills.   The Love was overwhelming. His strength was great.   I had to finally resign my job.   That hurt.   That week my husband went on "overtime" at work.   Just like that every need was met."

"Then came the day I could go home, but, with one drawback.   I thought it was all done. I thought I could just walk away and get better.   The doctor came in only to say it was "systemic lupus" (meaning it would not go away). My heart sank."

"I don't want it."   I thought.   "I want to go back to my old self. Take it away."

"The specialist said I had the worst -- the highest level of lupus.   He told me it was the kind of lupus that one could not even go into the sun.   I loved the sunshine. We had 4 children and we loved nearby beaches. Not to be able to share that with them tore me up."

"I needed comfort. I had a girl friend who had lupus. I called her immediately and cried for a long time. Then I called the pastor, but the phone was busy.   I hung up the phone and prayed. "Lord, you always comforted me before. Couldn't you comfort me now.   Before I even finished the prayer, my pastor walked through the door. Again I was comforted.   The pastor said he had not planned to come that day, because I was going to be leaving the hospital tomorrow.   But it was apparently the Lord who changed the pastor's mind." (This is the end of her narrative.)

MARITAL CRISIS REVIVES THE LUPUS PROBLEMS

M.J. was becoming healthier since the lupus diagnosis of 4 months ago. Then a marital crisis brought her and husband in to see me for counseling. The communication and trust between them had broken down. Counseling went on weekly for 3 months. She found it difficult to regain former feelings. Both were trying to work out differences, but conflict existed at multiple levels, and M.J. had some past negative feelings toward someone that kept undermining efforts to regain stability.

The crisis mounted.   M.J. was diagnosed as having pernicious anemia.   Many of the former symptoms were returning. This is now the 8th month from the lupus diagnosis, and M.J. is on Darvocet, Naprosyn, Prednisone, Tagamet, Plaquenil, a sleeping pill, a monthly shot to regulate her period, (and one drug I wrote down, but can't find in the PDR).

M.J. has physical symptoms of headaches, depression, constipation alternating with diarrhea, fatigue, sweating, nervousness, blood in her stool, ulcers, frigidity and unrelenting resentment toward her husband, felt helpless and hopelessly in the grip of her anger.

WHOLISTIC TREATMENT

On February 22,1983 M.J. began an integrated program which would eventually see her transcend both the marriage problem and the lupus. She came in for 3 sessions a week. She practiced the following wholistic skills.

Jan-83	**(SED RATE stands at 150)**
2-22-83	Introduction to Relaxation Training.
	Galvanic Skin Response (GSR) equipment.
	Introduction to Mind-over-matter concepts.
	Gave her Guidepost story, Heal Me Lord.
2-24-83	Visualization techniques introduced.
	Say "I am being healed" as though a prayer.
	Relaxation Tape used.
	Breathing relaxation excercise introduced.
2-25-83	Visualization and GSR practice.
	Breathing and relaxation practiced.
2-28-83	GSR training --
	Used tape of Image Rehearsal for Arthritis.
	She wrote letter of all hostilities to hus-
	band and sent the letter to a friend.
3-2-83	She read Reader's Digest article on Stress,
	and that made her talk about childhood.
	She began to write on childhood injustice.
	She used the trampoline to jog.
3-7-83	GSR practice
	Discussion of early life history.
3-8-83	M.J. wrote letter to the person who upsets
	her a great deal.
	She jogged on the trampoline.

Relaxation tape was used.
Temperature biofeedback used.

3-9-83   No response yet to the letter she wrote.
Music therapy practiced. (Koln concert)
She has been down. She read God's Waiting
     Room, by Joyce Landorf, felt good.

3-14-83   She owned (confessed) some childhood
     hurts, and let her husband know.
She jogged on the tramp -- used Psalms
She used the Relaxation tape again.

3-15-83   She read Dr. Simonton on POSITIVE
MENTAL IMAGES....
(SED RATE has dropped to 78)
(M.D. specialist is lowering the drug dosage)

3-17-83   She did isometric exercises.
She listened to tape, POSITIVE ADDICTION
We discussed forgiveness.

3-18-83   She finished tape on Positive Addiction
She jogged on the tramp, and relaxed.

3-21-83   We talked. Why didn't she get response
     to her letter?
She interrogated husband too much.
She jogged, prayed, relaxed.

3-22-83   She talked with the person who upsets her.
Today she feels bushed and depressed.
Music therapy -- Scripture tape used.
She feels it hard to forgive.

4-11-83   I had a conference with her husband today.
I suggested he "hug", not ask, "What's
     wrong?", help heal her.

4-15-83   M.J. wrote her feeling down instead of
     verbalizing them. She wants proof
     of his loyalty and love.

4-18-83   Some relaxation, some jog, some talk.
She plans to join the Computer Class at
     Community Ed. It will build self
     worth, thats good.
She is getting better, and getting bored.

4-20-83   Relaxation training, GSR, Tape,
She is reading Healing of Memories.

5-1-83   Friends are still calling.
Church people are still helping.
She is still using the relaxation tape at
     home.

She still has sore joints, but feels somewhat better. She still feels
put down by that one person.
She bought a bike.

5-8-83   She went to church but had to leave in a
panic.

5-18-83   **(SED RATE is now at 55)**
Practice Assertiveness with husband.

6-21-83   Letter written to the Mich Dept of Rehab
to keep M.J. mobilized in the
healing direction.

6-27-83   The person by whom M.J. gets upset called
me and wanted to talk about M.J. Now I
can understand some of the reason for the
lack of final resolution to the perpetual
unrest in M.J.'s life.   This person is very
powerfully able to intimidate. —

In the following weeks M.J. and her husband
used Matthew 18:15-17 and finally came to
some agreement with that person.

Aug-83   **(SED RATE is down to 35)**

1984   **M.J. is back to work. (SED RATE became
normal.)**
NUTRITIONAL ANALYSIS was carried out
during many weeks of this Wholistic treatment program.   A computer program was
used to analyse the level of nutritional balance. ——— Some attempt was made to
look at the possibility of FOOD ALLERGY
as well.

ADD PRAYER TO WHOLISTIC TREATMENT

Part of true wholistic healing involves prayer. M.J.
not only prayed, but had many people praying for her.
I assume that numerous prayers included a petition for
those who were helping her get well. I was one of them,
and believe that God was partly using me in this process
to mobilize faith, will, courage and the capacity to relax,
so that healing could happen.

M.J. gives much credit for her healing to those who
prayed. Here are more of her words.

"I used to pray, Lord, help us to get to know the people of our church better. Now, everyday I get a new face in my house, and get to know the people better. My daughter's whole school is praying for me. Two of the area churches, in addition to my own church, brought up my name in the congregational prayers. Bible study groups all over are praying for me. My family and friends and people who don't even know me. . . The Lord has always been in my life, and he let me know just recently that he is still there."

COOPERATION IN WHOLISTIC HEALING

This story of M.J. illustrates the need for mind-over-matter skills, faith, hope, prayer and medicine, all working in concert. At no time does wholistic thinking consider eliminating any of the healing arts. Wholistic tries to be inclusive, without including those skills which may seem to some to be quackery. So long as those who bring their arts to the person, have a healthy respect for each other, the cooperative efforts will be beneficial to the patient. If, however, those who bring their healing skills, look scornfully upon each other, there will likely be division, and the patient will pick that up. Such negative elements cannot be a part of that healing process. Healing requires a confluence of believing people, who love each other and the patient loves them. If we believe the proposition that stress causes some illnesses, then we cannot bring stress into the healing process.

HEALING AFTER PROBLEMS ARE RESOLVED

M.J. saw healing taking place during the entire time in which problems were being resolved. Yet, there was one final snag, one final hitch, to the complete resolution. When agreement or acceptance, was finally achieved, between M.J. and the person with whom she had difficulty, only then could the final healing take place. (M.J. recognizes the problem was hers, in that she didn't know how to handle the other person.) Recall from M.J.'s narrative that she saw herself doomed to a life of pain. Notice that M.J. did not accept that doom-spelling verdict of her doctor. After all, the doctor was only reflecting the statistical probabilities. The doctor did not know how many people would become mobilized, and reverse the statistical average. It is faith, will, courage and hope like that which makes changes in favor of the healing odds.   With Jesus spirit available to those who believe, almost nothing can stop us from achieving a greater than average statistical chance. Stress management skills can increase the odds in favor of health, and stress management which includes the healing power of Christ, can increase the odds toward healing by that much more.

M.J. has found healing, but it took a MULTIPLE IMPACT approach to beat the odds against her.

YOUR MARRIAGE PROBLEM CAN MAKE YOU ILL

Many research projects have now substantiated the notion that both mental and physical illness comes out of a multiple array of stress factors. It is relatively easy to understand how marital stress can bring on emotional problems, but less understandable that illness can be the result of marital stress.

Counselors see this phenomenon a lot. A young man had numbness on the outer side of his right leg. He saw a doctor. When all the tests ruled out a medical problem, the doctor asked about other sources of stress. The young man owned he had a marital problem, and the doctor referred him to me. After a few sessions the marital problem was resolved and the numbness in the leg went away.

HEALING AFTER PROBLEM RESOLUTION

It is not difficult to see the logical deduction from stress research, that removal of the stressor makes it possible for healing to take place. Medicine frequently reminds the victims of illness, that the doctor does not heal anyone.   The medical intervention simply removes the blockage preventing healing, or aborts the deteriorative process.   The body heals itself.   There is a homeostasis within the natural body, which seeks to bring itself back to the position it was supposed to be in in the first place. Therefore, once the overloading stressor which is producing deterioration, is removed, the body will return to its normal functioning.   If that overload is the conflict of the marriage, once that overload of conflict is resolved, healing can return the body to the homeostatic position it was intended to occupy. The same is true for almost every other stress factor in one's life.

RESOLVING MARITAL STRESS

Marriage counselors agree on a number of things about making marriages work. With each new publication familiar themes are developed in quite imaginative ways. I believe most counselors would agree on working toward the following goals to make a marriage sing.

1. Persons have to be willing to give more love than they get in return. Jesus said, "Love your enemies..." (Matthew 5:44)

2. Spouses need to learn how to communicate without "anger". "Anger" is a sin, says the Apostle Paul in Galatians 5:20. "A soft answer turneth away wrath." (Proverbs 15:1)

3. Spouses who suppress negative feelings and then blow up later are a menace to the marriage. Counselors spend much time on the communication skills, where feelings are shared at early stages. In the biblical sense, counselors are trying to help people learn to do what the Apostle Paul said, "Being angry, do not sin, do not let the sun go down on your wrath, (lest) you give opportunity to the devil." (Ephesians 4:26)

4. Much time can be spent on a variety of behaviors which are extremely stressful; "jealousy", "drunkenness", "carousing" (etc) (Galatians 5:19ff). Counseling therapy, may try to accomplish what a good "conversion" can accomplish much more quickly.

5. Therapy for spouses will almost invariably focus on the need for more "love, joy, peace, patience, kindness, goodness, faithfulnness, gentleness, and self-control". (Biblically, they are found in Galatians 5:22-23)

6. Issues of justice, or fairness abound in therapy sessions. Selfish spouses resist, or do not come to sessions to negotiate. "To do justice is more acceptable to the Lord than sacrifice." (Proverbs 21:3, See also Micah 6:8 and Colossians 4:1) These are hard words for the spouse who feels that "head of house" means to create injustice and stamp it "O.K."

7. Therapeutic intervention follows many roads and unfolds in many ways, but in each of these instances it follows the Biblical rules which Jesus set forth in Matthew 18:15-17.

"If your brother sins against (offends, trespasses against) you, go and tell him his fault, between you and him alone. If he listens to you, you have gained your brother. But if he (she) does not listen, take one or two others along with you, that every word may be confirmed by the evidence of two or three witnesses. If he (she) refuses to listen to them, tell it to the church; (Seek out a pastor or professional counselor.) And if he (she) refuses to listen even to the church, let him (her) be to you as a Gentile or a tax collector." (After several attempts at problem solving, it may be necessary to let the other person suffer the consequences of his or her behavior.)

ONENESS IN THE MARRIAGE

There is a paradoxical tension between being in a relationship of "oneness", while still maintaining our "individuality". In a paradox both sides of the proposition are true, and defy logical connections. Just as the humanity and divinity of Jesus are paradoxical truths, so are "oneness" and "individuality" in the marriage. Marriages need two persons working on their "oneness" and their "individuality", and holding on to these spiritual polarities.

God ordained such a "oneness". After God created Eve, He said, **"Therefore, a man leaves his father and his mother and cleaves to his wife and they become one**

flesh." (Genesis 2:24) This is repeated 4 more times by Jesus and the apostle Paul. (Matthew 19:5, Mark 10:7, I Corinthians 6:16, Ephesians 5:31) Considering this repetition, one has to recognize its importance.

Husbands have difficulty allowing themselves to become "one" with their wives, other than at times of sexual interaction. They are psychologically capable of allowing their emotions to determine their behavior. Yet, macho mentality, resistance to things spiritual, inferiority feelings, narcissism and pride, inhibit men from sharing their feelings of pain, hurt, failure, unfairness, low self-worth, and defeat. Not sharing this creates emotional distance. Hence, a husband appears to be a strong "individual", but at the expense of "oneness" in the marital relationship. Harmony in the marriage requires a vigilant attention to keeping oneness and individuality in balance.

Harmony among the children results from oneness in the marital relationship. When the values, behaviors and discipline of the parents are similar, you seldom see acting-out children. Rebellious behavior, or acting-out behavior that is not nutritionally fostered or chemically fostered, seldom comes out of a home where there is oneness between husband and wife. Only when one parent is overly strict, and the other parent is overly lenient, do you find severe problems with children's behavior. I have counseled many families, and its always true. Rebellious children come out of excessively polarized homes. Too much emphasis on our "individual" points of view at the expense of "oneness", creates trouble.

Healing of the whole person -- the body, the marriage, and family's rebellious child -- relies heavily on the willingness to go for oneness. In the story of M.J. , the return to oneness in the marriage was a powerful healing factor. In the lives of parents dealing with wayward children, the return to oneness in the marriage is fundamental to the healing of the defiant-filled relationship. In counseling a great deal of family therapy seeks to put the husband and wife on a similar frequency to produce oneness that the child can understand. Many therapists counsel children who are defiant. I work better at spending more time counseling the parents of those children than counseling the child. I think I have more success doing it this way. Tough Love is an organizational approach, which brings in parents of rebellious children. The parents discuss their problems in the group of parents, and find, both support and guidance in getting the marital act together again. Healing can come when persons are "one" with themselves and with others.

MARITAL EQUALITY vs. DOMINANCE — DEPENDENCE

I love the way God has revealed his messages to mankind so that Biblical truth applies to so many situations. There are happy persons who have an equalitarian marriage. There are marriages where two persons live in a semidominant-dependent relationship. They are happy too. These two sides launch their missiles at each other from time to time. They play a "star war" game for spacial control of their point of view. Neither side has yet won the battle for "truth". There is less tendency to fight for "right" or "wrong" points of view when you view things paradoxically. God is "three" and God is "one". That is O.K. That is a paradox with no logical connectedness. We simply live with that. We believe both. We do not let ourselves get pushed into denying one or the other. Another paradox is found in the historical controversy over "faith" and "works". We have to operate our lives from 100% of both sides of the issue, not just 50-50. The minute you clip some points off "faith" or "works" you are in theological trouble. As human beings we live between those paradoxical polarities. Humanly speaking we may fluxuate a bit more today to the one side, and a bit more to the other side tomorrow. God will not condemn us for this flexibility. We are on the "straight and narrow" path of life, but the concept of paradox makes the "narrow" wide enough to walk on without falling off the theological knife's edge of right and wrong.

You need to approach God's Word in Ephesians 5:21-33 with just the same mentality. There is enough in this passage to fortify the persons who preach "equality" and those who preach "submission".

> "**Be subject to one another** out of reverence for Christ. Wives, **be subject to your husbands,** as to the lord. For the husband is head of the wife as Christ is head of the church, his body, and is himself its Savior. As the church is subject to Christ, so let wives also be subject in everything to their husbands. Husbands, love your wives, as Christ loved the church and gave himself for her, ... Even so, **husbands should love their wives as their own bodies.** He who loves his wife loves himself, for no man every hates his own flesh, but **nourishes and cherishes it,** as Christ does the church... Let each one of you love his wife as himself, and let the wife see that she **respects** her husband."

Hold two things in mind. There is as much need for the male to treat the female respectably as there is need for the female to think respectfully.

Postscript

In July, 1984, at a meeting of Womens Aglow, a woman, having a "word of knowledge" that someone was going to be healed of arthritis, declared that in a public meeting. M. J. received it for herself, since there were still some symptoms of arthritis in her. She felt a "fire" run through her body, after which she has not experienced that pain again.

On January 4, 1985 her doctor found no trace of lupus and wrote in his notes, "Healed by faith."

M. J. beleives that her "standing on God's Word" and "living the promises" is the major ingredient of the healing process.

DISCUSSION

1. In the story of M.J. there is a combined program of medical, psychological, and spiritual treatment. How can we go about getting more of this kind of treatment?

2. Were all the treatment modes or tactics necessary?

3. Who gets most of the credit for the healing? Was it M.J., or the physician, or the counselor, or God's praying and helping people?

4. What do you think of the idea that we are responsible for some of our own healing?

5. Marital conflict may contribute to degenerative illnesses. What other kinds of conflict may contribute to degenerative diseases?

6. Jesus gave four steps for problem-solving between two persons. Can you remember them? (You will find them in Matthew 18:15-17)

7. We are not accustomed to make a connection between marital conflict, conflict with the boss, or family conflict, and degenerative illnesses. The Holmes and Rahe Stress Test in Chapter 1 shows there is a connection. Discuss what might be some of the clues to help us understand when conflict is a major stress factor.

8. Which kind of marriage is best for for you, equalitarian or dominant-dependent?

9. If God is "just", and we pattern ourselves after God, should we teach more justice for marriages? Is there any difference between justice and equality? Can a relationship be "just" without being "equal", and vice-versa?

10. "Oneness" is important to marriage and family harmony. How much "individuality" do a person need to give up to gain "oneness"?
    How does the gospel help you decide this one?

Chapter 5

HEALING BY EXPRESSION

OF NEGATIVE FEELINGS

"Therefore, confess your sins to one another, and pray for one another, that you may be healed."   James 5:16

I believe that medicine and surgery bring healing. I believe that God heals in response to prayer. I have rediscovered that healing is a result "confession". Stress management theory does not say it exactly that way. Research just says that holding too much anger inside, is one of the contributing factors in high blood pressure, heart pain, and heart attacks. Psychology has long ago seen the connection between negative feelings and mental illness. Both physical and mental health are affected.

Fill out the following inventory to analyse the degree to which you either express or suppress your feelings.

STRESS FROM THE SUPPRESSION OF NEGATIVE FEELINGS

Pick out the most appropriate response. Write the number of that response in the space provided by that statement.

0. Never   1. Rarely   2. Occasionally   3. Sometimes
4. Frequently   5. Almost always

1. _____ I keep hurt and upset feelings in side.
2. _____ I back off from verbal combat.
3. _____ I keep my temper under control.
4. _____ People take advantage of me.
5. _____ I try to keep peace even if I have to keep still.
6. _____ I remain calm under criticism and do not speak up.
7. _____ I give others the benefit of the doubt.
8. _____ If people tease me, I can be hurt but do not speak up.
9. _____ When my boss is critical I simply keep still.
10. _____ When my father or mother upset me I keep still.
11. _____ I avoid people who offend me.
12. _____ I am gloomy; I grumble, pout or sulk when I am mad.
13. _____ I am patient when others make mistakes.
14. _____ I am bitter from things that happened in the past.
15. _____ I am depressed for a day when someone is rude .
16. _____ I get silent when I am angry about something.
17. _____ When I have an urge to get even, I suppress it.
18. _____ I have problems making quick "come back" responses.
19. _____ I keep a smile even if I am angry or upset.
20. _____ I keep quiet if someone steps in front of me in a line.
21. _____ I am patient when others are late.
22. _____ I keep silent rather than hurt someone's feelings.
23. _____ I let others do the planning and leading.
24. _____ I try to be diplomatic in what I say, rather than
speaking bluntly and to the point.
25. _____ If I am evaluated and receive a poorer report than
I thought I deserved I do not speak up about it..
26. _____ If you have been treated harshly, unfairly, rudely or
critically by someone in the past, and it continues to bother you, add the following points.
25 points for a small hurt that still bothers you.
50 points for small upsets that keep coming.
75 points for severe pent-up hurt feelings.
100 points for aggravations that have produced a lot
of hate for that person(s).

_____ TOTAL (Range 0 - 225)

(Enter this score in the summary SCORING on Page 358)

INTERPRETATION

0 - 40   Your score on SUPPRESSION OF NEGATIVE FEELINGS indicates that you could be too quick to respond to irritations by other persons. You need to find a balance between not responding at all and responding somewhat defensively. Having a score in this range is essentially good, but passive persons may not know how to react to your assertiveness.

41 - 85   Your score on SUPPRESSION OF NEGATIVE FEELINGS shows a moderate assertiveness. You are probably quite respected for your opinions. You apparently do not suppress your negative feelings too much. Assertiveness is a fine quality unless it runs rough-shod over someone else.

86 - 125   Your score on SUPPRESSION OF NEGATIVE FEELINGS shows a good amount of balance between speaking up and keeping quiet when you are hurt. You are probably working out of a formula in your mind which keeps both yourself and others happy. Expression of feelings and suppression of feelings are counterbalance weights to maintain peace.

126-150   Your score on SUPPRESSION OF NEGATIVE FEELINGS shows you to be somewhat passive when someone else hurts or offends you. It would be good for you to learn that it is OK to speak up regarding unpleasant experiences. You do not need to blow-up, just say how you feel as a result of someone's abusive attitude or behavior.

Above 151   Your score on SUPPRESSION OF NEGATIVE FEELINGS is too high. You seem to be keeping an excessive amount of feelings inside. You need to resolve some problems. You need to talk much more to or confront those who hurt or offend you. Keep your anger level down when you speak up. Perhaps you could even write a note to those who hurt you.

THE ANGER — ILLNESS CONNECTION

Believe it or not, some illness is the result of bottled-up negative feelings. Mental, physical and spiritual illness is frequently traceable to guilt, fear, loss, etc. Hurts from favoritism, neglect, sarcastic ridiculing, mockery, etc., are anatomically destructive. However, anger, which is either suppressed (consciously) in large amounts, or repressed (unconscious activity) for a long period of time, is the largest offender.

Of all the sins listed in the Bible, I would suggest that suppressed and repressed anger bring on more spiritual, mental and physical illness than any other single factor. We look at the list of the sins of the flesh, and some of them are, "Immorality, impurity, licentiousness, idolatry, sorcery, _enmity, strife_, jealousy, _anger, selfishness, dissension, party spirit,_ envy, drunkenness, carousing and the like." (Galatians 5:19-21) Some say that all sins are the same size. Before God, I am sure that is true. My clinical experience tells me that the anger from unresolved conflict is the most destructive. Counselors deal with a great deal of client "anger". It comes in many sizes and manifests itself in kalaidoscopic patterns. Invariably, the hurts, and the anger they cause, de-stabilize mind, body and soul.

Jesus healed the lame man who sat beside the pool of Bethesda for 38 years. Afterward, Jesus met him in the temple and said;

> **"See, you are well! Sin no more, that nothing worse befall you."** **(John 5:14)**

Jesus knew the effect of sin upon human mental, physical and spiritual processes. We have to be exceedingly careful to point out that not all illness, however, comes from sin. Job, of Old Testament fame, was a righteous man, who suffered illness, but not due to sin. God simply let satan buffet Job for a while, with troubles which included illness. In the New Testament, Jesus and his disciples observed a man born blind. In that incident the disciples asked whose sin had caused this problem, the man's or his parent's. Jesus, in this instance, said, "Neither did this man sin, nor his parents." (John 9:1-41)   Thus, we have to face the hard fact that sin causes some illness, but not all illness is from sin.

KARL MENNINGER ON ANGER AND ILLNESS

The Menninger Foundation in Topeka, Kansas was started by Karl Menninger M.D., a Psychiatrist, a Presbyterian layman, and an author.   In his book, Man Against Himself, published in 1938, he wrote about the effect of repressed anger.

> "The existence of fierce but repressed hate is strikingly apparent in several forms of somatic disease, instances of which have been psychologically studied. In the study of heart disease previously mentioned, for example, my brother and I found evidence for concluding that heart symptoms and presumably heart disease were sometimes a reflection of — or expression of — strongly aggressive tendencies which had been totally repressed. Heart disease is very apt to occur, as is well known, in externally mild, gentle people, and in our series, in men who had been strongly attached emotionally to their fathers, and often more or less definitely hostile to their mothers. The conscious affection for the father usually completely obliterates the deeply buried hostilities to him." (p. 375)

In addition to heart disease, Karl Menninger spoke of the connection between repressed hostility and such things as depression, frigidity and impotence (pp. 343-344). We are speaking of repressed anger (the flip side of hurt) in quantities which the person finds unmanageable. We all have the capacity to absorb some negative experiences in life.   However, each person has a breaking point, or a point at which stress begins to convert into mental, physical or spiritual deterioration.

PAUL TOURNIER ON NEGATIVES AND ILLNESS

Paul Tournier is almost a household term, known by Christians around the world.   As a practicing physician he has dealt with the negative feelings persons experience which incite or induce their illnesses. Tournier took seriously the moral and spiritual issues of person's lives, and counseled his patients to change their behavior in order to facilitate the healing processes.   He seems to have had great success in turning people's character around, so healing could take place.   In his book, The Meaning of Persons, first published in Switzerland in 1940, he gives several illustrations of physical illness brought on by attitudes or experiences.   I would like you to see some of the connections he observed many years ago.

THE ILLNESS	THE NEGATIVE FEELINGS
"arthritis"	(Is caused by)"overwork, lack of exercise, wrong eating, (and)...60% of arthritis cases have their origin in moral conflict."
"neuritis"	"showed itself shortly after a bereavement which left the patient in a rebellious state of mind."
"rheumatism"	"Genevieve" wanted badly to be "independent". She married. Her husband went bankrupt. She was "compelled to accept assistance. . .soon her health gave way. . .arthritis (set in)..."
"Athero-sclerosis"	(These persons) "have a long history of digestive and moral indiscipline. . .They enjoy the excesses of diet."
"high blood pressure"	Albertine "lived in a state of perpetual agitation, unable to relax. . .She trusts no one and has no friends. She is imprisoned in grim inner tension."
"angina"	"is susceptible of being provoked by various causes, moral as well as physical..."

"phlebitis"   "usually occurs in subjects who are physically and morally fatigued."

"skin disease"   "in a patient troubled by a hopeless marital conflict. . .recovered rapidly as a result of a religious conversion."

"boils"   "A patient said, I get a new boil every time I have an argument with my wife."

"heart disease" "I was called to an old lady of 86 who had tachycardia. . .(When asked about what emotional trauma might have caused the tachycardia, she said,) "They killed my cat."

"The exact frontiers between functional and organic troubles are not always easy to establish in everyday practice. One is often amazed at the remarkable way in which the body can bear serious organic disorders, while other very minor disturbances obtrude themselves on the attention, because of the functional troubles they trigger off." (The Healing of Persons, p. 38)

The connection between such negative feelings as anger, guilt, fear, worry, fright, etc., and the onset of mental, emotional, or spiritual illness, is clear. Persons like Tournier are validating what our instincts have been telling us for a long time.

RESEARCH ON ILLNESS CONNECTIONS

The body of research on the connection between stress and illness, has had a powerful impact on my theological awareness. Repeatedly, I saw the scientific world validate the propositions of the Bible, regarding health from a variety of mind-over-matter, or non-indulgent behaviors. Each chapter in this book calls persons to be aware that they have some responsibility for their health and healing. That is message of scientific research and stress management experts. It is also the message of the Bible.

The Framingham study, dating continuously from 1949 until the present, has been producing statistical data on the life-style of people of the city of Framingham,

Massachusetts. In an 8 year study of the incidence of Coronary Heart Disease, they discovered that "not discussing anger" was an "independent predictor" of Coronary Heart Disease. Often, there are many factors which come together to produce a problem. The study focused on "Type A" (the more aggressive type of behavior), "work overload", "suppressed hostility", and "frequent promotions". Yet the study concluded that the extent to which people fail to talk about their feelings of anger, is the extent to which people experience "angina", "myocardial infarction", and Coronary Heart Disease in general". (Am. Jrnl. of Epidemiology 111:37-58)

Biblically, the sin of "anger" is not punished directly with Coronary Heart Disease, but the Apostle Paul says, by Divine inspiration, "I warn you, as I warned you before, that they who do such things shall not inherit the kingdom of God." (Galatians 5:21) The kingdom of God, starts in this world and continues on into eternal life. The kingdom of God is the good life here on earth and in heaven. We begin to taste the blessings of heaven here and now, with our participation in conversion, sanctification, growing in the grace of Jesus Christ. We will be spiritually, mentally, and physically healthier when we speak up and resolve problems of anger.

HIGH BLOOD PRESSURE — NEGATIVE FEELINGS

People are killing themselves with anger, or at least shortening their life with unresolved conflict, and then wonder why God won't bail them out when they get sick "nigh unto death". The Department of Medicine, White Medical Center, and the Hypertension Service, Department of Medicine, and the Department of Psychiatry and Neurology, University of Southern California School, of Medicine, in Los Angeles, California, published a study in the Journal of Clinical Studies (1981) 61, 389s-392s. They concluded

> "Patients with primary hypertension,
> (high blood pressure), had more anger,
> anxiety, and guilt."

The researchers tested the subjects for anxiety, depression and repressed anger. They had the subjects do isometric handgrip exercises (IHE) for 3 minute periods, and then tested blood pressures. They concluded

> "Subjects with the combination of
> increased anxiety scores and suppressed
> anger had an enhanced increase of
> their systolic pressure after the IHE."

You will statistically pay a price for anxiety and anger if you leave it untended. Put more faith in God. Cast your cares on Him for He careth for you. Learn how to meditate, eat properly, relax and trust. Each chapter in this book will help you.

ADAPTATIONS TO KEEP YOU HEALTHY

You cannot violate the homeostatic balance of the body, mind and spirit for very long without illness setting in. The human reservoir which accepts the flood waters of overwhelming negative experiences can only take so much. Either the dam will burst, or the overflow will wash out the structure built to retain an appropriate amount of hurt. Putting that in psychological terms, we can say that the psyche is the storehouse of our emotions. It can contain both positive and negative charges. When the charge becomes more negative from hurts, than positive from happiness and joy, there is a drain on the human system. People have many ways to fight off the dissipation resulting from negative input. Some yell. Some hit. They ventilate their feelings on to others, so the negative is discharged on another person. Some find positive substitutes for every negative they experience, and those substitutes can be good or bad for the person. Some seek out the aid of religion. Others get into purchasing objects, etc. Other groups of persons change their values to adapt to the input of negatives. Instead of suffering scorn for not drinking alcohol, they turn to alcohol. Rather than taking abuse from a harsh person, another will run away. People will do many things to dissipate the accumulating effect of negative experiences. Some discharges of negative feelings are moral, and some may not be very honorable, but persons automatically fight against living with an inner turmoil which can have serious effect upon their health. The natural instincts of the body, mind and spirit are to preserve themselves, to maintain a homeostatic balance, so the body will not become ill. When all the defense mechanisms have failed, the person will experience illness.

DO NOT TURN THE OTHER CHEEK TOO MUCH

"Turning the other cheek" is both Christian and self-destructive. I have seen some of the finest examples of Christian grace, who "turn the other cheek". My father is one of them. My mother is another. There are millions of these absolutely delightful people who "turn the other cheek". Yet as a counselor, I listen every day to persons who have "turned the other cheek" too much. I see the broken persons who do not know how to speak up without blowing up, so they begin to learn to simply suppress their hurts, disappointments, put-downs, "anger", "wrath", "strife", "enmity". More mental illness comes out of the suppression of hurt feelings than imaginable.

The heavy emphasis on "turning the other cheek" is very Biblical. Jesus' Sermon on the Mount conveys this idea strongly. It starts out with "Blessed" are those who "are poor", "mourn", "are meek", "hunger for right-eousness", "the merciful", "the pure in heart", "peace-makers", "persecuted", and "reviled". No one is charged up for justice, righteouness, and fairplay by these words. Rather, we are calmed. There is not much encourage-ment to speak up, from these placards of Christian virtue.

Jesus did not mean to make Christianity soft, and spongelike. The Sermon on the Mount is not simply promoting a "turn the other cheek" style of living for Christians. Only improper interpretation has allowed this conclusion. Look at the 12 propositions of Matthew 5:21-43, set in juxtaposition to one another, six to six.

THE OLD TESTAMENT	THE NEW TESTAMENT
"You shall not kill."	"But I say unto you, that every one who is angry with

	"his brother shall be liable to judgment."
"You shall not commit adultery."	"But I say unto you that every one who looks at a woman lustfully....."
"It was also said, Whoever divorces his wife let him give her a bill of divorce."	"But I say to you that every one who divorces his wife, except on the ground of unchastity, makes her an adulteress...."
"Again, you have heard it said ... You shall not swear falsely..."	"But I say to you, Do not swear at all...."
"You have heard it said, An eye for an eye, and a tooth for a tooth."	"But I say unto you, Do not resist one who is evil. But if any one strikes you on the right cheek, turn to him the other also...."
"You have heard it said, You shall love your neighbor and hate your enemy."	"But I say to you, Love your enemies, and pray for those who persecute you."

I do not see how you can begin to select the "eye for eye" and the "tooth for tooth" verse, and theologically throw it out. That verse is just as much a part of the Old Testament as are the other five verses in the left hand column, and all 6 verses in the right hand column.

Too many persons listen to sermons in which the "eye for eye" ventilation of feelings is preached as totally unChristian. I recognize that to even suggest a bit of "eye for eye" may simply turn loose the "wife beaters", "child abusers", and hostile maniacs, to do what would be very demonic. Yet, as long as preaching soft-pedals the concepts of fighting for justice, righteousness, and fairplay, we will continue to have good Christian persons being hurt by their own suppression and repression of negative feelings. It will keep counselors busy. That may be good for the economy, but not for the image of the church, and the health of its members.

CHAR WAS SICK FROM SUPPRESSED HURTS

Char (not her real name) told me of a long history of suppressing her hurt, anger, disappointments, and repeated hospitalizations. Her presenting complaints included headaches, stomach pains, rhumatoid arthritis in the fingers, constipation alternating with diarrhea, periodic chest pains, nightmares, etc. Periodically, stomach pains required hospitalization.

Psychologically, she was having equally difficult times. The Minnesota Multiphasic Personality Inventory (MMPI) revealed the following.

- — "Evil spirits possess me at times."
- — "I have strange experiences."
- — "I believe I am being plotted against."
- — "I am afraid of losing my mind."
- — "Persons are trying to steal my thoughts..."
- — "I have blank spells in my activities...."
- — "I have felt like someone was making me do
        things by hypnotizing me...."
- — "I hear strange things when I am alone."

The MMPI did not show psychotic deterioration, but elevations of anxiety and depression. The test also pointed a finger at "father conflict", "mother conflict", and "sibling conflict". She was on Limbitrol, Darvocet and Tagamet. She also took Dilantin for treatment of an inherited condition of cerebral palsy. She was referred by her "doctor", her "pastor" and the "yellow pages".

I listened to feelings of "rejection", "placement in a children's retreat at age 9", "alienation", "seizures", and innumerable "put downs" due to this combination of problems. I heard of psychological distance from parents (not their fault), and the longing to have "warmth" from them. Her "shyness", "learning disability", and "left out" feelings were slowly draining her vitality. In spite of all of this, there was character, will, backbone and fight in this fine young woman. She belonged to a very evangelical church, and it was obvious that God was working overtime to prevent a complete breakdown.

Her husband is a gem. His smile, faith, patience

and intestinal fortitude were significant therapeutic benefits for Char. I calculated that he would be a good buffer in the therapeutic process.

TREATMENT FOR CHAR

I generally use the type of treatment dynamics that I find Biblically acceptable. Making sure you hear the problem accurately and empathetically is of primary importance, but I usually follow that up with some verses from the Bible. I quote Ephesians 4:26

> **"Be angry, but do not sin; do not let
> the sun go down on your anger, and
> give no opportunity to the devil."**

There are also four problem-solving steps which Jesus set forth in his Sermon on the Mount. Psychology does not describe them in this sequence, but could very well take a lesson from Jesus. Matthew 18:15-17

> **"If your brother (any person) sins against (trespass
> against or offend) you, go and tell him (her)
> his (her) fault between you and him (her) alone.
> If he hears you you have gained your brother."**

> **"But if he (that person) does not listen, take
> one or two others along with you, that every
> word may be established in the mouth of two
> or three witnesses."**

> **"If he (that person) refuses to listen to them,
> tell it to the church (professional capacity)."**

> **"If he (that person) refuses to listen even to
> the church, let him be to you as a Gentile and
> a tax collector." (Let him go to hell!)**

These verses set up the structure in which suppressed negative feelings can be brought forth. I am very careful to teach that such negative feelings do not come out improperly.

TREATMENT WHICH USES CONFESSION

I understand very clearly that the "sharing of feelings" which psychology uses, is geared to enable a person to speak up without accusation, blame, condemnation, bad words, angry charges, and all the behaviors which incite more of a riot than bring peace. I proceed to teach very precisely, what Tom Gordon teaches in Parent Effectiveness Training, that all this should be done with confessional "I sentences". Psychology uses the term "own". We have to "own" how we feel, rather than say what we think of the person whom we believe hurt us.

Three weeks after we started therapy, Char was hospitalized for recurring violent stomach pains. While in the hospital one of the medical doctors spoke harshly to her about all the "pains in your head". Char was angry after she got out of the hospital. The doctor who layed the long and painful "put down" on her was a medical person covering for her regular doctor.

She believed me that this was a valid situation in which to speak up. In that session I helped her put her feelings down on paper, in letter form. She rewrote the letter and sent it, with a copy to her regular doctor. That took a lot of courage and belief in my interpretation of the message Jesus gave us about speaking up. She was tickled she wrote the letter, but when the doctor left town a month later, she did acknowledge some guilt feelings about writing the letter.

CHAR WRITES TO HER PARENTS

Six weeks into therapy she had the courage to write about her past hurt feelings to her parents. She had practiced on the doctor. She had also practiced on a local dishwasher repairman, who said, "Well, you do not have to be nasty about It." Slightly miffed, she did get heard and got the repair. Next, she needed to "own" and "confess" the anger (Galatians 5:19) (sin) she had been carrying around for years. The following letter was written. Some details are altered to preserve anonymity.

Dear (Parents)

I want to write something to you that I have wanted to say for years, but I never knew how to write it. I hope I can say it right. I have been hurting for quite a while. It happened again in the hospital the other day when I was there for my stomach pains. I was glad you came, but I felt so distant from you. I did not feel warmth from you, and I wanted so much for you to touch me and pray over me.

Something is wrong with our relationship. I feel so loved by my husband, but that same feeling is not there with you, my parents. I do not feel accepted, appreciated or loved when I am home. For a long time, I thought you were happy that I was married and no longer at home. I have felt like I was the black sheep of the family. Yet, I never could figure out what I did wrong. I'm sorry to report that I felt I did not belong in our family. I felt I was a burden to all of you.

My physical handicap seems to stand in the way. I felt criticized for my way of talking. I'd try to change to please you. I could not do better so I felt like a failure. I always felt I was blamed for my talk, but I had a problem trying to figure out how come I was blamed when I was born that way.

The other thing is my hay fever. The doctors diagnosed it, yet I never felt right about the attacks. I felt I was not supposed to get them, but I could not stop them, so I would feel guilty.

I feel my brother and my husband accept me. Neither of them knock me down. These are my feelings. I cry a lot. I am tense and cannot relax, so I get sick a lot.

I have tried to honor my father and mother, but the Bible also says I should not bottle my feelings. (Ephesians 4:26) The Bible says I should speak up. Matthew 18:15-17. I still want to honor you, but I also have to speak up. I want your love and care more than anything in the world.

Love, Your daughter

EFFECTIVE BIBLICAL THERAPY FOR CHAR

The letter touched deep emotions and created a predictable stir. Persons who receive such "confessions" and requests for change become hurt. They personalize it as intensely as the one who failed to speak up for years. The pent up emotions need to blow off. They do. They always do. But that is a requirement for healing. What stayed inside for so many years had to come out. You can go to a psychoanalyst for 2 years and not have as much benefit as going through 1 week of Biblically oriented confrontation.

Char's husband listened to much of what was communicated over the telephone, and played the "buffer" role until he went over to talk face to face. Then he set up a time for them all to talk about their feelings, and for Char to stake a claim for more love and warmth. In that session, the parents, brothers and sisters also stated their hurts over the years gone by. It was predictably beneficial, for all of them claimed to be Christians.

I have gone through this procedure innumerable times and have never had it backfire. I have a file full of letters that I have helped people write. Some sent them. Some memorized the "I sentence" ideas, and went over to the person whom they felt "bugged" them, sharing the ideas, and finding peace. Never, has the word of God fallen short for the believers that used it in all its power to bring peace between themselves and another.

Char has not been in the hospital in the past 3 years. Her relationship with her parents and siblings is superb. There is love, warmth and peace.

Char could have saved herself years of hurt, if she had been taught, from the Bible, to assert herself, and confess that she was living in the sin of "anger", "strife", and "enmity" (Galatians 5:20). Clergy need to preach more sermons on the effect of suppressed (conscious) and repressed (unconscious) negative feelings. Protestant clergy preach on confession to God, but we need to return to direct face-to-face confession for problem-solving here on earth.

Char's husband commented later, "I spent $50.00 a month on vitamins before my wife went into counseling and learned how to eliminate the anger she had learned to keep inside." This underscores the need for persons to look for help from wholistically oriented treatment programs. There are new clinics opening where the medical and psychological therapists work together. They are creating Wellness Centers or Wholistic Health Centers to help persons become well. These centers focus on multiple factors and treat the person with multiple impact treatment programs.

CONFRONTATION, CONFESSION, FORGIVENESS

Imagine, one day you are out playing football. Your team wins. You are on your way back to the locker room. Your sweetheart makes her way through the crowd and rushes to plant a proud kiss. You have heavy shoes and you step on her feminine clad foot. Suddenly, she is in pain. What does she say?

"You big Jerk, where are your manners? You are just a dumb clod. You do not deserve to win. You are just stupid."

I rather doubt she would say that; not unless there was a long history of such behavior. I rather think she might say,

"Hey Honey, you're hurting my foot. **(Confrontation)**

This is a mind confrontation. It is giving feedback on behavior. The comment has anger in it. There is caring in it. It is reminiscent of David Augsberger's book, entitled Caring Enough to Confront. After this mild confrontation I would expect the football player to say,

"Oh, sorry, I didn't mean to; these big shoes, you know." **(Confession)**

This is a confession. He quickly saw his problem, and out of love and an awareness of imperfection, said, "I'm sorry." Now, I expect the final comment to come from the sweetheart,

"Oh, I understand. That's alright." __(Forgiveness)__

In miniature, this is what I see as the appropriate interchange when someone feels put down or hurt. There should be no slam, no blast, no Vesuvius erruption of anger. The offended person needs only to use self-control while __confronting__ the person who did the hurting. When the person being confronted "owns" or __confesses__ their wrong doing or accidental behavior, then the offended person can __forgive.__

If you do not tell a person he or she is hurting you, how can he say "I am sorry.", and then how can you forgive? Forgiveness is the end result and maintains the relationship. Unforgiven negative feelings have a detrimental effect on a person's health, so go forth today and resolve those negative feelings you have been carrying around too long. You can probably save some pain now, or prevent some future illness.

I LEARNED THE HARD WAY

I was in my first church as an associate pastor, in full charge after the senior pastor left for another church. That made me extremely busy. One day, I received some membership papers in the mail from another church, for people I had never seen. I was impulsive and quite unthinking when I dashed off a note, saying something like, "I do not know who these people are, and I do not appreciate having people I do not even know, want to be members of my church. Sounds like trash membership and I do not need that." I mailed it.

Two weeks later, a well dressed stranger stood at my office door, with a Bible in his hand. I went to inquire, and the first thing he did was introduce himself. Then he pointed to Matthew 18:15 and began to read.

> "If your brother sins against you, go
> and tell him his fault, between you
> and him alone."

I listened and was totally dumbfounded as to what was going on. This gentleman identified himself as the clergyman from the church to which I had returned the membership papers with the untasteful note. He asked if he could come in and talk. We must have talked for an hour, after he "confronted" me, I "confessed" (repented is a better word here), and he "forgave. I had not remembered ever hearing a sermon on Matthew 18:15-17. This was the best lesson. It surpassed in value, many psycyology classes I had taken.

Since that time, I have both used it for myself, and taught it to countless others. I have used it with my father, mother and family. I speak up in countless ways. From time to time, I am kindly chided by my wife and children that it is still possible to "turn the other cheek" a bit more. Yes, I believe that, and I try to hold the speaking up and the shutting up in balance. I confess, it is a struggle, but I work at holding myself within the confines of the paradox, or the polarities of "turn the other cheek" and "let not the sun go down on your wrath".

"He who conceals hatred has lying lips."
Proverbs 10:18

DISCUSSION

1. In the story of the man healed at the pool of Bethesda, Jesus said, "See, you are well. Sin no more, that nothing worse befall you." Try to speculate on what sin or sins he might have committed.

2. In Luke 5:17-26, there is the story of Jesus healing the man stricken with "palsy" who was lowered through the roof. Jesus said, "Son, thy sins are forgiven." Jesus went on to say that it is as easy to heal as to forgive sins. Did Jesus mean to say that the man's sins had caused his "palsy"?

3. This chapter focused on illness coming from suppressed negative feelings. How big or how long do you think people have to endure negative feelings before illness sets in?

4. This book helps to define a number of stress factors which can overwhelm us. Read the titles of the chapters again. Then discuss how many of these areas have to be stressful before a person becomes ill.

5. In the story of Char, we see someone who had never been taught to speak up. What percentage of the people in the church do not speak up?   at work? in a bar?   on the beach?   in the classroom?   in congress? etc.

6. Would anyone be willing to share how they learned to speak up, and what success you have had?

7. The Bible seems to tell people both to speak up and turn the other cheek. How can we decide when to do which one?

8. Is the idea of speaking up about 50% and keeping silent about 50% of the time a good way to handle things?   How about speaking up 1 in 2, or 1 in 3, or 1 in 4, or 1 in 5 times, or 1 in 10 times?   How much can you absorb before you have to speak up?

Chapter 6

JOB BURNOUT

"Come unto me all you that labor and are heavy laden and I will give you rest." Matthew 11:28

If you do not like your job your chances of Job Burnout increase. The logic is simple. Suppressed negative feelings are destructive. The Apostle Paul warned about the destructive effect of letting "the sun go down on your wrath". Therefore, a person needs to deal with the negative feelings on the job. Perhaps it will require settling injustice feelings, cleaning up contaminated relationships, verbalizing instead of suppressing feelings, or finding compensating positive input in "off hours" so that the job is tolerable.

Fill out the inventory on the following page to analyze the extent of your Job Burnout symptoms.

JOB STRESS

(Burnout Inventory)

Pick out the most appropriate response. Write the number
of that response in the space provided by that statement.

0.Never   1. Rarely   2. Occasionally   3. Sometimes
4. Frequently   5. Almost always

(Housewives, please substitute "home" or "housework".)
(Students, please substitute "school" or "schoolwork".)

1. _____ I have headaches at work.
2. _____ I feel moody, restless or depressed at work.
3. _____ I feel discouraged. I work harder and enjoy it less.
4. _____ I have lost interest in my work.
5. _____ I see myself withdrawing and less social.
6. _____ I get irritated with the demands of people.
7. _____ I am making more mistakes or am more forgetful.
8. _____ I get upset about the way things are going at work.
9. _____ I get tired and drowsy at work.
10. _____ I miss work due to illness, colds and flu.
11. _____ I have gained or lost weight.
12. _____ I get tired of all the rules or obligations.
13. _____ I think about looking for a different job.
14. _____ I am bored at work.
15. _____ I am on tranquilizers or anti-depresant medication.
16. _____ I stop to have a drink with friends after work.
17. _____ I do drugs after work. ("pot", "uppers", "downers")
18. _____ I am having trouble sleeping.
19. _____ I feel in bondage at work; no way up or out.
20. _____ I have an elevated blood pressure.
21. _____ I have indigestion, heartburn.
22. _____ I dred getting up to go to work.
23. _____ I use my time less efficiently.
24. _____ I have been blowing up at people.
25. _____ I feel like a failure, or feel inferior.

_____________TOTAL   (Range 0 – 125)

(Enter this score in the summary SCORING on Page 358)

INTERPRETATION

0 – 25   Your JOB STRESS score shows very little stress. There may be times when your job does not give you the satisfaction you want, but the lack of stress-related symptoms indicates that you are coping fairly adequately.

26 – 50   Your JOB STRESS score indicates mild stress at work. If your score is closer to 26, there is a mild stress, but if it is closer to 50 you are reaching serious levels. The human body can tolerate sizeable amounts of stress in one area such as a job. However, if stress levels in other areas of your life are exceeding normal limits the compounded effect may be serious enough to bring on illness.

51 – 75   Your JOB STRESS score is above average for your work. This may not be a problem if stress levels are not elevated in other areas of your life, or if this level of stress at work is temporary. If, however, you have felt the way your score shows for many months, you should do some more evaluation of all the stress areas in your life. Nutritional levels may be poor enough to make you not like work. Lack of exercise or lack of sleep may set you up for some of the symptoms you checked. Poor interpersonal relations could be undermining your coping capacity. Check all the areas in your life for elevated stress scores and work on elimination of those stresses.

Above 76   Your JOB STRESS score shows that you are under more stress than you should be. There may be other factors causing you to have some of your symptoms. Poor nutrition, lack of exercise, poor communication with others, suppression of negative feelings, marital conflict and medical problems are some of the possible compounding factors. It might even be adviseable for you to think of changing jobs.

JOB BURNOUT FOR MANY REASONS

Victor was a client, age 31, single, living at home, plenty of money, shy, and hard working. But Victor was depressed. He had turned to reading the Bible, and was searching for a church that might help him solve his problems better than his own church. He even thought about mission work. He was searching for health and happiness.

After several sessions I administered a paper-and-pencil test for Hypoglycemia. His scores were high enough to refer him for a 5 hour Glucose Tolerance Test for low blood sugar. He was diagnosed a hypoglycemic, and began to use the nutritional treatment. Victor got his old self back. He retained interest in spiritual matters, and became happy at work once more.

Victor was going through Job Burnout, but not from the traditional reasons like disliking the boss, or disliking work conditions, marital conflict, poor pay or benefits. He was suffering burnout due to fatigue, restlessness, indecision, mood fluctuation and other symptoms of hypoglycemia. It affected his body, mind, and spirit.

CAUSES OF BURNOUT

Multiple factors are prevalent in persons who feel "burnout", and the list of those factors can be quite lengthy. Frederick W. ILfeld, Jr., of the University of California (Davis), made of a study of 2,299 persons in the Chicago area, and the report is published in Psychological reports, 1976. His team used the following items to make an evaluation of Job Stress.

1. "income is not right for my job"
2. "a chance I may be out of a job."
3. "work has   (bad) fringe benefits..."
4. "work that you cannot handle"
5. "under pressure to keep up with new ways..."
6. "in danger of illness or injury on the job."
7. "do the same thing over and over again."
8. "cannot count on a steady income."
9. "(The work is not) preparing me for a better job."
10. "have to do tasks no one else wants."
11. "lot of noise on your job."

12. "work too many hours."
13. "treated unfairly by another person."
14. (treated) "as you are a person without feelings."
15. (less) "chances for increased earnings..."
16. "work in a lot of dirt or dust."
17. "people....unfriendly."
18. (being) "told you are doing a good job."
19. "people (do not) come to you for your opinion..."

Each of these is a stress factor in itself. It would be an enormous task to identify every possible stressor. Nevertheless, job stress, and the burnout from it, is one fundamental category, and it has been researched a great deal. Hopefully, as you look at this list, it may help you determine whether or not you suffer from Job Burnout.

SYMPTOMS OF BURNOUT

As yet, there is no universal set of symptoms and scales to judge accurately the buildup and critical stages for burnout to occur. There is a Staff Burnout Scale for Health Professionals (SBS-HP), available through London House Management Consultants, 1550 Northwest Highway, Park Ridge, Illinois 60068. Their test includes the following symptoms.

1. fatigue
2. missed work due to colds
3. headaches on the job
4. increased alcohol consumption after work
5. more marital or family difficulties
6. feeling the desire to take tranquilizers
7. loss of interest in the work
8. frequent thoughts of quitting
9. increased anger or irritation with people
10. trouble getting along with fellow employees
11. very concerned regarding personal welfare
12. avoidance of the supervisor
13. lowered work performance
14. rules and regulations seem to reduce interest
15. work environment seems depressing
16. feel uncreative and understimulated
17. often think about finding a new job

18. worry about job interferes with sleep
19. feeling of little room for advancement
20. avoidance of interaction on the way to work

Listen to your feelings. Do they tell you that you are either "burned out" or burning out? While this inventory may not have been made for your type of work, the issues may be the same for you. Take seriously what is happening to you. Stress at work may truly be coming from your job, but the stress on the job may not necessarily be the cause, but the effect of other problems. Insufficient sleep is a problem, because the body's neurotransmitters are re-manufactured during the time of sleep. With lack of sleep, the chemicals such as serotonin, actecholine, and dopamine, may be in short supply. Such short supply may bring on irritability, fatigue, or other symptoms. Poor nutrition, with lots of calories, but low in vitamins and minerals can add to, and compound the "burnout" potential. Do not blame your job, until you have made sure that you are eating, sleeping, exercising, relaxing, and resolving conflict.

MOSES — THE FIRST CASE OF POTENTIAL BURNOUT

The Israelites had safely passed through the Red Sea, after escaping Egypt. God had provided Manna for food, and water from the rock. With victory over Amalek, they settled down, and began to bicker.

> "On the morrow Moses sat to judge the people, and the people stood about Moses from morning til evening. . . .(Jethro, Moses' father-in-law, said,) You and the people with you will wear yourselves out, for the thing is too heavy for you. You are not able to perform it alone. . . .Choose able men who are trustworthy and who hate a bribe; and place such men over the people as rulers of thousands, of hundreds, of fifties, and of tens. . . . If you do this, and God so commands you, then you will be able to endure, and all this people also will go to their place in peace."
>
> Exodus 18: 13-23

I never cease to be amazed at the wisdom of the Godly men of the Bible. Jethro is the first "One Minute Manager", which idea is enjoying a revival in the current best selling literature. Not much credit is given to Jethro for today's lucrative sales of the same idea, and that is somewhat of an embarrassment for the church's lack of initiative.

COMBATING BURNOUT THROUGH MANAGEMENT

Jethro had the "bigger picture". Jethro saw the "forest", while Moses could only see the individual "trees". Moses had to get the bigger picture in order to survive. Part of the reason persons do not survive today, is that they do not ever look for the bigger picture -- the "forest". Burdened with "nose to the grindstone" dedication, they cannot look up and catch a vision of a thousand grind stones. Fearful, from "short-sighted" preoccupation with details, there is no time to dream, plan, organize, structure, and burst ahead.

I can be like Moses; so busy with the daily work of counseling that I fail to manage myself. I can get into such one-on-one interaction, that the larger task of helping others become equipped for counseling, slips by. My current endeavors, embodied in my writing, are the result of forcing myself to look at a "bigger picture". It is actually very strenuous and very rewarding to transcend day-to-day demands.

You need to get the "bigger picture" -- the vision that enables you to transcend daily demands and become a manager. I know that circumstances prevent us at times, but these situations should not tie us down perpetually. Dream a bit. Let your fantasy go. Ask God what else there is in the world for you to do. Pray about it. Talk to your Christian friends, to your pastor, to your family, and to significant people who, themselves, have demonstrated a self-management style.

Your vision or goal may not be in your work. You may indeed catch the spirit of service or involvement. There is nothing like giving away what you do not have, to get back what you wanted in the first place. That is what happens when you serve. If you cannot get out of yourself, your own preoccupation with yourself may be your worst enemy. Our narcissistic bent to this preoccupation is a part of our sinful human nature. The mind can be so bent inward. The spirit can be so bent toward regression, that pro—gression spins, with no forward movement. The healthy people of this world catch visions, and pursue them. They serve, help and get involved. They structure what it takes to carry out the vision. They manage personal and family schedules, money, will, and put a structured schedule of the steps it takes to achieve the end result. Like Moses, they manage themselves better so they can serve better.

KING DAVID COUNTERACTS POTENTIAL ILLNESS

King David always had problems with the Amalekites. A band of Amalekite soldiers raided Ziklag, in the Negeb (southern Palestine), and carried off all the citizens, cattle and property, including two of David's wives. When others heard, and wanted to "stone" David, David took 600 men and pursued the Amalekites. David followed them with the help of an abandoned servant of an Amalekite. In the pursuit 200 of King David's men became too "exhausted". David left them with the "baggage", and went on to find and kill every one of the Amalekite soldiers. There was considerable "booty" to take back, but the 400 fighting soldiers did not want to share with the 200 who had stayed with the "baggage".

King David saw two potentially conflicting groups in his army. David made a decision to promote unity.

> David said, "You shall not do so, my brothers, with what the Lord has given us; he has preserved us and given into our hand the band that came against us. Who would listen to you in this matter? For as his share is, who goes down into the batle, so shall his share be who stays by the baggage; they shall share alike. And from that day forward he made it a statute and an ordinance for Israel to this day." (I Samuel 30:23-25)

David did not want to see a disgruntled minority. David wanted to preserve the "whole". David did not want injustice feelings to grow large in a disenfranchised group. David did not want such feelings to lay smoldering inside the hearts of his people. David knew how to prevent the rebellion which comes from repressed anger.

Scientists have determined that good relationships between working persons is a central factor in individual and organizational health. (Argyris,C, Integrating the Individual and the Organization. N.Y., Wiley, 1964) and (Cooper,C.L., Group Training for Individual and Organizational Development, Basel, Switz., S. Karger, 1973) King David seems to have known this instinctually, or divinely, and covertly set forth a health law for his people.

JESUS COUNTERACTS ILLNESS—PRONE TYPE A

Current research into the causes of Coronary Heart Disease (CHD), points to the more aggressive person as the one with the largest incidence of CHD. Type B personality is more passive. It sounds like Martha and Mary.

> "(Jesus) entered a village; and a woman named Martha received him into her house. And she had a sister called Mary, who sat at the Lord's feet and listened to his teachings. But Martha was distracted with much serving and she went to him and said, Lord, do you not care that my sister has left me to serve alone? Tell her to help me. But the Lord answered her. Martha, Martha, you are anxious and troubled about many things. One thing is needful. Mary has chosen the good portion, which shall not be taken away from her."
> (Luke 10:38-42)

Martha appears to me to be much like the Type A personality, which is researched, and shown to be more prone to illness.   I'll let you make up your own mind about Martha. We do need her kind in this world, just as we need the Type B personality, but the Type A personality does have higher incidence of Cardio-vascular illness.   Here is an abbreviated list of the characteristics.

TYPE B (Mary)				TYPE A (Martha)		
1	2	3	4	5	6	7

Leaves things unfinished — Must get things finished
Calm, unhurried about appts. — Never late for appts.
Not competitive — Highly competitive
Listens well — Anticipates other's conversation
Never in a hurry — Always in a hurry
Able to wait calmly — Uneasy when waiting
Easygoing — Always going full speed
Takes one thing at a time — Does several things at once
Slow and deliberate in speach — Speedy, vigorous speech
Concerned about self satisfaction — Wants recognition
Slow doing things — Fast doing things
Easygoing — Hard driving
Expresses feelings openly — Holds feelings in
Has large No. of interests — Few interests outside of work
Satisfied with job — Ambitious, wants advancement
Never sets own deadlines — Often sets own deadlines
Feels limited responsibility — Always feels responsible
Never judges things in terms of numbers — Often judges performance in terms of numbers
Casual about work — Takes work very seriously
Not very precise — Very precise (about details)

If you wish to score yourself choose a number between
1 and 7, which represents where you are between 1 (Mary
type) and 7 (Martha type). Thon add up your score for
the 20 characteristics.

ANALYSIS OF YOUR SCORE

Total score of 110 – 140 You are Type A.
      High risk of developing cardiac illness,
      especially if you smoke.
Total score of   80 – 109 You are a Type A^2.
      You are prone to cardiac problems.
Total score of   60 – 79   You are Type AB.
      You are a mixture of A and B patterns.

Total score of   30 – 59   You are Type B².
        Your behavior is on the less–cardiac–prone end
        of the spectrum.   You are more relaxed.
Total score of   0 – 29   You are Type B₁.
        You are quite far removed from the high risk
        persons who are prone to Coronary Heart Disease.
(Credit: Dr.   Howard I. Glazer, director of behavior
management systems at EHE Stresscontrol Systems.
Inc.)

WHAT SCIENCE HAS TO SAY REGARDING TYPE A

Cardiologists, Meyer Friedman and Ray Rosenman spent 10 years (1960-1970) investigating 35,000 men, aged 31-59 for Coronary Heart Disease (CHD).   Of the 257 who had developed CHD, 70 percent of them were classified as Type A.   Type A's were three times more prone to have cardiac problems than Type B's, even if Type B's smoked, or had high blood pressure, or had a family history which included heart attacks. (see Type A Behavior and Your Heart, by Friedman and Rosenman, New York; Knopf, 1974)

WHAT JESUS HAS TO SAY ABOUT TYPE A

Research science is saying that illness results from a life style which includes a multiple number of factors. Jesus did not warn Martha about impending illness if she kept her style of life.   Yet, Jesus did say, "Mary has chosen the good portion."   Clergymen are inclined to press home the conclusion that Mary was more spiritual. That may well be true. Scientific research might suggest that the "good portion" Jesus spoke about, may be enjoying a healthier life.

HEALING RESULTS FROM STRESS REMOVAL

Healing results from surgery, medication, and therapeutic treatments of many kinds.   Never neglect them.   Moreover, use them, but do not stop there.   There are times when others can "rescue" you from the folly of your life-style which has brought on your illness.   There are other times when only God may be able to rescue you from your indulgences.   But finally, there are times when your systematic exorcism of debilitating stress factors in your life may be the final weight which is lifted from the overload of your life. Healing results from stress removal. Your stresses may come from multiple sources. Your job may be a large source of your stress, or stress in other areas of your life may show up in decreased performance on your job. Whatever the source. Go after your stress and scuttle it, for your health's sake.

DISCUSSION

1. Name as many factors as you can which contribute to Job Burnout, or illness on the job.

2. Name as many symptoms of Job Burnout as you can.

3. Jethro, Moses father-in-law, forsaw Moses becoming overloaded with "judging" the people. Jethro suggested that Moses break up his responsibilities, and delegate them to others. How can that advice help you in your home? In your job? And in the church?

4. Jethro could see the "big picture", while Moses was bogged down. Who helps you when you are bogged down? Who are the persons we can turn to when we get bogged down?

5. What makes people fail to seek help when they get bogged down with the daily job routines?

6. When King David declared that the soldiers who protected the baggage would have equal share with the soldiers who fought in battle, he was promoting good relations. What is the connection between good relationships on the job and health?

7. King David promoted justice and fairness on the job. How much stress from unequal or unfair treatment can the average person stand? Can you stand more if you are a Christian?

8. Martha seems to be a Type A personality, and Mary a Type B personality. Jesus favored Mary. Did he commend Mary for her spirituality or for her life-style that would make her less prone to Coronary Heart Disease?

Chapter 7

ELIMINATING FINANCIAL STRESS

"Blessed is the man who fears the Lord, who greatly delights in his commandments. . . Wealth and riches are in his house. . . "   (Psalm 112:103)

"I love those who love me, and those who seek me diligently find me.   Riches and honor are with me, enduring wealth and prosperity."   (Proverbs 8:17–18)

On the next page there is a Financial Stress inventory for you to fill out.   How burdensome is your financial situation?   Score yourself.

FINANCIAL STRESS

Pick out the most appropriate response. Write the number
of that response in the space provided by that statement.

0. Never 1. Rarely 2. Occasionally 3. Sometimes 4. Frequently
5. Almost always

1. _______ I/We spend more than ¼ of my/our monthly income
for rent or house payment.
2. _______ I/We spend more than 1/3rd of my/our monthly
income for rent (or house payment) and install-
ment payments.
3. _______ I/We have unpaid debts like medical, dental, loans
for school, utilities or other.
4. _______ I/We cannot afford the kind of food I/we should have.
5. _______ I/We cannot afford the medical care I/we should
have for myself/ourselves.
6. _______ I/We cannot afford the clothing I/we should have
for the various seasons of the year.
7. _______ I/We cannot afford to eat out in a restaurant.
8. _______ I/We cannot afford the dental repairs I/we need.
9. _______ I/We cannot afford a vacation.
10. _______ I/We cannot afford to replace some furniture or
a car that is not working well.
11. _______ I/We cannot afford a home large enough for
myself/our family.
12. _______ I/We do not have any money saved or left over at
the end of the month.
13. _______ My/Our financial troubles come from using credit
cards.
14. _______ I/We spend too much money on alcohol, or cars,
or cigarettes, or lottory, or sports, or hobbies,
or eating out.
15. _______ I (or my spouse) buys costly items without consulting
(the other partner).
16. _______ I (or my spouse) gets layed off from work.
17. _______ I (or my spouse) has a low paying job.
18. _______ I (or my spouse) has a seasonal job.
19. _______ I am divorced.
20. _______ I am retired.   (Enter this score in the summary
                                    SCORING on Page 358)
_______________ TOTAL (Range 0 – 100)

INTERPRETATION

0 - 20   Your FINANCIAL STRESS score indicates a very low level of stress. Your very low score shows that you seem to be a fairly self-controlled person. Congratulations!

21 - 40   Your FINANCIAL STRESS score indicates that you are operating within a safe range. You appear to be moderately self-controlled and are able to curb your purchasing to fit within your limits. Hold on to your present style of money management. It seems to be neither too rigid nor too liberal.

41 - 60   Your FINANCIAL STRESS score indicates you are getting into the danger zone, or may already be there. Unemployment is some person's problem, but careless spending or excessive appetite for "things" can get control of persons and create financial stress. Focus on relationship. Budget so that money is spent on "relationship" more than on "things".

61 - 80   Your FINANCIAL STRESS score indicates that your lack of control over spending may be putting too much stress in your life. Perhaps unemployment has been a problem. With research suggesting that stress causes illness, you need to bring your income and expenses closer together. Bring your spending under control. Use a budget. Seek credit counseling.

81 - 100   Your FINANCIAL STRESS score shows you are not operating responsibly with your money. You need to cut out a number of your purchases or find the kind of work that can support your life style. You cannot overextend yourself to this extent, without eventually feeling stress in your body. and having that contribut to illness.

GOD DOES NOT INTEND CHRISTIANS TO BE POOR

If you are poor, and you are a Christian, then you should not be poor for very much longer. Conversion turns persons around from selfishness to sharing. Conversion turns persons around from "Poor Me" to faith and hope. Conversion turns persons around from their previous venting of hostility, to be givers of love, joy, peace, patience, kindness, goodness, faithful, gentleness and self-control. Such persons get hired more quickly and keep their jobs longer. The defeatism of the past becomes triumphant transcendence. The slothfulness of the previous existence spins into purposefulness and a sense of direction. False and deceptive excuses are replaced with honesty and commitment. Such persons are hireable, and soon they are no longer poor.

God wants you to be dedicated to His life-style, and when you walk with Him, He promises you will enjoy what He enjoys. Obviously, you cannot cheat very much without paying a price. Maybe you have been cheating a bit too much. The promises are clear. You must be dedicated to the Lord.

> "Therefore, I tell you, do not be anxious about your life, what you shall eat or what you shall drink, nor about your body, what you shall put on. Is not life more than food, and the body more than clothing? Look at the birds of the air; they neither sow, nor reap, nor gather into barns, and yet your heavenly Father feeds them. Are you not of more value than they? And which of you by being anxious, can add one cubit to his span of life? And why are you anxious about clothing? Consider the lillies of the field, how they grow; they neither toil nor spin; yet I tell you, even Solomon in all his glory was not arrayed like one of these. But if God so clothes the grass of the field, which today is alive and tomorrow is thrown into the oven, will he not much more clothe you, O men of little faith? Therefore, do not be anxious, saying, What shall we eat?, or What shall we drink?, or What shall we wear?

> **For your heavenly Father knows that you need them all. <u>But seek first his kingdom and his righteousness, and all these things shall be yours as well.</u>"** (Matthew 5:25-33)

Can you consider yourself a "born again" Christian if you are constantly poor and unemployed, so that you do not have food, clothes and shelter. People do have spells of hard luck, or "purging", but Jesus promised (above) in the Sermon on the Mount, that His Father would supply our needs, if we were faithful to Him.

POOR HEALTH AND FINANCIAL STRESS

There is a connection between your socio-economic level and your health. Poor income is stressful and all excessive stress produces illness. Therefore, a poorer income can precipitate a larger amount of illness. That makes excessive poverty one of the multiple factors which produces illness. This has been demonstrated in research projects. The Midtown Manhattan Study, conducted from 1952 - 1962, researched the causes of mental and emotional illnesses. This multi-factoral study interviewed a 1600 person cross-section of counseling cases in the New York -- New Jersey Metropolitan area. They investigated 8 childhood factors and 6 adulthood factors. The "economic" and "health" factors were analyzed in both. "No matter what the number of stress factors reported (with the exception of "none"), the low Socio-Economic-Status group consistently runs a higher risk." (Life Stress and Mental Health, by Thomas S. Langner and Stanley T. Michael, London, Free Press of Glencoe, 1963, Pg. 152) Persons in the lower Socio-Economic-Status (SES) levels had poorer "Physical Health" in childhood and currently. Their parents had "Poor Physical Health". They suffered more from "Childhood Broken Homes", from "Parent's Character Negatively Perceived" and from "Parents Quarrels". They had more "Work Worries", "Poor Interpersonal Affiliations", more "Marital Worries", and more "Parental Worries". (pp.104-105) In other words, there were greater numbers and higher incidence of multiple stress factors in the lives of persons in the lower Socio-Economic-Levels. "On questions where health is estimated, then, we find the low SES reporting poorer health." (p.273) Poverty and Illness go together, so healing and health require some relief from poverty. God promises to give that if we are committed to Him.

PERMANENT POVERTY IS NOT IN THE DIVINE PLAN

Christ gives you the good life. If you are committed to Christ and his life-style, you should not always be poorer and sicker. The promises of the Word of God are that the power of faith in God and His Son Jesus Christ, should enable you to get on top -- to transcend poverty and illness. There are oppressive forces, but Christ gives power to break out of financial bondage.

I cited the Midtown Manhattan Study to show that illness and poverty go together (statistically). But if the Lord God has promised to reward his faithful followers with both their needs and some degree of "prosperity", then the health level should rise with the rise in the income. Thus, you get some healing from being faithful to God. Strange as it may seem, healing and health are going to come to those whom God rewards with a higher income. This may seem like a somewhat circuitous route, but health and healing are result of a multiple number of factors, good finances being just one of them.

The Gospel has the power of elevating persons from poverty to prosperity. Dr. Elton Eenigenburg, of the Western Theological Seminary in Holland, Michigan, pointed out in a classroom lecture, that revivals start, usually, among persons in the lower income levels. The Reformation was not simply a religious reformation, but political and economic as well. The poor and disenfranchised declared their independence from the oppressive religious system. Zwingli, Luther and Calvin gave the poor a religious system which enabled them to transcend their plight. The converts first fled to the Netherlands and England in the mid 1500's, but within two generations the transcending and transforming power of the Gospel of Jesus Christ had given rise to a mighty migration to America, where the internal power of mind-over-matter, the transcendent Gospel, gave rise to a country that still seems to be transcending. There is power in the gospel, to lift people out of poverty. One hundred years of reformation then brought about a fairly middle and upper-middle class church. But now they could not minister to poor people.

So after one hundred years, approximately, another group of persons felt the need of reforming some of the malpractices of the stagnating churches. The intervening 100 years had seen some complacency creep in, so a movement of Anabaptists, coming from the poorer socio-economic levels, came to be born. That group of poor persons found the power of the Gospel, and they were transformed into middle class persons.

By the 18th century, state churches had become havens for the middle and upper-middle class people. Another revival among the poor was lead by persons who broke off from state churches, and began independent churches. The annals of revivalism are filled with stories of tent-crusades, saw dust trails, and altar calls as well as splits from the state supported churches. Those churches have again become our middle class churches.

In the 19th century, John and Charles Wesley preached to the poor, and began a Methodist movement, which, after about 100 years, is a middle to upper class church.

Now in the 20th century, the pentecostal movement is working mightily, and it finds its role largely among poorer persons. Let another hundred years go by and these churches will be middle or upper class churches, and God will have to start another revival among the newly poor and disenfranchised persons of the 21st century.

The Gospel simply lifts people out of poverty and poor health. You need to believe that, even though you may be temporarily troubled about your financial problems.

GOD WANTS YOU TO BE WEALTHY AND HEALTHY

The success of God's program depends on born-again winners. God has given his Word and Spirit to a small percentage of the world's population; to the ones who have agreed to carry the ball for Him. With that small band of persons He transformed Western Civilization from a band of Northern European barbarians into people who at least try to be helpful in this world. With an equally small band of the faithful, God has brought education and medicine to African and South American tribes. God gave them a spirit of freedom, and these peoples have thrown off the yoke of foreign oppression. Missionaries brought these things. Someone paid those missionaries. Money was needed and is still needed. God needs persons with love in their hearts, to make money and share it so that the Gospel can be communicated. Therefore, God wants you to be wealthy, and to share that wealth. God cannot have a group of poor and sickly people waiting around for Heaven to take them out of their misery. His program would become defunct. God needs you to make enough money, so that the proportion you give can become higher and higher. In that way the "yeast", the "salt" and the "light" of the Gospel can make this a better world in which to live. God wants you to be wealthy. It is a mutual blessing for Him and for you.

JESUS WAS WEALTHY

Carpentry contracting has made many person's prosperous. Jesus was a carpenter's son and supported himself and his spiritual ministry. He hob-nobed with the wealthy, befriended wealthy Lazarus, Mary and Martha, dined with wealthy Zaccheus, and used a wealthy man's tomb at his death. He wore a seamless robe, for which soldiers gambled, because it was too valuable to cut in pieces. During his ministry he likely received some contributions from believers and recipients of his healings. Judas held the money. He was the treasurer. It appears that Jesus disciples were wealthy enough to be self-supporting throughout the three year campaign ministry. Paul, the apostle, writing of Jesus, once said, "...though he was rich, yet for your sakes he became poor, that ye through his poverty might be rich." (II Corinthians 8:9) Jesus took his wealth and used it in service of the Kingdom of God. He did it all in three years. We need to share our wealth over a lifetime. It is not sinful to want to be wealthy, as long as the reason for your wealth is the glorification of God, as Jesus did.

RULE NUMBER ONE FOR PROSPERITY

You have to be committed to God and the Godly life-style for ongoing prosperity. That is the repeated message of the Old Testament. Abraham, Isaac, Jacob and Joseph were all rewarded with prosperity as a result of their divinely prescribed life-style. Then, after the Exodus, the recorded Word of God reminds the people that prosperity comes from a commitment to God and all that is righteous.

> **"You shall remember the Lord your God, for it is <u>he who gives you power to get wealth</u>, 'that he may confirm his covenant which he swore to your fathers, as at this day. And if you forget the Lord your God and go after other gods and serve them and worship them, I solemnly warn you this day that you shall surely perish."**
> **(Deuteronomy 8:18–19)**

For the next 1000 plus years, the children of Israel either prospered when they were faithful to God, or skidded downward toward poverty and extinction when they strayed from living the divine life-style. There were peaks of prosperity and power under Saul, David and Solomon, but God allowed the Philistines, Syrians, Assyrians, Babylonians, Medes and Persians to reduce the sinful people to poverty and misery for their lack of living the divine life-style. We have one short sentence, recorded regarding Uzziah, about 780 B.C. "As long as he sought the Lord, God made him prosper." This is essentially a major theme of the people of God. Solomon reduced it to a general principle, applicable to anyone.

> **"The reward for humility and fear of the Lord is riches and honor and life."** **(Proverbs 22:4)**

The principle of living the divine life-style is written deep in the scriptures. It is promised so often that it is small wonder that more persons do not take it more seriously. Listen to the Psalmist.

> "Praise the Lord. Blessed is the man
> who fears the Lord, who greatly delights
> in his commandments! His descendants
> will be mighty in the land; the generation
> of the upright will be blessed. <u>Wealth
> and riches are in his house,</u> and right-
> eousness endures for ever." (Psalm
> 112:1-3)

The Bible promises prosperity to those who live a divinely directed life-style. There may be times when prosperity gets washed away in natural disaster or personal calamity such as Job experienced. That is only a temporary setback. The faithfulness of the Job variety is eventually rewarded. In the meantime, continue to hold on to your faith like Job did. Meditate on the promises of God. Claim the promises of God. Recite the promises of God. Affirm the promises of God. Take all the scripture verses in this chapter and memorize, visualize, conceptualize, and actualize them.

LISTEN TO A SPECIALIST ON PROSPERITY

"Jack Hartman is a self-employed businessman. In 1974, when his business was on the verge of bankruptcy and he was on the verge of a nervous breakdown, he gave his life to Jesus Christ and started studying the Bible in great detail to learn what God said about solving financial and emotional problems. Jack put what he learned to good use. Today his business is growing very well. The Bible study which started with four people in his office in 1975 now has grown into a church with an average Sunday morning attendance of 1000 people." In his book Trust God For Your Finances (Word Associates, P.O. Box 3293, Manchester, NH 03105) Jack Hartman describes the laws for prosperity.

> 1. **Start every day with prayer, quiet time and reading the Bible.** (Matthew 6:33 and Luke 9:23)
>
> 2. **Surrender totally to God, and put Him in charge of everything.** (Proverbs 22:4 and Exodus 20:3)
>
> 3. **Mentally acknowledge that everything**

is God's, and we only have use of things. We are to share, not hoard. (I Timothy 6:7, Deuteronomy 10:14, Haggai 2:8, Mark 10:24-25)

4. Meditate (murmur, mutter) on the promises to enable the soul to be transformed into the kind of person God can bless. (Psalm 1:1-3, Joshua 1:8, Psalm 112:1-3)

5. Work hard. With spiritual stimulation people can rise earlier and accomplish more. (II Thessalonians 3:10, Proverbs 10:4, Proverbs 6:6-11)

6. Do not expect to get paid more than you are worth. Go the second mile. (Matthew 5:41, Proverbs 20:4, James 1:25)

7. Use strong faith. Constantly affirm God in the process of living. (Hebrews 4:2, 10:23)

8. You need to sow to reap. You must start giving money away to get it back. Practice the Golden Rule. (Matthew 7:12) (See also Mark 4:26-27, Matthew 7:20, Obadiah 1:15, II Corinthians 9:6-8, II Corinthians 9:10, Proverbs 11:24)

9. Contribute charity ("tithe") on the basis of what you would like to earn, rather than what you do earn. (Jack Hartman)

10. You cannot outgive God. (Luke 6:38, Galatians 6:7, Malachi 3:10, Ephesians 4:28, Psalm 41:1-2, Proverbs 22:9, Proverbs 28:27)

Jack Hartman has ups and downs in his business. When financial strains begin to appear and cash-flow isn't looking good, Jack asks his secretary to write checks for larger amounts and to greater numbers of needy, beginning with his church. He "sows" more "seed". Invariably, the tide of business turns and his income reaches larger and larger amounts.

You need to read Mr. Hartman's Biblically substantiated work, to appreciate his commitment and the rewards of that dedication. If you are in debt, and

in financial trouble, I recommend that you start with
the purchase of his book.

DISCUSSION

1. In the Sermon on the Mount (Matthew 5) Jesus says
   a Christian's needs will be supplied. Other scripture
   says we can be prosperous. Is there a formula that
   the more righteous a person is the more prosperous
   he may become?

2. If you can trace the economically transforming
   power of the Gospel from revivals, can you see it
   in born again people in the church?

3. If it is true that poor persons have more illness (See
   Midtown Manhattan study.) should the church fulfill
   Jesus' healing ministry by helping their church
   members get on top financially, by assisting, advising
   or giving loans?

4. Are there ways to become prosperous without being
   Godly?

5. If you do become temporarily wealthy through other
   than righteous means, how long will such wealth
   last?

6. Jack Hartman says you can "Give your way out
   of financial problems." Do you know anyone who
   has tried that, and been successful?

7. Which way to prosperity is most asssured, by living
   a divine life-style, or by getting an advanced education
   or degree?

8. Are Christians generally wealthier than
   non-Christians?

9. With wealth goes a lot of responsibility. What
   percentage of people simply will never become
   wealthy because they do not carry responsibility
   well?

10. If you have been sick, have lots of doctor bills and
    are behind on bills, would you send $5.00 to some
    other poor person this week?

Chapter 8

HEALING THE STRESS

FROM ALCOHOL

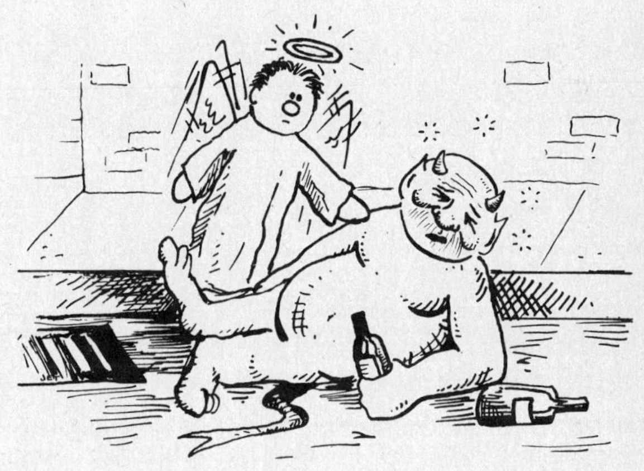

"Who has woe?
Who has sorrow?
Who has strife"
Who has complaints?
Who has needless bruises?
Who has bloodshot eyes?
THOSE WHO LINGER OVER WINE."
Proverbs 23:29–30

The symptoms of excessive alcohol consumption reflect problems for the excessive drinker and for the families of persons who consume excess alcohol. Take the following Alcohol Stress Inventory to analyze the intensity of this stress factor.

ALCOHOL STRESS INVENTORY

Pick out the most appropriate response. Write the number
of that response in the space provided by that statement.

0. Never 1. Rarely 2.Occasionally 3. Sometimes 4. Frequently
5. Almost always

(Put an "0" in all the spaces if you do not drink alcohol.)

1. _____ I have had to stay home from work after drinking.
2. _____ My family criticizes me for drinking.
3. _____ I am bolder and more talkative when I am drinking.
4. _____ My reputation is affected by my drinking.
5. _____ I feel remorse after I have been drinking.
6. _____ I spend money on alcohol that should go for bills.
7. _____ I drink with people below my economic standing.
8. _____ I neglect my wife and children when I drink.
9. _____ I have less ambition after I have been drinking.
10. _____ I have a special time of day that I really like to drink.
11. _____ I have an urge to drink the morning after drinking.
12. _____ I have difficulty sleeping after I have been drinking.
13. _____ My efficiency increases after drinking.
14. _____ My drinking affects my job or business.
15. _____ I like to drink to ease my worries or troubles.
16. _____ I drink when I am alone.
17. _____ I have some loss of memory, "blackouts" of what
            happened while I was out drinking.
18. _____ I have been treated or warned about my drinking.
19. _____ I feel more confident when I am drinking.
20. _____ I have been hospitalized for drinking.

_________________TOTAL (Range 0 – 100)

(Items in this list are adapted from The Chicago Program
For The Prevention of Progressive Alcoholism.)

(Enter this score in the summary SCORING on Page 358)

INTERPRETATION

0 - 15   Your ALCOHOL STRESS score is either zero, or so modest that you could hardly be stressing yourself with alcohol consumption. If you are honest with yourself on this inventory you are in a safe zone. You might have a low score but still get drunk. Be careful that your drinking does not produce stress in someone else's life. Do some reading about nutritional approaches to the prevention of alcohol abuse.

15 - 25   Your ALCOHOL STRESS score is indicating that your consumption of alcohol may be putting a stress on your health as well as, possibly, putting a stress on your relationship with others. Your score indicates that you probably know of this stress already. The connection between consumption and illness has been researched, and there is a definite connection between excess alcohol usage and longevity of life. You can combat your need for alcohol through A.A., nutritional and personal counseling.

25 - 35   Your ALCOHOL STRESS score indicates you definitely have a problem with alcohol consumption, but are either ignoring it or hiding it. It is not really the amount you drink, but the effect of it on you. Alcohol dependency increases in time of stress, and the alcohol you consume drains your nutritional and emotional reserves. It alters your judgment and leads to further stress. You should definitely be in Alcoholics Anonymous until you get your alcohol consumption under control.

Above 35   Your ALCOHOL STRESS score suggests you probably need treatment for alcoholism in an inpatient setting (hospital treatment center). You need to have medical supervision and strong treatment programs. You need to learn about nutrition to fight off cravings. You need to join A.A. after you are discharged. You need a total treatment program.

ALCOHOL AND ILLNESS

The illness producing effect of alcohol has been known for a long time. Not until recently have we known the statistical effect. Health Hazard Appraisals are questionaires which industry is using to establish health risk among its workers. They resulted from studies during the 1970 census, and connect health risk with a variety of things like overweightness, cholesterol, smoking, alcohol consumption, nutritional intake, excercise, and family history. These Health Hazard Appraisals have been used to alert persons to the increased risk of sickness and early death for persons who are not using some self-control over the ingredients of their life-style. There is now a fairly well established coorelation between alcohol consumption, earlier illness and premature death.

ALCOHOL AFFECTS MORE THAN JUDGMENT

Alcohol affects the biochemistry of the body's cells, depletes the body of vitamins, upsets metabolism of food, distorts the mineral balance, confounds the activity of hormones and generally weakens the cell structure, making disease happen.

I have heard a thousand times that alcohol is destructive, affecting judgment, unleashing anger and abuse, using up the money which is needed for children, causing accidents and fires, leading to economic and professional ruin. But not until recently have I heard about the cellular destruction which induces illnesses, cancer being one of them.

In my training at the Institute of Religion at the Texas Medical Center, I became acquainted with a person who was doing research on cancer. He was looking for a virus, a mutation, a genetic aberation. Much of that was fruitless. Alcohol is now known to be a contributing stress factor to cell structure changes, along with stress, poor nutrition, etc. Smoking is another.

HEALING AND ALCOHOL DO NOT WORK TOGETHER

As Chaplain in the American Mission Hospital in Bahrain, Arabian Gulf, I visited with an American oil driller who had received a large gash in his leg from some equipment. He lay in the hospital waiting for the leg to heal.   When it didn't, investigation revealed that he was drinking alcohol excessively. This was producing high blood sugar (a diabetic condition) so the wound would not heal. I am sure the man was unaware of the conflict of alcohol and healing. You cannot expect God to circumvent His biochemical principles. You cannot expect healing when your alcohol consumption is setting the stage for the illness in the first place.

DON'T WASTE TIME PRAYING IF YOU DRINK ALCOHOL EXCESSIVELY

The following illnesses are strongly associated with drinking.

Cirrhosis
Hypertension
Gastritis
Pancreatitis
Cancer of the mouth
Cancer of the tongue
Cancer of the throat
Cancer of the esophagus
Cancer of the liver
Cancer of the pancreas
Cancer of the bowel
Diabetes

(1982 Report on Drug Abuse and Alcoholism)
(Joseph A. Califano, Jr.)

These are degenerative diseases. We bring them on by our life-style. They do not necessarily come from bacteria, germs, virus' and the like. These are life-style diseases which come more readily to those whose life-style includes large consumption of alcohol. You cannot expect healing, either from the doctor or from God, if you continue to irritate the biochemistry of your body with excessive alcohol.

"The alcoholic person lives 12 years less than the average person."

"The alcoholic person suffers twice

> the incidence of respiratory disease
> and cardiovascular disease as other
> people."

(Joseph F. Follmann, Alcoholics and Business)

Don't waste your time praying for health, happiness and long life if you plan to continue excessive alcohol consumption. However, if you now understand this healing problem, and you decide to cease, or at least drastically reduce your consumption, then I believe you are acting within the framework, within which God can work.

EXCESSIVE ALCOHOL — MORE THAN SIN

Sin can be forgiven. The price you pay for excessive alcohol consumption cannot be taken back, wiped clean, and totally forgotten. Alcohol speeds up the time clock of aging. Lines get drawn deeply. The skin becomes less resilient and will not regenerate as well. The fat which gets stored in the liver from excessive consumption of alcohol shunts off blood supply and a bit of the liver dies a little at a time. The hardening of the arteries, from excessive alcohol consumption (in part), is highly resistent to restoration, except perhaps, at times, when chelation therapy does help remove some of the plaque from inside the arteries. God can and does heal, but if you accelerate the process of aging through excessive alcohol consumption, you may never get that time back. Sin is easier on you than the effect of alcohol, for at least it can be removed through forgiveness. Ceasing alcohol consumption will generally halt the degenerative effect which has been put in motion, unless some "disease" process has already progressed too far.

Get off the notion that alcohol is only an offense to God. It truly is, but excessive alcohol consumption is an offense to yourself that you will pay for in some way. Alcoholism will force you to miss some of the "Good Life" of the Kingdom of God, here on earth.

In the Word of God we read of God's dislike for excessive alcohol consumption. The message comes through often.

> "Wine is a mocker, strong drink a
> brawler; and whoever is led astray
> by it is not wise.   Proverbs 20:1
>
> "The drunkard and the glutton will
> come to poverty."   Proverbs 23:21
>
> "The priest and the prophet have erred
> through strong drink, they are swollowed
> up of wine."   Isaiah 28:7
>
> "Nor drunkards . . . shall inherit the
> earth."   I Corinthians 6:10
>
> (Sins of the flesh) "Drunkenness".
> . . . . Galatians 5:21

There is no debate over the matter of excessive alcohol being an offense toward God. It is sin. God sent Jesus into the world, so that sin could be forgiven. Jesus was nailed to the cross for our sins. We are saved by grace, through faith, not of works. When we sin we have an advocate with the Father, Christ Jesus. All this never spoke to me like the the blazing facts of physical degeneration from excessive alcohol consumption. I am not a drinker, so I never had to worry, but I can now preach on the degenerative capability of alcohol stronger than most.

ALCOHOL — A GAME OF RUSSIAN ROULETTE

You do not know what chamber the bullet is in with alcohol. As you try to get your kicks out of this life, and load yourself with a bullet like alcohol, someone is going to get hurt.

> "One in every 2000 babies born has
> a physical or mental impairment because
> of alcohol the mother drank during
> pregnancy." (Joseph A. Califano)
>
> "Up to 64% of attempted suicides
> and 80% of those who succeed, involve
> alcohol." (Joseph A. Califano, Jr.)
>
> "Up to 64% of the drivers involved
> in fatal crashes in 1977, a year in
> which 50,000 people died in automobile

> accidents, had been drinking prior
> to the accident." (Joseph A. Califano, Jr.)

> "Falls are second only to automobile
> accidents as a cause of accidental
> death, and they account for more
> than 60% of injuries. Nearly one-half
> of those who die in falls have been
> drinking." (Joseph A. Califano, Jr.)

> "More than 50 percent of adult deaths
> from fires involve alcohol. Alcoholics
> are 10 times more likely to die in
> a fire than the population as a whole."
> (Joseph A. Califano, Jr. The 1982
> Report on Drug Abuse and Alcoholism)

We need to put some of our playfulness away, when there are serious health and longevity questions to deliberate. We need to turn to more of a mind-over-matter approach to life. Mind-over-matter is a simple notion of letting your ego listen just as much to your Superego (oughtness) as it tends to listen to the Id (want). Putting it in transactional analysis, the inner "adult" needs to take more command, and not let the inner "child" have so much power, so that the child-like inclinations are given their proper place, but no more.

SOMEONE SUBSIDIZES DRINKING COSTS

Non-drinkers subsidize drinkers indirectly, through paying their health insurance, but using it less than the problem drinker. We will never really know how much non-drinkers subsidize the health costs of drinkers. The cost is large, and it supports the persons who are hooked on alcohol.

> "The health care price tag for an
> alcoholic or problem drinker exceeds
> $2000 each year over and above the
> health care expenditures of the average
> non-alcoholic." (Joseph A. Califano,Jr.)

I was the therapist for the wife of a local alcoholic who spend his last days in the hospital. This alcoholic received all the heroics which were available by the local doctors. The bill came to over $100,000. Non-drinkers can not deduct part of their health insurance premium under "charity", but charity it is, for about 8,000,000 to 10,000,000 problem drinkers. We pay for the cleanup and repairs resulting from intoxication.

HEALING AS A MIND-OVER-MATTER SKILL

Stress management puts more responsibility back in the hands of the the person. We have such an in-trenched concept that illness comes from something outside of us, that we often sit back and do a "poor me" on the doctor, the preacher, and on God. We sit back psychologically, and say "Fix me", "Everyone else, help me." That is both irresponsible, and a violation of healing faith. Frequently, Jesus commanded an act of faith as part of the healing. **"Take up your bed and walk."** (to the paralytic at the Pool of Bethesda), **"Your faith has made you whole."** (To the woman who had an issue of blood for 12 years.) **"Go wash in the Jordan."** (To man born blind) THERE ARE SOME SITUATIONS WHEREIN, IF YOU DO NOT GET OFF YOUR DUFF AND DO SOMETHING, YOU SIMPLY WILL NOT BE HEALED. Faith is not simply a pacifier, but a guts approach to life and healing.

> **See, you are well! Sin no more, that nothing worse befall you." John 5:14**

The man at the Pool of Bethesda was warned about reverting to previous behavior which made him become ill. Since excessive alcohol consumption plays such a strong role in certain illness, healing and permanent health from that disease are dependent on a mind-over-matter approach. You either develop a moderate life-style, or you pay. And if your life-style must include excesses of alcohol consumption, then do not bother God, unless you are sorry enough to do everything to change your behavior.

DISCUSSION

1. Is alcohol consumption bad? Was alcohol consumed by Jesus? (Both wine and beer were available in N.T. times. Distilled liquor was not known until about the 800-900 A.D. when Scottish Highlanders used the process to make whiskey.
2. Why did the Apostle Paul allow Timothy to use wine "for your stomach sake"? (I Timothy 5:23)
3. If excessive consumption of alcohol sets persons up for a variety of illnesses, why don't people see this, and work harder at moderation?
4. The author is suggesting that a person whose life-style includes too much alcohol consumption, is wasting his time praying for healing from pancreatic cancer, cirrhosis of the liver, and the diseases that are alcohol related. Do you agree that that person is wasting his time praying? Is the church wasting its time praying for healing of an alcohol-related disease if the person will not quit drinking alcohol?
5. Sin can be forgiven, and sin can be cleansed from our lives. Is there a difference between the effect of sin and the effect of alcohol? The soul can be renewed. Can the body be renewed after alcohol's effect?
6. Should persons adopt a policy of total abstinence to keep from becoming problem drinkers or alcoholics?
7. There is a low rate of alcoholism among Jewish, Chinese American, and Italian-American people. What factors do you think contribute to that?
8. MADD is an organization of Mothers Against Drunk Driving. Do you have an organization like that in your community? How about organizing one?
9. What do you think of Alcoholics Anonymous? How can the church create more awareness about the illness and suffering created by excessive alcohol consumption?
10. Jesus' first miracle was to turn water into wine. (John 2:1-11) What can be done to teach people to maintain a mind-over-matter attitude like Jesus'.

Chapter 9

HEALING IF YOU SMOKE

SMOKING

"A custom lothsome to the eye,
**   – hateful to the nose,**
**   – harmful to the braine,**
**   – dangerous to the lungs."**
KING JAMES OF ENGLAND, 1604 A.D.

"Do you not know that your body is a temple of the Holy Spirit within you, which you have from God.?"
GOD, 65 A.D.

The following Inventory lists both the symptoms of extensive smoking and the hazards of smoking in combination with other factors. Fill out the Inventory, if you smoke, and let it help you identify the potential problems of your smoking activity.

STRESS FROM SMOKING

Pick out the most appropriate response. Write the number
of that response in the space provided by that statement.

0. Never 1. Rarely 2. Occasionally 3. Sometimes 4. Frequently
5. Almost always

(Put an "0" in all the spaces if you do not smoke.)

1. _____ I smoke 20 cigarettes a day.
2. _____ I smoke more than 30 cigarettes a day.
3. _____ I smoke and take birth control pills.
4. _____ I smoke and drink alcohol.
5. _____ I smoke and work   around gas fumes, fabric smells,
          waxes, detergents, factory chemical fumes or
          other environmental odors.
6. _____ I smoke and eat very few vegetables or fruits.
7. _____ I have an elevated cholesterol level.
8. _____ I have high blood pressure.
9. _____ I have a resting pulse rate above 80. (Check it now.)
10. _____ I cough and need to get rid of sputum.
11. _____ I have sinus drainage or sinus headaches.
12. _____ I have shortness of breath.
13. _____ I have chest pains .
14. _____ I have nausea and vomiting.
15. _____ I have indigestion or ulcer.
16. _____ I have leg cramps or pains.
17. _____ I have laryngitis.
18. _____ I have blood in my urine.
19. _____ I have reduced sperm count.
20. _____ I have low sexual interest.
21. _____ I have hardening of the arteries .
22. _____ I have dry , ashen skin.
23. _____ I have facial wrinkles.
24. _____ I have poor sensitivity of taste and smell.
25. _____ I miss work due to colds and flu.

_______________ TOTAL (Range 0 – 125)

(Enter this score in the summary SCORING on Page 358)

INTERPRETATION

0 – – – –   Your STRESS FROM SMOKING score was zero. This indicates that you are not currently smoking. Research conclusions suggest you will live longer and have fewer medical problems.

1 – 20   Your STRESS FROM SMOKING score indicates that you smoke only a minimal amount, or you have not been smoking very long. If you must smoke, just remember that you are asking for a greater number of health problems.

21 – 40   Your STRESS FROM SMOKING score suggests your smoking is giving you some health problems. If you stop now, you will be putting yourself in a safe zone. Read books to give yourself motivation for stopping.

41 – 60   Your STRESS FROM SMOKING score suggests that you need to cut out this stress factor in your life. Smoking may not be the only stressor, and the accumulation of several stressors may be compounding the effects of smoking, or smoking may be compounding the effects of other stressors, producing the symptoms.

61 – 80   Your STRESS FROM SMOKING score is much too high. Your body is trying to tell you that it is irritated by the way it is being treated. It is reacting to the overstimulation, and is having difficulty coping. There may be other reasons, too, why your body is showing this amount of stress under "smoking". Quit smoking and see if some of your physical problems will heal.

Above 80   Your STRESS FROM SMOKING score is in the critical range. You cannot continue with these symptoms, and continue to smoke, without having serious consequences. Overload of stress factors will eventually cause a breakdown in the defense mechanisms of your body.

HISTORY OF SMOKING TOBACCO

Smoking tobacco was unknown in Bible times. The earliest evidence of smoking tobacco comes from a 5th century bas-relief found in the pyramidal ruins of the ancient Mayan civilization in Palenque, Mexico. This civilization was at its peak from 470 — 620 A.D. Tobacco is indigenous to the western hemisphere, and was used extensively in religious rites and sacred ceremonies. The Indians of the Americas smoked, chewed and snuffed tobacco. Pipestone, Minnesota takes name from the type of rock available there for making pipes. The Indians often blended their tobaccos with sumac and dogwood bark.

Christopher Columbus was probably the first person from the eastern hemisphere to observe the use of tobacco. The plant in Cuba, called "Caoba", was used, and Cuba was to become the cigar capital of the world years later.

Tobacco was brought to the eastern hemisphere sometime around 1550 or 1559. A Frenchman, named Andre de Thevet, in 1550, allegedly brought back tobacco seeds from South America, grew tobacco and distributed the seed. Others credit Francisco Hernandez de Toledo, physician to Philip II of Spain, as the first person to cultivate the seeds of tobacco in 1559. In 1560 tobacco was brought to the Fench court by Jean Nico de Villemain, the French ambassador to Lisbon. We get the name "nicotine" from this event and this person. Tobacco showed up in English ports in about 1565 A.D. and by 1614 London had 7000 tobacco shops.

Initially, tobacco was believed to be partly a medicine, and was used to treat migraines, colds, fever and the plague. This soon proved to be ineffective, and by the early 1600's it was opposed heavily by King James I of England, and banned in Spain, with the sentence of death to those who were caught. In less than a century after being introduced into the eastern hemisphere the Ottoman Emperor, Amurat IV, sentenced smokers to death. The Czar of Russia reintroduced whippings for smokers. A Shah had smokers impaled.

Settlers in Jamestown, Virginia, about 1600, found the local tobacco too bitter, and imported seeds from Spain which were milder. Tobacco growing flourished, and with the high demand for tobacco, settlers moved out from that Virginia colony in search of other land for the cultivation of tobacco. Delaware was founded as a colony for the primary purpose of exporting tobacco. The colony failed, due to Indian opposition, but Maryland was founded in 1634, again for the purpose of growing and exporting tobacco. Slowly pioneers pushed west and south for more and better land for tobacco.

Medical problems from the use of tobacco were being cited in the 19th century, but scientific investigation of the connection between cancer and smoking began in the 1920's. In the 1950's researchers began to find a statistical correlation between smoking and cancer. In late 1959 and early 1960 the American Cancer Society undertook a study of one million persons. By 1964 the Advisory Committee to the Surgeon General of the U.S. Public Health Serviced published,

> **"Cigarette smoking is causally related to lung cancer in men; the magnitude of the effect of cigarette smoking far outweighs all other factors. Data for women, though less extensive, point in the same direction. The risk of developing lung cancer increases with the duration of smoking and the number of cigarettes smoked per day and is diminished by discontinuing smoking."**

In 1965 the Federal Trade Commission enacted a law placing a warning on the package of cigarettes. In 1971 it became illegal to advertise cigarettes on television or radio. In 1985 smoking was no longer done on "prime time" television in the evening on the three major networks, except for characters portrayed which were less than respectable.

Latest data suggest that smoking is a "contributory factor" in cancers of the bladder, pancreas, kidney, stomach and cervix, as well as cancer of the lungs.

Legislation is being passed in states to give the right of clean air to people. Hospitals are setting policies of not hiring smokers (Chicago, 1985). Smokers will, in all likelihood, retain their freedom to smoke, so long as it does not interfere with the rights of others. This is a phenomenal reversal in public polity, but the lack of mind-over-matter mentality will freely allow persons to be self-destructive.

FACTS ON SMOKING AND ILLNESS

— Smoking 20 cigarettes a day shortens life 2 years.
— Smoking 30 cigarettes a day shortens life 4 years.
— Smoking 50 cigarettes a day shortens life 6 years.
— Smoking 1 pack a day doubles heart attack risk.
— Death rate from coronary heart disease is 9 times
    greater in smoking women.
— Heavy smokers have 20-30 times greater risk
    of developing lung cancer.
— Lung cancer victims number 100,000 annually,
    of which 98% are smokers.
— Smokers have 26 times the number of lung problems.
— Death rate from emphysema is 5 times greater
    for women who smoke, and 7.4 times greater
    for women who smoke a pack or more.
— Smoking during pregnancy increases stillbirth
    risk by 24%.
— Miscarriages in England were double for
    smokers.
— Smoking mothers have 50% more miscarriages.
— Babies born to smoking mothers are 6-7 oz. lighter.
— Children born to smoking mothers have higher
    risk of birth defects and susceptibility to
    disease.
— Female smokers have lower fertility rates.
— Active sperm count is lower in men smokers.
— Use of oral contraceptives and smoking increases
    the risk of stroke by 21.9%.
— Smoking promotes blood clots.
— Persons who live with smokers have 3 times the
    risk of lung cancer.
— A combination of cholesterol over 300, no exercise,
    above average stress, and 40 cigarettes a day,
    delivers a 96% chance of Coronary Heart Disease,

and a life expectancy of age 51 for men and
60 for women (Lower the cholesterol to normal,
eliminate stress, exercise, cut out smoking
and the life expectancy rises to 83 in men,
and 84 in women.
-- (For references to these facts, see HEALTH
THROUGH STRESS REDUCTION by Darrell Franken)

THE TOBACCO CONFLICT

Federal govenments and tobacco interests are waging campaigns over tobacco advertising, sale, and use. It is a war for freedom from some diseases, and freedom for some diseases. Governments do not want to risk what happened when alcohol was prohibited in the U.S.A. Thus, the campaigns for and against tobacco use are arming themselves with research projects and scientific studies. Mostly it is a battle for getting at the truth, and making the truth known.

Sweden began in 1963 with a campaign to have a "Cigarette-Free Society by the Year 2000." Advertising is limited to a 15 centimeter square, without scenes, and carry warnings, of which there are 16 such messages. Cigarettes are taxed so heavily they cost $2.00 a package. Sale from vending machines has been outlawed. Children are taught the facts of smoking and illness in schools.

Norway started its campaign in 1964, and has trained field workers, and equipped them with video equipment, to crusade against smoking. "The Tobacco Act prohibits the advertising of all types of tobacco products, including cigarette paper." Their ban on advertising is an almost total ban on all public media.

England banned adds from television in 1965. Increased taxes on cigarette sales now make them cost $2.00 Newspaper and magazine ads are not allowed to suggest or allude to any success-making qualities in cigarettes. Packages of cigarettes must also bear warnings specified by the government.

West Germany banned TV ads for cigarettes in 1973. Billboards warn of the hazards of smoking. While West Germans have been heavy smokers, along with their neighbors, the Dutch, their Federal Center for Health

Education is active in getting out the mind-over-matter message of health through smoking-stress reduction.

France began its war on smoking in 1974. Like most countries they require the tar and nicotine content to be printed on the package, along with a health warning. Smoking is prohibited in schools where students are under age 16. It is prohibited in hospitals, clinics, grocery stores, public elevators, cable cars, and in vehicles where children are transported. Smokers must use restricted areas in buses, planes, trains and ships. There is now a total ban on advertising tobacco electronically in France. Printed ads have restrictions.

(Source: Curtis W. Casewit, QUIT SMOKING, Para Research, Inc., Rockport, Mass. 01966)

THE FAITH HEALING CONFLICT

Whether to smoke or not, to quit or not, or to judge those who do or not, requires wisdom and grace. There is enough good wisdom in the Word to condemn smoking, but there are tobacco raising and smoking Christians who would defend their right to be both a smoker and a Christian. The Christian debate between smokers and non-smokers had stalemated, until more recent research and data has substantiated the illness-contributing factor of smoking. Now the non-smokers are capable of wielding some clout with their arguments.

The real question becomes this. "How can a person ask God for healing of a disease, which comes from smoking, if s/he does not plan to stop smoking?" How can I pray, in faith, believing, asking God for special favors, when I have set myself up for the problem in the first place, and do not intend to stop setting myself up through smoking? This is essentially the same question which exists throughout this book. If you now see the connection between your illness and you decide to quit, that is fine. Now pray in faith, believing, and receive God's healing.

What value is there going to a healing crusade conducted by a great healer, with the laying on of hands, when your particular type of illness was precipitated

by a number of life-style errors, ignorances and/or
indulgences? Prepare yourself for God's healing. Use
your judgment regarding the road-blocks you put in God's
way. Remove your life-style indiscretions which
over stress your body and make you susceptible to illness.
Make it easier for God to heal.

There are stress factors in life over which we have
no control; death of a loved one, financial crises, accident,
etc. Such factors bring terrible stress to bear upon
our lives, and sometimes the overload of stress brings
on illness. God knows these too, and He must certainly
look down with mercy, love, care, compassion and healing.
But what can God think of a person who willingly,
knowingly, and boldly continues a behavior that will
eventually get him/her into trouble with his/her health?
Can God be as merciful to this brazenly executed
indifference toward the consequences of his/her indulgent
behavior?

I believe this is why some prayers are not answered.
Every ill person deserves to live. However, if God would
answer the prayers of the irresponsible, an indirect
message is given to mankind. The message is, "Go ahead
and indulge. God will bail you out if you get sick." I
do not think God needs a message like that to be generated
to the world. God brings healing to the humble, to
the contrite heart, to the repentant sinner.

MIND-OVER-MATTER THINKING

Curbing the impulses, whether they be impulses for
smoking, excess alcohol consumption, excess spending,
yelling, fighting, or whatever, requires spiritual power.
Conflict exists between the forces which would make
us want to indulge, and the forces which would enable
us to rise above the impulses. The Apostle Paul called
this a war between the "flesh" and the "spirit". Intertwined
with Paul's discussion about the value of the "law" is
God's revelation about how the "law" helps us see our
sin, and rise above it.

> **"I am carnal, sold under sin. I do not
> understand my own actions. For I**

> do not do what I want, but I do the
> very thing I hate . . . So I find it to
> be a law that when I want to do right,
> evil lies close at hand. For I delight
> in the law of God, in my inmost self,
> but I see in my members another law
> at war with the law of my mind and
> making me captive to the law of sin
> which dwells in my members.
> (Romans 7:14, 21–23)

Every person, whether born-again like Paul was, or totally in the other direction, has this inner struggle. Paul sees it as a dichotomy of choice, a split of allegiance, a polarization of contending forces.

> "Wretched man that I am! Who shall
> deliver me from this body of death?
> Thanks be to God through Jesus Christ
> our Lord! So then, I of myself serve
> the law of God with my mind, but
> with my flesh I serve the law of sin."
> (Romans 7:24–25)

You visualize a stalemated battle if you stop here. That is what one faces without some spiritual power to transcend deterioration. If you have ever tried to give up something that gives as much pleasure as smoking, then you know the power of the impulses and the biological determination of addiction. Paul speaks in terms of transcending power.

> "There is therefore now no condemnation
> for those who are in Christ Jesus.
> For the law of the Spirit of life in
> Christ Jesus has set me free from
> the law of sin and death. . . .For those
> who live according to the flesh set
> their minds on the things of the flesh,
> but those who live according to the
> Spirit set their minds on the things
> of the Spirit. . . .If the Spirit of him
> who raised Jesus from the dead dwells
> in you, he who raised Christ Jesus
> from the dead will give life to your

**mortal bodies, also through his Spirit
which dwells in you." (Romans 8:1,2,5,11)**

There is mind-over-matter power when you have the Spirit of Jesus Christ in you. It is not simply a strength to overcome smoking. It is a strength to overcome almost any force. In the Christian faith we do not deny the "flesh". We simply keep it under control. The psychological "Id" impulses are not stamped out, just monitored and given their fair share, no more. The Christian faith recognizes the psychological Ego as the master controller. The Ego listens to the "Superego" and the "Id" and holds them justly accountable for a fair distribution of influence. For the Christian, the indwelling Christ, living within the human heart, manages the "flesh" and the "spirit". Ultimately, there is a triumph of the "spirit". This is different than early psychology, which usually spoke on behalf of the "Id" impulses, granting them freer pasturage than most Christian therapists were willing to allow.

You have power to rise above the addictions of the body. You may need help, but you can win. You can use auto-suggestion techniques. You can use meditation techniques. You can use relaxation techniques. You can use mental imagery. You can use the mind power of knowledge. You can use self-hypnosis. You can use repetitive conditioning. You can use subliminal messages on tapes. You can use group support. You can use substitute gratification. You can use nutritional manipulation. You can use tapering. You can use prayer. You can use power from the Spirit of the living God. If you have the will and the faith, you can regain control. You can save yourself money and prevent a great deal of pain, misery and anguish.

P.S.————"Dr. Albert J. Tuyns, of the International Agency for Research on Cancer in Lyon, France found that a person. . . who both smoked and drank heavily increased the risk (of esophageal cancer) 44 times." Lowell Ponte, in Readers Digest, April, 1985

DISCUSSION

1. American wealth is partly gained through the export of tobacco. How do we solve the smoking problem, which is so deeply imbedded in our agriculture, commerce, and social customs?

2. If we spent more time in high school teaching about the effects of smoking, would we cut down on smoking?

3. What is it in human nature that wants temporary kicks, even though there are potentially serious results in the long run?

4. How should we go about preventing our children from taking up smoking?

5. If your pastor were interested in preaching against smoking, what scripture could he use?

6. How well would faith healing, with the laying on of hands, work with a smoker?

7. If the tar of cigarettes induces lung cancer and the nicotine affects the heart, why do some smokers still live quite long lives?

8. Has the tobacco industry become necessary to America'a prosperity?

9. Why have some churchs gotten away from preaching against the social issues of smoking, drinking, gambling, pornography, etc.

10. If a smoker prays for healing from an illness which results, at least in part, from smoking, why would God heal the smoker just as quickly, or not as readily, as someone else?

Chapter 10

WEIGHT CONTROL FOR HEALTH

AND HEALING

Obese persons, 20% – 40% overweight, have
— 3 times the normal incidence of high blood pressure.
— 3 times the normal incidence of diabetes.
— increased risk of heart disease; shorter life span.
— unusually high risk of respiratory disorder.
— unusually high risk of arthritis and cancer.
Severely obese women, more than 40% overweight, have
— 5 times the normal risk of cancer of the uterine
lining, heightened risk of breast and cervical cancer.
Severely obese men have increased risk of cancer of
the colon, rectum and prostate.
(Source: National Institute of Health, in Time, Feb 25,1985)

The following questions in the Overweight Inventory
will help you determine the stress of excess weight.

OVERWEIGHT

Pick out the most appropriate response. Write the score
for your response in the space provided.

The following table shows acceptable weights for most
persons. Find your height on the chart and calculate
how many pounds overweight you are.

MEN		WOMEN	
Height	Weight	Height	Weight
5'3"	118-141	5'0"	100-118
5'4"	122-145	5'1"	104-121
5'5"	126-149	5'2"	107-125
5'6"	130-155	5'3"	110-128
5'7"	134-161	5'4"	113-132
5'8"	139-166	5'5"	116-135
5'9"	143-170	5'6"	120-139
5'10"	147-174	5'7"	123-142
5'11"	150-178	5'8"	126-146
6'0"	154-183	5'9"	130-151
6'1"	158-188	5'10"	133-156
6'2"	162-192	5'11"	137-161
6'3"	165-195	6'0"	141-166

(Source: U.S. Department of Agriculture)

Put   0 (Zero) in the blank if you are less than 30 pounds
overweight.
Put 30 in the blank if you are 30 pounds overweight.
Put 40 in the blank if you are 40 pounds overweight.
Put 50 in the blank if you are 50 pounds overweight.
Put 60 in the blank if you are 60 pounds overweight.
Put 70 in the blank if you are 70 pounds overweight.
Put 80 in the blank if you are 80 pounds overweight.
Put 90 in the blank if you are 90 pounds overweight.
(Add 10 points for every 10 pounds beyond this.)

___________ SCORE (To be added to the score on
the next page.)

The "skinfold test" is a measurement of the amount of fat
you can pinch between your thumb and forefinger.   Locate
the first "skinfold" site on the back side of the right arm.
Pinch the fat and not the muscle, and estimate the thickness (¼inch, ½ inch, 3/4 inch, 1 inch, etc.) —— The second
place to take the "skinfold" test is on either the left or
right side of the navel. Estimate the thickness of that
fat. Combine both estimates (or calculations) for the total
thickness in inches.

Put a 0 in the space if the combined thickness is less than
            3/4ths of an inch.
Put a 10 in the space if the combined thickness is between
            3/4ths inches and 1¼ths inches.
Put a 20 in the space if the combined thickness is between
            1¼ ths inches and 1-3/4ths inches.
Put a 30 in the space if the combined thickness is between
            1-3/4ths inches and 2-¼ inches.
Put a 40 in the space if the combined thickness is between
            2-1/4th inches and 2-3/4ths inches.
Put a 50 in the space if the combined thickness is more
            than 2-3/4ths inches.

_________ SCORE FOR SKINFOLD TEST

_________ SCORE FOR OVERWEIGHT (Previous page)

_________ TOTAL SCORE

(Enter this score in the summary SCORING on Page 358)

INTERPRETATION

0 – 30   Your WEIGHT is within a relatively safe zone. "Obesity" is defined as being more than 15% overweight. Persons who are 20% overweight or less are statistically less prone to illness from overweight.

30 – 60   Your OVERWEIGHT condition is one of the risk factors creating poor health, disease and early death in general. If you are a male and you are at least 20% overweight you have "twice the risk of developing coronary heart disease" (Framingham Study, Dawber, 1980). You have a "78% greater risk of hypertension" (Paffenbarger). If you are a male you have a "42% chance of dying sooner than normal men", and if you are a woman over 30 you have a "30% chance" of dying sooner than women of normal weight (Tear and Lindsey, 1978). If you are a female you have an increase in the risk of developing endometrial cancer (Charles Simone M.D., 1983). Obesity increases the risk of colon cancer, breast cancer, infections, gall bladder problems, respiratory problems and wear and tear on the joints (Simone, 1983). Obese persons have two to three times higher risk of diabetes (Simone, 1983).

Above 60   Your OVERWEIGHT condition is a serious detriment to your health. Overweight-ness, high blood pressure and heart attacks are related. The higher the overweight condition, the higher the risk of high blood pressure, and the greater the risk of stroke (Framingham Study, Dawber, 1980). Men who are 40% or more overweight "show an increase of cancer of the colon, rectum and prostrate". "Women who are 40% or more above their ideal weight have an increased risk of cancer of the uterus, ovaries, gall bladder, and breast." (Dr. Kenneth Cooper, The Aerobics Program for Total Well-Being, 1982).

FAT, CHOLESTEROL AND ATHERIOSCLEROSIS

Coronary heart disease is the leading cause of death in men over the age of 40 and women over the age of 55. Thirty-four percent of the people who die in the United States, are victims of coronary heart disease (CHD). That percent was climbing steadily until 1967, but has been declining somewhat, due to the massive interest in exercise. Persons who have Coronary Heart Disease, do not always have a bad heart. They have artherosclerosis, which is a clogging and hardening of the arteries in the heart from cholesterol deposits, which prevent the flow of blood to the heart. Lack of oxygen to the heart causes pain, called angina. Excessive consumption of fatty foods elevates blood cholesterol, which combines with the calcium in the blood stream, and forms a plaque on the inner walls of the arteries. Sweet treats contribute their share of fat to the blood stream. When blood sugar is excessively high from overconsumption of sweets, insulin is secreted, which turns blood sugar into fat to store it. Sweets and starches contribute to the overall fat level.

GOD'S ANCIENT ILLNESS PREVENTION PROGRAM

God set up a a Wellness program when he commanded the Children of Israel to worship Him by burning fat on the altar. The fatty parts of the sacrificial animals were to be burned on the altar. The animal's fat had to be burned for the "burn't offering", the "sin offering", the "guilt offering", the "consecration" and the "peace offering", whether that offering was a "bull", "goat", or "lamb". (Leviticus, Chapters 1 - 8) The several commands are summarized:

> **"The Lord said to Moses, Say to the people of Israel, You shall eat no fat of ox, sheep or goat. The fat of an animal that dies of itself and the fat of one that is torn by beasts, may be put to any other use, but on no account shall you eat it. For every person who eats of the fat of an animal of which an offering by fire is made**

to the Lord shall be cut off from his
people.   Moreover you shall eat no
blood whatever, whether of fowl or
of animal, in any of your dwellings.
Whoever eats any blood, that person
whall be cut off from his people."
(Leviticus 7:22-27

God has been in the nutrition and health food business for a long time.   The command to burn fat was given to the Israelites immediately after their emancipation from 400 years of Egyptian bondage.   Prior to this 400 year stop-over, the Israelites had suffered famine in the land of Palestine, and Joseph had been sold into Egypt to prepare a way to save them from starvation.   Joseph was commanded by Pharaoh to bring his family into Egypt so they could **"eat the _fat_ of the land."** (Genesis 45:18) We have frequently interpreted the word "fat" to mean "plenty", but perhaps we need to interpret it literally. There are health problems from eating too much fat and God would know that better than anyone.   God instituted an entire liturgical system, to help the people live longer.

GOD REWARDS OBEDIENCE WITH HEALTH

History records the growth of this band of people, until their number and their power spread from the Nile River in Egypt to the Tigris and Euphrates River in Assyria. God instituted fat-burning somewhere between 1900 B.C. and 1400 B.C. and by the time of David and Solomon in 1000 B.C. to 900 B.C. the Jewish nation outgrew boundary after boundary. They were a healthy and robust people. God gave them a bit of heaven here on earth.

Obedience and faithfulness to God and his Word produce immediate results.   People do not have to wait for death to translate them into the Kingdom of God.   That Kingdom of God, and of our Lord Jesus Christ, begins in time, not in eternity.   It begins when people are born-again, and make their commitment to live out of their salvation. Such rebirth plugs people into the source of truth and power that maintains and regains health.

A   lifetime   of   moderation-eating   has   statistically

life-extending power. Research proves again and again, that lowered cholesterol, from eating less fatty substances, adds years to life. At the Arizona Heart Institute, Edward B. Diethrich, M.D., and his colleagues, put together a HEART TEST, which incorporates 12 major factors as they relate to longevity.

1. Age	7. Cholesterol
2. Gender	8. Diet
3. Family History	9. Blood Pressure
4. Personal History	10. Weight
5. Diabetes	11. Exercise
6. Smoking	12. Stress

All these are contributing factors to heart attack, and a combination of 3 - 5 of these factors puts one in a "high risk" category of having a heart attack. High cholesterol gives 25% to the high risk. More than 25 pounds overweight gives another 10% of the high risk. Smoking gives another 25% to the high risk. Poor diet increases high risk of heart attack by 20%. High blood pressure, no exercise, and stress, each gives another 10% to the high risk. No exericise gives another 10% to the high risk. Family history of heart attacks gives another 10% to the high risk of having a heart attack. You can save pain, money, and be confident in a healthful life, by using some Biblical principles and mind-over-matter self-control.

God gave the Israelites a fairly complete system for regulating mental, physical and spiritual health. Then God layed promises before the people, and promised them that following these principles would bring results. In Deuteronomy we read,

> **"And when your son asks you in time to come, what is the meaning of the testimonies, and the statutes, and the ordinances. . . .(say). . . . The Lord commanded us to do all these statutes, to fear the Lord our God, _for our good_ always, that he might preserve us alive, as at this day."**
>
> **(Deuteronomy 6:20,24)**

The fat-burning ordinance is only one of the many statutes which God gave. That ordinance was observed by righteous persons for centuries, and no doubt, persons who followed it were less prone to Coronary Heart Disease. They experienced "for our good" because they maintained self-control over their appetite. Now, with growing affluence in many countries, people are more able to afford foods with higher fat content. For this reason Coronary Heart Disease began to become epidemic. That drove researchers to discover, what God had set forth in history many centuries ago. Reduced fat consumption is "for our good".

GLORIFYING GOD BY FAT REDUCTION

God blessed His people with health for a reason. He was using the Children of Israel as examples. His Children became the "yeast", the "light", and the "salt" of the earth, to be a testimony to the nations of heathen and unbelievers. In Deuteronomy we see this written.

> **"The Lord will establish you as a people
> holy to himself. . . . And all the peoples
> of the earth shall see that you are
> called by the name of the Lord, and
> they shall be afraid (respectfully)
> of you. . . . The Lord will open to you
> his good treasury. . . . The Lord will
> make you the head and not the tail..."**

God wants you to be a leader and not a follower. God works out his plan for the human race through his people. To accomplish that God needs "heads" and not "tails". God can only use people who use their head. God needs mind-over-matter thinking. He is calling you and me to be moderate in our life-style, including the eating of fat.

MULTIPLE FACTORS CREATING ILLNESS

People are extremely resilient, and can bend a great deal before they break. The body is filled with an amazing capacity to adjust and adapt, but the human body has tolerance limits. As Children of God, we cannot fly in the face of truth and not expect to suffer when truth won't bend for us. We believe in a gracious and merciful God, but He is not a push-over. God set forth some major principles and dynamics which are structures within which we need to operate. God has been known to lift those dynamics and work miracles. Yet, when persons continue to violate such principles as excessive eating of fatty foods, which do not get burned off with work or exercise, can they expect to come to God in prayer, and be heard?

There are some hard facts being turned out by epidemiological studies, and scientific fact-finding that are forcing us to admit that some of our illness may be our own fault.   Take the multiple factor analysis of Forrest H. Blanding, in a book entitled The Pulse Point Plan. This former Exxon analyst and his colleagues studied 200 of the current pieces of research on stress and illness. They see the resting "pulse" rate as an indicator of fitness. And in addition they see a need to be alert to reducing multiple stress factors to maintain health.   They see "cholesterol" as a major problem, especially in combination with other stress factors.

FOUR STRESSORS	RISK OF Coronary Heart Disease	LIFE Expect- ancy	
Serum Cholesterol of over 300 No exercise Smoking 40 cig/day Above average stress	77% 96%	Female Male	Age 60 Age 51
Serum Cholesterol of under 180 Fine fitness No smoking Below average stress	1.5% 3%	Female Male	Age 84 Age 83

Excessive fat consumption, coupled with three other factors, increases the risk of Coronary Heart Disease from 1.5% to 77% in women, and from 3% to 96% in men.   Excessive fat consumption, coupled with three other factors, reduces life expectancy by 24 years in women, and by 32 years in men. (Source: Forrest H. Blanding, The Pulse Point Plan)

Fat consumption (and cholesterol elevation), by itself, is not severly destructive. If you have a cholesterol level of over 300, but you are physically fit, do not smoke, and live with below average stress, then the risk of CHD is only 25% for males and 11% for female. It usually takes multiple factors to set people up for degenerative disease.

STRESS ALSO RAISES SERUM CHOLESTEROL

The fight against the overweight condition needs to be fought on multiple fronts, because serum (blood) cholesterol also rises from stress. Think of the mad-dog fight-flight problem. In such stressful situations, the body is mobilized through adrenaline, through glucose oxidation, and through glucogenesis, which is a process of releasing stored fat, and processing it in the liver to make glucose which is to be used in the fight-flight situation. If a person is constantly under stress, the body constantly needs fat cells to be processed by the liver. Stress puts more fat cells in the blood stream, getting ready to be processed. While in the blood stream such fatty substance is in limbo. It is made available and ready to be used, but is not used, so it is measurably high. Under such circumstances it has no place to go, but wanders through the arterial system, and finds itself attracted and bound into plaque on the artery wall. This is just a picture view. Let us look at the research.

"One of the earliest studies investigating the relationship between stress and cholesterol level was carried out by Friedman, Roseman and Carroll. Subjects were accountants who, because of their work, were required to meet specific deadlines during the year. Forty accountants were followed for a six-month period. These accountants were physically relatively inactive throughout the year, and neither level of physical activity, weight, nor eating habits appeared to differ between relaxed and busy work periods of the year. The most strenuous work periods coincided with the highest levels of cholesterol. The average serum cholesterol level was 252 mg% at the time subjects considered themselves under the greatest stress (as measured by the questionaire), and only 210 mg% during the periods in which they felt most devoid of tension or a sense of urgency. . . .This stress induced increase equals that which would result from a 70 percent increment of nutritional cholesterol." (Lorenz J. P., Van Doornen, and Orlebeke, Journal of Human Stress, December, 1982) Stress inducement of elevated cholesterol has been substantiated by others. Medical students were found to have an increase of about 20% in their cholesterol during exam time. Deep Sea Divers have shown 20% elevations from the stress of their tasks. Men who have lost their jobs and have been unemployed for months, had a drop of 10% in their cholesterol after they found work. Military pilots were studied, and a 19% (mean level) rise of cholesterol level was found at the start of training, but went higher during examination periods. Both the cholesterol levels and the triglyceride levels have been shown to rise in people being interviewed. Racing drivers, however, do not show a rise in cholesterol, but have an increase of triglycerides

(Source: Lorenz, Van Doornen, and Orlebeke, in Journal of Human Stress, December, 1982, Vol. 8, No. 4.)

Stress elevates cholesterol (in many situations). Eating high cholesterol foods elevates cholesterol levels in the blood. Cholesterol hardens the arteries. Cholesterol clogs the arteries. Cholesterol creates pain, illness and early death. Also, smoking excessively, and no exercise, raise the odds of pain, illness and early death. Do you see the sense in developing a balanced mind-over-matter perspective on life. It will deliver a bit of heaven to you, even while you are on earth.

DEVELOP FAITH TO FIGHT FAT

God wants you to surrender your anxieties, fears and will to Him. Let the Spirit, teachings, principles, expectations, and guidance of God, take over your life. Commit yourself to a life of faith, so that destructive stress may be calmed. This will reduce the cholesterol levels inside your arteries, and enable you to live a less painful life.

There are women involved in a "3-D" program of weight reduction. The three "D's" stand for DIET, DEVOTION AND DISCIPLINE. Women who are struggling with the problem of weight-control, join in a mutual-support and Bible-support group. These support groups have a positive influence. They provide the spiritual, mental and emotional support to regain lost mind-over-matter. There are thousands of these groups meeting in homes and churches; each seeking to reduce the "distress" of human existence.

DEVELOP AWARENESS TO FIGHT FAT

Television is educating us to eat the fad, fast and fat foods. Our educational system has not been strong enough, or educated enough, to counteract the power which attracts impulse food buyers. Add to this the problem that every person burns up a different daily total of calories, minerals and vitamins. Compound this with genetic personal differences in metabolism, and you have a disheartening task of choosing! Finally, people say, **"So, what the heck! I'm just going to eat what I want."** This becomes the attitude of even the fattest person, and it is very self-destructive.

People need to know the facts, and be willing to regulate themselves. Not a diet in existence demands a total deprevation of everything that is "good". Courses in high school ought to teach information like this.

A fast food hamburger, or two hot dogs, or two Danish, have a little more than 1 oz. of fat. Here is what you would have to eat of more natural food to get the same amount of fat.

- — one halibut filet
- — ½ lb boiled and skinned chicken
- — a whole head of Bibb lettuce
- — one onion
- — six scallops
- — a cup of cooked beans
- — a cup of brown rice
- — a pound of green beans
- — one sweet potato
- — an ear of corn
- — a cup of raisens
- — an orange
- — two red beets
- — four asparagus spears
- — ½ lb green peas in the pods

--a cup of popcorn
— a cup of cooked spaghetti
— two slices of whole wheat bread

(Source: Alexander Schauss)

You would have to eat all that to get the fat you would get in one fast food hamburger, or two hot dogs, or two Danish. If nutritional information were drilled into the minds of our children, like reading and mathmatics, behaviors and life-styles would have a chance to change. At present there are a few sincerely dedicated parents, who themselves, have had to learn some nutritional lessons the hard way, now live by and teach some of the principles that will save their children some pain.

God's revelation to Moses, regarding the burning of fat, needs to be reinstated in the minds and hearts of His people, and others. This presents theological problems to some persons, who tend to view the Old Testament as having been fulfilled by the coming of Christ. It is difficult to understand and follow the distinction between what was worship and what was a health practice. For the Israelites their worship liturgy was tied in with their health practices. In Leviticus we read God's instructions for religious liturgical practices, rules for eating the proper meats, quarantine rules to keep disease from spreading, etc. We have felt justified in dropping the religious liturgical rules like sacrificing, but we can now see that in dropping the sacrifice of animals, we have dropped our awareness about the problems of eating too much fat. Christ came to displace the liturgical rules, but did not replace the health rules. We need to be diligent to interpret the Old Testament with intellectual integrity.

COUNT CALORIES IN -- CALORIES OUT

People should know what amount of exercise will expend the calories they have just eaten. This requires some idea about the calorie content of foods, as well as how many calories are burned up by certain types of exercise. It takes about 3000 - 3500 calories to make a pound of human body fat. Simply substituting more fish and poultry for red meats, doubling up on vegetables, while cutting back on breads and sugars will, almost invariably, produce a 3500 calorie per week cutback.

Add a one mile per day walking-exercise program and the calorie expenditure can produce weight-reduction. Leisurely bicycling, like leisurely walking, will use up 210 calories per hour, and bicycling at 13 MPH will burn up 660 calories per hour. Brisk walking for 1 hour will use up 300 calories. Tennis will consume 420 calories per hour. Running at 10 MPH will burn up 900 calories per hour. Domestic work uses an average of 180 calories per hour, which is considerably less, yet persons in low-calorie-consumption jobs will eat as much as persons on high-calories-consumption jobs. People need to become more aware of the proper regulation of calorie intake and expenditure.

FASTING

For some persons, illness and aging are the result of "biochemical suffocation", which can be cured by fasting. Fasting is safe and beneficial to healing. There are eighty six references in the Bible which speak of fasting. History is filled with persons who fasted.

- Hippocrates (b. 460 B.C.) fasted and wrote, "Abstinence and quiet cure many diseases."
- Moses fasted for 40 days during his stay on Mount Sinai, when God gave 10 commandments. (Exodus 24:18)
- Hanna, mother of Samuel, conceived her son after fasting. (I Samuel 1:7,18)
- Samuel gathered the Israelites at Mizpah where they fasted one day to show their repentance. (I Samuel 7:1-6)
- The Israelites fasted one day after a bitter defeat and a loss of 18,000 men. (Judges 20:26)
- King Saul observed a one day fast, just before his last battle. (I Samuel 28:20)
- King David learned of Saul's death, "mourned and wept and fasted until evening". (II Samuel 1:12

-- King David went into fasting when his son
      was ill. (II Samuel 12:16,22,23)
-- Ahab was embarrassed and remorseful, after
      Jezebel had committed murder to get a
      vineyard for Ahab. Elijah confronted Ahab
      who felt sorry for the act of murder done
      for his benefit. He fasted. (I Kings 21:27)
--Jehoshaphat and Ezra proclaimed a fast, and
      the Lord won the battle for them.
      (II Chronicles 20:3,15, Ezra 8:21)
-- Ezra fasted and prayed for his personal sin
      and the corporate sin of his people.
      (Ezra 9:5)
-- Nehemiah and his people prayed and fasted
      in a public confession for their sins.
      (Nehemiah 1:4, 9:1)
-- Daniel fasted to gain "wisdom and understand-
      ing". (Daniel 9:1-22)
-- Jonah preached repentance to Ninevah, and
      when the city repented, they proclaimed
      a fast. That saved the city. (Jonah 3:5,10)
-- Zechariah proclaimed a routine quarterly
      fast for the Israelites. (Zechariah 8:19)
-- Jesus fasted in the wilderness, where the
      devil came to tempt him. (Matthew 4:10,11)
-- Jesus prescribed private, non-displayed fasting
      for people. (Matthew 6:16-18)
-- The early church leaders "fasted and prayed,
      and laid their hands on" Paul and Barnabas
      before sending them out. (Acts 13:2,3)
-- The early church marked the ordination of
      the elders by prayer and fasting.
      (Acts 14:23)
-- Paul, the apostle, was ". . in fastings often."
      (II Corinthians 11:27)
-- Tertullian, church leader in 210 A.D. spoke
      of the benefits of fasting vs. feasting.
-- Polycarp, church leader in 110 A.D., fasted.
      He advocated it to fight temptation.
-- Greeks like Socrates and Plato have fasted for
      reasons not currently known.
-- Moslems practice 28 days of fasting from
      daybreak to sundown. (28 days annually)

-- Martin Luther fasted from time to time while
  he was translating the Bible.
-- John Calvin favored the practice of fasting
  but spoke with caution.
-- John Wesley called for fasts and practiced
  it himself personally.
-- Mahatma Ghandi fasted for personal and
  public reasons.

You are a friend and compatriot of saints and leaders when you adopt fasting practices. The length of the fast may vary, as well as the purpose of the fast. In most cases the "fast" is a spiritual tool to gain further insight, wisdom, and power, for oneself and for the benefit of others. For Christians, the goal must be to glorify God, and grow spiritually. When you fast, you practice mind-over-matter. Your fasting is an effort which is expended to gain or regain something lost or something new. The weight loss is only secondary to the primary goal of obedience and subservience to God. Excessively heavy people are a burden to themselves, and to those who must take care of their more frequent infirmities. They drain off the energy and resources which could go to save, redeem or improve the plight of those who do not know Christ. Therefore, to adopt "fasting" as a practice, benefits both self and the Kingdom of God.

FASTING AND HEALING

The final decision by the judges of history are not available on this one. George Blackburn M.D., Ph.D., a Harvard Medical School professor of surgery, has studied some of the physical aspects of fasting and says, "There are no known therapeutic reasons for a total fast, not even weight loss, because the dramatic change in body metabolism it creates could cause organ failure and disease, and the composition of weight loss would be an unacceptable amount of body fluid and tissue protein from muscles and organs."

In the ring, fighting for the orthomolecular physicians, is Dr. Alan Cott, author of Fasting, The Ultimate Diet (Bantam Books), saying, "I've fasted about 300 chronically ill schizophrenics, people who would have ended up in the back wards of mental hospitals." He fasts these patients from 25 to 32 days in length. He reports that 65% had improved with adequate functioning to be on their own again. These patients were taught to eat a diet high in vegetables and whole grains. Those who were faithful to the diet had the least amount of relapse. Dr. Cott cites Russian and British researchers who report that fasting raises the level of serotonin, a neurotransmitter in the brain that influences and controls mood. Therefore, fasting helps heal mood variations.

Fasting treatment for arthritis is a popular treatment in Sweden. A 7-14 day fast is followed by a vegetarian diet. Swedish researchers conclude, also, that "fasting seems to have a fairly potent anti-inflammatory effect". (Acta Dermato-Venereologica, vol. 63, no. 5, 1983) That is why it helps arthritis.

Paavo Airola, in Every Woman's Book, recommends a one day juice fast to cleanse the system, and thereby restoring the health of the skin, and especially good treatment for acne. He claims great success in using the juice fast as the most practical way of weight reduction without problems. The range of benefits from fasting are not being systematically researched so that one can be sure of the healing effects. Yet, reduction of weight, by fasting under medical supervision, for short periods of time, improves health. Weight reduction results in reduced blood pressure and all the problems associated with Coronary Heart Disease. Reductions in food intake, through a weekly 24 hour juice fast, will ease the tasks of the esophagus, stomach, duodenum, colon and rectum. With reduced stress the body ought to rejoice and be happier.

THE FAST — A DIVINE PROGRAM

Truth is truth, from wherever it comes. The scientific and the divine cannot conflict. There is so much evidence that fasting is good for us. We simply need to know how, when, where and why to use it. Fasting is a mind-over-matter skill, which, if learned in relation to food, may help us control other behaviors.

THE STRUGGLE TO HOLD OUR WEIGHT DOWN

Please do not expect me come up with the "final
solution" to the problem of "overweightness" in this book.
Everyone must be aware that diets abound, and promises
galore have not yet stemmed the tide of the overweight
problem.

There are many factors influencing human nature's
enjoyment of eating, and there are many eating problems
stemming from person's attempts to bring appetite under
control.   Finding the balance between caloric intake
and caloric expenditure is as hard as finding the balance
between many competing temptations and obligations.
The victory belongs to the person who can finally achieve
a mind-over-matter perspective, in which the heart and
mind (like the ego) take control.

KNOWLEDGE NEEDS EXPANSION

Knowledge is our best ally.   We need to know the
power of the indwelling Christ to help us with weight
control.   We need that spiritual knowledge.   However,
we also need a greater amount of knowledge fed into
our total population, regarding nutrition intake and
expenditure.   It would be nice to see our educational
processes deliver this along with reading, writing, and
arithmetic.

The church has often pioneered in bringing a new
awareness of some need into our society.   The church
established nearly all the first schools, hospitals, social
services, etc.   The church is always seeking to deliver
knowledge of truth to the world. Perhaps the church
can be persuaded to again collect a new body of wholistic
health care knowledge, and disseminate it to the world.

DISCUSSION

1. The author suggests that the sacrificing of fat on the altar was a thinly disguised health rule. Is that acceptable to you?

2. Would you prefer to think of the sacrifice on the altar as having spiritual significance, educational significance, or significance for health? or all three?

3. Can we draw a parallel between the health and growth of Israel due to obedience, and our health and growth due to obedience to God?

4. Fat burning was done to glorify God. If people lose weight through exercise, are they glorifying God in some similar spiritual way?

5. Do you remember what stressful life-style behaviors, added to overweightness, elevate the risk Coronary Heart Disease?

6. Cholesterol is a killer. Stressful work and responsibilities raise cholesterol in certain situations. How do you lower your cholesterol, if you have a stressful job?

7. Is there an organization in your community called "3-D" for Diet, Discipline and Devotion?

8. Does your high school teach nutrition information to the students? Should they? When will they?

9. From memory, try to mention all the instances you recall where persons in the Bible fasted.

10. Have you ever fasted? Would you be willing to try a 24 hour juice fast? Why? Why not?

Chapter 11

NUTRITIONAL THERAPY FOR HEALING

"Too much good food does more harm than too little bad food."   Shem-Tov Falaquera   1225-1290 A.D.

In June, 1978, Dr. Anthony J. Sattilaro, M.D., was told that he had prostatic cancer which had metastisized to his skull, shoulder, spine, sternum, and ribs. He was 47 years old. His medical awareness told him this was a diagnosis with a death sentence. Two hitchhikers introduced him to a macrobiotic diet, which consists of 50% whole grains, 25% lightly cooked, locally grown vegetables, 15% beans and sea vegetables (seaweed), soups and condiments (herbs). Dr. Sattilaro conquored cancer. His book Recalled by Life, chronicals his experiences with these life-giving nutrients.

Evaluate your Stress from Poor Nutrition with the following Inventory, and let it begin to give you clues regarding a health-enhancing nutritional life-style.

STRESS FROM POOR NUTRITION

Pick out the most appropriate response. Use the scoring
instructions with each question.

1. _____ How many servings of DAIRY PRODUCTS do you
eat per day of the following?

      Milk (8 oz. glass)   Pudding (1 cup)
      Cheese (2 slices)   Cottage cheese (½cup)
      Yogurt (1 cup)   Ice Cream (1 cup)

If you eat 0 daily servings give yourself 20 points.
If you eat 1 daily serving give yourself 10 points.
If you eat 2 daily servings give yourself 0 points.

2. _____ How many servings of MEAT and other HIGH
PROTEIN foods do you eat per day?

      Beef (3.5 oz. - hamburger size)
      Ham or pork (3.5 oz.)
      Chicken turkey, duck (3.5 oz.)
      Fish, shrimp, seafood (3.5 oz.)
      Liver, heart, kidney, tongue (3.5 oz.)
      Cold cuts or luncheon meat (3.5 oz.)
      Peanut butter (3-5 tbsp.) or nuts (3 0z.)
      Eggs ——— or beans (lima or navy in chili)

If you eat 0 daily servings give yourself 20 points.
If you eat 1 daily serving give yourself 10 points.
If you eat 2 daily servings give yourself 0 points.

3. _____ How many servings of FRUITS or VEGETABLES
do you eat per day of the following?

      Salads or cabbage (½ cup serving)
      Beans, corn, carrots, peas, beets, asparagus
      Brussel sprouts, broccoli, spinach
      Potatoes, tomatoes, peppers
      FRESH FRUIT: apple, orange, grapefruit,
           peach, pear, melon, grapes, apricot, etc.

If you eat 0 daily servings give yourself 40 points.
If you eat 1 daily serving give yourself 30 points.
If you eat 2 daily servings give yourself 20 points.
If you eat 3 daily servings give yourself 10 points.
If you eat 4 daily servings give yourself 0 points.

4. _______ How many servings of BREAD and CEREALS do
you eat per day?
     Bread (No. of slices)
     Cereal (No. of bowls of boxed or cooked)
     Waffles, corn bread, tacos, rice (No. of servings)
     Potatoes or chips (No. of servings)
     Macaroni, spaghetti, noodles (No. of servings)
     Crackers (6 crackers is one serving)
     Doughnuts, pastries, sweet rolls (No. of)
     Pie, cake, brownie, cookies (2)
If you eat 0 daily servings give yourself 40 points.
If you eat 1 daily serving give yourself 30 points.
If you eat 2 daily servings give yourself 20 points.
If you eat 3 daily servings give yourself 10 points.
If you eat 4 daily servings give yourself 0 points.

5. _______ How many of the following SNACKS do you eat in
an average day? Give yourself ten (10) points for
each of the following.
     Malt, milkshake, sundae, soda
     Candy bars or equivalent in other candy
     Pop — carbonated and sweetened only
     Beer, wine, whiskey, gin, rum (No. of drinks)

6. _______ How many cups of COFFEE (caffeine) TEA or HOT
CHOCOLATE do you drink in an average day? Give
yourself five (5) points for each cup.

7. _______ How much BUTTER, MARGERINE or OIL do you
consume in an average day? Give yourself five (5)
points for each tablespoon.

8. _______ How many times a day do you add EXTRA SALT
to your food? Give yourself ten (10) points for
each time.

9. _______ How many times a day do you add CATSUP, or
MUSTARD or SAUCES to your food?   Add ten
(10) points for each time you do per day.

10. _______ How many glasses of WATER do you drink per day?
If you drink 0 glasses per day give yourself 40 points.
If you drink 2 glasses per day give yourself 30 points.
If you drink 4 glasses per day give yourself 20 points
If you drink 6 glasses per day give yourself 10 points
If you drink 8 glasses per day give yourself 0 points.

_______________ TOTAL (Range 0 – 200 approx.)

(Enter this score in the summary SCORING on Page 358)

INTERPRETATION

In general, higher scores mean higher levels of nutritional deficiency and unhealthy eating patterns. Be careful to interpret that a higher score in Questions 1, 2, 3, & 4, means a higher risk of vitamin deficiency diseases and problems resulting from unhealthy metabolism of foods.

0 - 80   Your STRESS FROM POOR NUTRITION score is excellent, meaning you eat properly. You seem to know about the necessity of a proper balance of dairy products, meat, fruits, vegetables, bread, cereals and liquids. You are to be congratulated.

80 - 120   Your STRESS FROM POOR NUTRITION score suggests your nutritional intake is average for Americans, but actually below the U. S. Dept. of Agriculture Recommended Daily Allowances. Persons with your score should improve nutritional intake by increasing servings of fruit and vegetables, and by decreasing sugar-laden and flour-laden snacks.

120-150   Your STRESS FROM POOR NUTRITION score says you need to learn more about eating the right balance of the four basic food groups: dairy products, meat, fruit/vegetables, whole grains. You also need to understand the vitamin and mineral deficiencies in snack foods. The long range probability of poor nutrition causing illness, is serious, but not alarming.

Above 150   Your STRESS FROM POOR NUTRITION score suggests you need to make some major changes in what you eat. You may not be aware of the problems of inadequate vitamins and minerals in processed foods, high in sugar and white flour content. Such foods fill people up but lack the micronutrients needed for good health.
Read books, or find a class where good nutrition is taught. Nutritional deficiencies and excesses are the causes of many illnesses of body and mind.

DEGENERATIVE DISEASES FROM POOR NUTRITION

If you were a sailor, 200 or more years ago, and you did not get into port for some weeks, you soon became ill with a disease called "scurvy", and died. This dreaded Vitamin C deficiency disease had a number of symptoms.

- poor healing
- bleeding gums
- loss of appetite
- sore joints
- anemia
- fatigue
- apathy
- sore mouth
- loosened teeth
- brusing easily
- restlessness
- irritability
- listlessness
- feebleness
- death

You could "pray without ceasing", get others to pray, or even have a laying-on-of-hands-with-prayer service, but without Vitamin C, you died. The body cannot function without Vitamin C. People did not know that until about 200 years ago. God can work miracles. He can suspend the laws of nature if He wishes. Perhaps God can even allow a human body to function without Vitamin C. Yet, I will not, knowingly, push my luck on God supplying my Vitamin C or making me capable of life without it.

Beriberi, which is a Vitamin B_1 deficiency disease, and Pellagra, which is a Vitamin B_2 and Vitamin B_3 deficiency disease, plagued Southeast Asia a century ago. Many of the early symptoms of these diseases resembled the symptoms of emotional disturbances. Nutritionally oriented (orthomolecular) physicians are aware of the deteriorative effect of poor nutrition. However, traditionally trained (Allopathic) physicians, are not trained in nutritional awareness. It is good that there is a new surge of interest in determining the connection between nutrition and illness.

PHYSICAL ILLNESS AND POOR DIET

That improper nutrition can help induce cancer, is a substantially growing proposition. Studies which compared the Japanese diet of fish and rice with the American heavy-fat-consumption diet, point to excess consumption of fat as one of the causes of cancer. Giant multi-factoral studies are currently in progress to discover the truth. The connection between colon cancer and a low-fiber diet is fairly well established. Further connections between illness and diet appear daily in our newspapers and magazines.

Osteoporosis is a disease condition from insufficient calcium intake. Deficiency of Vitamin D causes rickets. Low potassium affects the heart beat. Insufficient iron causes anemia and fatigue. These are the most commonly understood deficiency diseases that substantiate the fact that there is a connection between poor diet and diseases.

EMOTIONAL ILLNESS AND POOR DIET

Dr. Warren Levine, nutritionist and director of the World Health Medical Group, New York, treated a woman who came to him on Friday afternoon. He wanted to run tests, but it was too late in the week. He noticed that she stuttered, and gave her some B complex vitamins. On the following Tuesday, Dr. Levine got a phone call from the woman's psychiatrist. "What have you done to my patient?" Dr. Levine told him he had given her some vitamins. The psychiatrist replied, "She is not stuttering anymore." A larger and larger number of emotional mood states are being treated with orthomolecular (nutritional) methods and many successes are being reported.

Insufficient calcium is a frequent cause of hyperactivity in children. Likewise, excessive sugar consumption in either children or adults, can result in a hypoglycemic condition, which has many similarities to emotional disturbance. All these diet-illness connections are forcing the medical world to understand the role of nutrition in the wellness process.

WHOLE GRAINS, FRUITS AND VEGETABLES

That is the essential answer to health. Whole grains, fruits and vegetables have more health giving power than much of our highly processed, fat-saturated, sugar-laden, starch-bound, heavily-salted, overly-cooked food. "High consumption of fruits and vegetables and whole-grain products appears to lessen the risk of getting cancers of the mouth and throat, according to a National Cancer Institute Study." (Cancer Research 44:3, 1216, 1984 reported by Medical Update, November, 1984)

> "Cancer is the second leading cause of death in the United States and accounts for close to one out of five fatalities. The causes of cancer are many. But a common factor appears to be what we eat, drink, and breathe as well as where we live and work. With estimates that approximately one half of cancer cases might be linked to diet, can we wait until all the data are in before suggesting preventive steps to the general public?" (Tufts University Diet and Nutrition Letter, October, 1983)

The message to get persons to eat whole grains, fruits and vegetables is in the public media frequently. That message is probably on the "other channel" or competing for your attention with the "fast food" and "gormet" eating establishments. But if you have had a lot of illness, and your life is at stake, my guess is that you have at least some inkling that "food" creates "mood", etc.

BACK TO THE BIBLE FOR MOTIVATION

SHADRACH, MESHACH, ABEDNEGO, DANIEL

> "In the third year of the reign of Jehoiakim king of Judah, Nebuchadnezzar, king of Babylon came to Jerusalem and beseiged it. And the Lord gave Jehoiakim king of Judah into his hand, with some of the vessels of the house of God; and he brought them to the land of Shinar, to the house of his God, and placed the vessels in the treasury of his God. Then the king commanded Ashpenaz, his chief eunuch, to bring some of the people of Israel, both of the royal family and of the nobility, youths without blemish, handsome and skillful in all wisdom, endowed with knowledge, understanding learning, and competent to serve in the

king's palace, and to teach them the letters and language of the Chaldeans. The king assigned them a daily portion of the rich food which the king ate, and of the wine which he drank. They were to be educated for three years, and at the end of that time they were to stand before the king. Among these were Daniel. . . .Shadrach. . .Meshach. . .Abednego."

"But Daniel resolved that he would not defile himself with the king's rich food, or with the wine which he drank; therefore he asked the chief of the eunuchs to allow him not to defile himself. And God gave Daniel favor and compassion in the sight of the chief of the eunuchs; and the chief of the eunuchs said to Daniel, 'I fear lest my lord the king, who appointed your food and your drink, should see that you were in poorer condition than the youths who are of your own age. So you would endanger my head with the king.' Then Daniel said to the steward whom the chief of the eunuchs had appointed over Daniel, Shadrach, Meshach and Abednego, 'Test your servants for ten days; let us be given <u>vegetables</u> to eat and <u>water</u> to drink. Then let our appearance and the appearance of the youths who eat at the kings's rich food be observed by you, and according to what you see deal with your servants.'"

"So he hearkened to them in this matter, and tested them for ten days. At the end of ten days it was seen that they were better in appearance and fatter in flesh than all the youths who ate the king's rich food. So the steward took away their rich food and the wine they were to drink and gave them vegetables."
(Daniel 1:1-16)

This Biblical story sounds like it came out of the most current wholistic textbook, Jane Brody's Nutrition Book, or something like the Pritikin diet program. I am enamored with the 20th century's repeated scientific validation of the Biblical record and principles. The search for truth invariably finds religion and science closer than the skeptics would have us think.

FOUR HEALTH FOOD ENTHUSIASTS

Daniel, Shadrach, Meshach and Abednego are more famous for their "lion's den" and the "firey furnace" escapes. I rather doubt that eating vegetables and drinking water will enable us to escape the persecution of this world, but nutritionists assure us that a life-style which includes an adequate amount of vitamins and minerals will help us escape from some of our own bio-degradeable tendencies.

Throughout history and throughout the world, there are persons who see the problems of a food-indulgent life-style. They see food-indulgent persons cater to their inner "Id" impulses. Their aversion to this liberal life-style makes them swing in the opposite direction, becoming very conservative. Such persons begin to deny their "Id" and go more with their "Superego", the conscience. They swing from a life-style of doing what they "want" to doing what they feel "ought" to be done. Thus, they live by an inordinate amount of self control.

John the Baptist was such a conservative person. He was a Nazirite; a person who likewise practiced a highly disciplined life-style. You will find these types of persons in nearly every political, social, philosophical and religious system in the world. They may appear to be too far out for us, but they do act as a moderating and educating influence.

MODERATION AS A MORE ACCEPTABLE LIFE-STYLE

We need to take a lesson from these persons who react strongly against liberal and indulgent excesses. Abraham Maslow has written profoundly about the homeostatic inclinations of the biological processes. Wellness and healing are natural phenomena, unless stressors impede or stretch the homeostatic processes. Biological, psychological and spiritual processes will fight to return to their natural state. They will maneuver in such a way as to resist the stressor's attempts to drive them too far left or right, too far from the norms. The processes of the body, mind and spirit will only adapt and fixate at the extreme ends of the polarity, if forced to by the stressors of life. Appropriate activity which contains some leftism and some rightism, giving man freedom to move and be creative, is part of the doctrine of moderation.

It is this concept of moderation which, likewise, needs to be applied to food, and almost every other part of the human life-style.

DIET OF DANIEL, SHADRACH, MESHACH, ABEDNEGO

These four health food enthusiasts ate only vegetables, and drank only water. Eating a primarily vegetarian diet seems "nutty" to most persons. People generally perceive "vegetarians" as obscessive, right-wing, and slightly radical. Today, however, among wholistically oriented persons, there is an increase in the consumption of vegetables, along with whole grains and fruits. Our Christian brothers, the Seventh-day Adventists, have been advocating a health-giving diet of vegetables for years. The National Institutes of Health studied the people of this denomination in California. Dr. Mervyn Hardinge reports: "Our studies have revealed that the Seventh-day Adventist vegetarians are healthier than the average Californian. . . .There is a lower incidence of all forms of cancer. Heart disease is significantly less and, when it does occur, it is an average of ten years later than in other Californians." All these are benefits from a vegetarian diet, combined with abstinence from alcohol and smoking.

Vegetarians are of three types. 1. Lacto-ovo-vegetarian; in which meat, fish and poultry are dropped from the diet. 2. Lactovegetarian; in which eggs are dropped from the diet, along with the meat, fish and poultry. 3. Total vegetarian; in which milk products are excluded from the diet, along with eggs, meat, fish and poultry. The soy bean has been the staple of the vegetarian diet for centuries, because of its high protein content, and capacity to produce the nutrients necessary for health. Other high protein foods are oats, potato and broccoli, etc. Vegetarians use these as protein substitutes. The green leafy vegetables are high in vitamins and minerals. Calcium is found in the soy, in green leafy vegetables, in whole grains and in seeds (nuts). All the nutrients are there, but vegetables, whole grains and fruits may have to be eaten in different quantities to get the proper balance.

The heroes of the "lions den" and the "firey furnace" apparently understood nutrition better than we do. They had learned it in their home land, Palestine, so the value of water and vegetables must have been known to the Chosen People of God, who did not always act like Sons and Daughters of the Most High.

NEBUCHADNEZZAR'S LIFE-STYLE BRINGS ILLNESS

The King who offered his "rich food" and "wine" to Shadrach, Meshach and Abednego, suffered from a mental-physical regressive disorder - lycanthropy. Lycanthropy is a psychotic disorder in which a person imagines himself as a wolf or other wild animal, and behaves that way. This illness was reported in the literature of the past up until about the end of the 17th century. This mental condition came upon Nebuchadnezzar.

> "I, Nebuchadnezzar, was at ease in my house and prospering in my palace. I had a dream which made me afraid; as I lay in bed the fancies and the visions of my head alarmed me. Therefore I made a decree that all the wise men of Babylon should be brought before me, that they might make known to me the interpretation of the dream. Then the magicians, the enchanters, the Chaldeans, and the astrologers came in; and I told them the dream, but they could not make known to me its interpretation. At last Daniel came in before me. . .and I told him the dream. . . (Daniel interprets the dream). . . . .All this came upon king Nebuchadnezzar. At the end of twelve months he was walking on the roof of the royal palace of Babylon, and the king said, 'Is not this the great Babylon, which I have built by my mighty power as a royal residence and for the glory of my majesty?' While the words were still in the king's mouth,

there fell a voice from heaven, 'O King
Nebuchadnezzar, to you it is spoken: The kingdom
has departed from you, and you shall be driven
from among men, and your dwelling shall be
with the beasts of the field; and you shall be
made to eat grass like an ox; and seven times
shall pass over you, until you have learned
that the Most High rules the kingdom of men
and gives it to whom he will.'   Immediately
the word was fulfilled upon Nebuchadnezzar.
He was driven from among men, and ate grass
like an ox, and his body was wet with the dew
of heaven till his hair grew long as eagles'
feathers, and his nails were like birds' claws."
(Daniel 4:4-33)

Most interpreters have seen Nebuchadnezzar's arrogance and pride as the cause of his downfall. That certainly is a strong contributing factor, but not necessarily the only precipitating factor. Nebuchadnezzar's general unrighteous behavior was a factor. Here is the warning Daniel gave to Nebuchadnezzar one year prior to his mental-physical breakdown.

"Therefore, O king, let my counsel be acceptable
to you; break off your sins by practicing
righteousness and your iniquities by showing
mercy to the oppressed, that there may perhaps
be a lengthing of your tranquility." (Daniel
4:27)

Daniel was practicing a righteous life-style which included a form of eating quite different from King Nebuchadnezzar's nutrition. Thus, when Daniel mentions that the king should be more "righteous", Daniel could have mean't that Nebuchadnezzar should adopt a less indulgent life-style which includes a less indulgent food consumption pattern. We probably could not have come to this interpretation until recently. We now know that "food" changes "mood", and that poor nutritional patterns are being implicated in both physical and mental illness. Current research seems to again be validating what people like Daniel have known for a long time.

HOWARD HUGHES AND NEBUCHADNEZZAR

Nebuchadnezzar seems to be an adequate illustration of total deterioration from factors which could include poor nutrition. Physically, mentally, spiritually Nebuchadnezzar became what persons become when poor nutrition and personal sin combine to destroy everything good in someone. And even to this day we still see some animalness in emotionally disturbed persons. We may not see them eating grass, but just as degraded. The late Howard Hughes is pictured from time to time as a person whose mental, emotional, and physical deterioration reached depths which resemble what we picture of Nebuchadnezzar. There is no exact parallel here. We know that Howard Hughes did not eat nutritionally adequate foods. We see both Hughes and Nebuchadnezzar having similar empires of power and wealth. Beyond this, we must be cautious in comparing or diagnosing. Yet, a life-style which combines multiple stressors to the body, mind and spirit, almost assuredly produces a regressively destructive influence towards animal-like existence.

ASTOUNDING NUTRITIONAL THERAPY

Nebuchadnezzar regained his sanity. His "reason returned" after he returned to a diet of natural foods and liquids. In his emotionally disturbed condition of "lycanthropy", he **ate grass**. Nebuchadnezzar got away from the "rich food" and the "wine" (with all its sugars). He was forced back to natural foods. He ate mother nature's prime vegetable - grass. He drank mother nature's liquid - water. He returned to a "macrobiotic" diet. We may never know how much of the healing came from God or how much healing came from the avoidance of certain kinds of foods. Yet, between God's direct healing power and the healing which comes from returning to fundamental principles, Nebuchadnezzar was restored. Abraham Hoffer, M.D., says that when he has "fasted" patients and "taught them a vegetarian diet" he has returned 65% of would-be back-ward psychicatric patients to be on their own. ----- Listen to the rejoicing and the praise Nebuchadnezzar gives to God.

"At the end of the days, I Nebuchadnezzar lifted up my eyes to heaven, and my reason returned

to me, and I blessed the Most High, and praised and honored him who lives forever; . . . At the same time my reason returned to me; and for the glory of my kingdom, my majesty and splendor returned to me. My counselors and my lords sought me, and I was established in the kingdom, and still more greatness was added to me. Now I , Nebuchadnezzar, praise and extol and honor the King of heaven; for all his works are right and his ways are just; and those who walk in pride he is able to abase." (Daniel 4:34-37)

Even Nebuchadnezzar probably did not understand how he had been recycled through mother nature. He cites "pride" as the cause of his troubles. It is still true that when people are proud and arrogant, they tend not to listen to good advice. They tend to be preoccupied with their "Id" (wants) and avoid their "Superego" (oughts or conscience). They are not spiritual enough to work at the fruits of the spirit, one of which is "self-control". Pride is probably still the main problem, and if one is too proud to improve his/her nutritional intake, then s/he may have to suffer the consequences.

Until I became familiar with the nutritional component of psychotic illness, I did not ever help a psychotic. I referred them all to a mental hospital. I do not need to refer such persons now, if they are willing to work with me. Using all the multi-variable factors which are in this book, I have been having larger and larger success with schizophrenic behaviors. Psychiatry is being forced to consider nutritionally oriented treatment programs. One of our local psychiatrists has done some treating with "nutritional" alteration and supplementation after trying conventional medical approaches. These are encouraging signs.

JOINING THE INCREASED FIBER MOVEMENT

Do you know what dietary fiber is? Most people do not. Fiber is the hull of wheat, rice , and most grains, which contains about 2 dozen vitamins and minerals. We call it bran. We used to throw it away because people thought it was undigestible. White flour and polished rice, from about 1850 to the 1930's, contained no vitamins, until U.S. Government forced the addition of few vitamins to white flour. Fiber is found in beans, vegetables, fruits, seeds and nuts. Wheat, oats, barley, rye and other whole grain cereals are abundant in dietary fiber. There are two types of fiber, soluble and insoluble. Soluble fiber disolves in water, and insoluble fiber absorbs water. They work together. The gel of the soluble and the gums of the insoluble interact to foster health.

Fiber slows sugar absorption into the blood through the action of the apple's pectin, which is a soluble fiber, turning the sugars into a gel for slower absorption. Soluble fibers are therefore, very important to decrease diabetes.

Cholesterol and triglycerides are trapped, worked over, metabolized, blocked, and in other ways prevented from forming plaque on the artery walls through soluble and insoluble fibrous foods. Therefore, dietary fiber is good prevention for atheriosclerosis and other heart problems.

Fiber, with its bulk, speeds up the passage of food from the stomach, cutting down risk of diverticulitis, colon cancer, constipation, etc.

You can overtreat yourself by adding too much bran, which will speed up evacuation beyond what is desireable. There is a natural way to know whether you are eating the right amount of bran. If your bowel movement floats, you are eating enough bran!

The National Cancer Institute has some strong conclusions about the benefits of a diet high in fiber. Dr. Vincent DeVita, director of the NCI says, "I believe the data are overwelming when you look at all the people in all the populations that we've studied around the world who have low incidence of colon cancer: The Finns, the Mormons, the Seventh-day Adventists, just to mention a few. People who live in the Third world countries — you can always find that the fiber in their diet is high. It's not always the same kind of fiber. In some cases it's fruits-and-vegetables type fiber, and in other cases it's wheat-grain type fiber. And in many cases, fat is low. . . .If fiber were put back into Western diets, the incidence and mortality from diseases like colon cancer most certainly would come down. . . ." (Medical Update, October, 1984)

Here is a graphic way to understand how to shift to a diet which is higher in dietary fiber. In a shift to a high fiber diet, higher vitamin and mineral levels will bring more nutrition to the body, and food-fat levels will decrease by about 25%. Calorie and protein levels remain the same. Such a shift accounts for a 400% increase in "all dietary fiber". That is a major contribution to helath, because it represents a large increase in vitamin and mineral levels as well.

TWO SAMPLE MENUS

CURRENT TYPICAL DAY	Calories	All Dietary Fiber*	Soluble Fiber*	HIGH-FIBER DAY	Calories	All Dietary Fiber*	Soluble Fiber*
BREAKFAST							
1 cup orange juice	112	-	-	1 medium orange	88	4	3
2 large fried eggs	258	-	-	1 cup oatmeal	170	7	4
2 slices bacon	151	-	-	1 slice whole-wheat bread	59	2	-
1 slice white bread	64	1	-	1 tbsp. peanut butter	97	1	-
1 tsp. butter	35	-	-	1 cup skim milk	88	-	-
Total	620	1	0	Total	502	14	7
LUNCHEON							
4 oz. hamburger	313	-	-	2 cups beans & pasta	472	21	2
1 roll	121	1	-	2 slices Italian bread	170	2	-
20 pieces French fries	274	2	1	1 tomato with oil dressing	145	3	1
12 oz. cola	145	-	-	1 cup skim milk	88	-	-
1 large apple	96	7	4	1 large apple	96	7	4
				2 tsps. margarine	70	-	-
Total	949	10	5	Total	1041	33	7
DINNER							
6 oz. chicken (no skin)	280	-	-	4 oz. chicken (no skin)	186	-	-
1/2 cup rice with dressing	145	1	-	1 cup brown rice/margarine	290	5	-
1/2 cup broccoli	20	3	2	1 cup broccoli	40	6	4
1 cup apple juice	120	-	-	1 cup apple juice	120	-	-
2 medium white rolls	150	2	-	2 medium whole-wheat rolls	132	3	-
2 tsps. butter	70	-	-	2 tsps. margarine	70		
1 medium brownie	97	-	-	1 medium pear/almonds	80	5	1
Total	882	6	2	Total	918	19	5
Grand Total	**2451**	**17**	**7**	**Grand Total**	**2461**	**66**	**19**

CARBOHYDRATE	FAT	PROTEIN		CARBOHYDRATE	FAT	PROTEIN
41%	40%	19%		52%	29%	19%

*In grams

PARADE SEPTEMBER 5, 1982

VITAMINS FOR PREVENTION AND HEALING

Daniel, Shadrach, Meshach and Abednego knew that certain foods made them feel good and function better. There are millions of people taking vitamins because they feel good and function better. Most traditional schools of nutrition still advocate a "balanced diet of the four food groups". That's fine for persons who are majoring in nutrition, but the average person does not even know what the four food groups are. They resort to the use of vitamin supplementation, out of shear defense against the absolute neglect of training regarding nutrition. It is now known that roughly half of the American adult population takes vitamins. They may take them out of fear of food oversight, because of habit, or for specific medical problems. Some take too much of too many. Others not enough. Some vitamin companies package genuine rip-off formulas, and other companies attempt to be very responsible. Considering the size of the market, certainly the value of vitamins exceeds the possible detrimental factors.

Norman Cousins, former editor of the Saturday Review of Literature, used Vitamin C as one of the treatments for his illness in 1964. He uses some vitamin and mineral supplementation yet. (Read the story of his healing in Chapter 19.) Dr. Linus Pauling, Nobel laureate, founder of the Linus Pauling Institute for Science and Medicine, takes 10 grams of Vitamin C per day in divided doses. He also uses super-B-complex, extra niacin, extra zinc, Vitamins A and E. Usually, people take vitamins and minerals for their own therapeutic reasons, and not superstitiously. Be careful of word-of-mouth advice. If you seriously wish to use vitamin supplementation, read some books from your local library on vitamins. Then decide why you should take them, and in what amount. Vitamins A, D, E, and K can be harmful in excessive amounts, because they are fat-soluble vitamins and are held in the liver where they can become toxic if stored in large amounts. B-complex vitamins and Vitamin C are water soluble, and are not toxic even in large amounts.

Richard A Kunin, M.D., has written a book entitled Mega-Nutrition, in which he cites nutritional treatments for cancer, heart disorders, digestive disorders, mental disorders,, allegy disorders, etc.

Lendon Smith, M.D., has written Foods For Healthy Kids, in which he cites nutritional manipulation as treatment for children's hyperactivity, and other behaviorial disorders.

Paavo Airola, N.D., Ph.D., has written several books including Every Woman's Book, in which you find much information on nutritional ways to resolve medical and emotional problems.

Carolton Fredericks, Ph.D., wrote Nutritional Guide for the Prevention and Cure of Common Ailments and Diseases.   From Acne to Vericose Veins, you are given nutritional treatments for a variety of medical problems.

Michael Lesser, M.D., born in Mitchel, South Dakota, near where I grew up, wrote Nutrition and Vitamin Therapy. This book is very helpful, because in it, Dr. Lesser suggest the amounts of vitamins and minerals needed to have a therapeutic effect.

The list is long, and getting longer, of notable persons writing about the benefits of proper nutrition.   Each writer expands and expounds the gospel practiced by Daniel, Shadrach, Meshach and Abednego.   No writer suggests that people be as radically different as these Old Testament men of God.   Neither do I believe in that degree of radical behavior, unless you are trying to prove a point or get well.

Chronically ill persons should buy all the above books and read them from cover to cover. Find a nutritionally oriented physician. Work with him on your nutritional approach (possibly combined with medicine) to regain your health.   Between the two of you, with your new awareness and his understanding, you may just be able to make some forward steps toward health.

BACKSLIDING DUE TO POOR NUTRITION

You will have difficulty being spiritually powerful if you eat rotten. Your best spiritual intention will fall flat if your brain does not get enough nourishment, from the right kinds of food. This is due to the fact that we are made up of body, mind and spirit, and they all influence each other. You may go for a long time on spiritual power holding up the body and the mind, but spirituality can not hold up both body processes and mind processes forever, if they are not fed properly.

The brain needs serotonin, norepinephrine, and acety-choline. These are neuro-transmitters, brain food. They are used in our neurological functioning, and are primarily re-manufactured during our sleep. The body manufactures them out of amino-acids. Tryptophane is needed for serotonin which helps sleep, pain and appetite. Tyrosine is needed for norepinephrine which helps regulate pep and stamina. Choline is needed for actycholine which helps memory. These are generally supplied in various quantities in many foods. Soy, lima beans, cottage cheese, sea food, and meat have the highest content of the various amino acids. For example soy flour has 5 times more tryptophane than wheat flour. Lima beans have 10 times more tryptophane than green beans. Soy beans have 20 times more tryptophane than mushrooms, pumpkin, squash, egg plant, carrots, or cabbage. (Source: Nutrition Almanac, McGraw Hill, 1979) If a vegetarian diet does not include peas, beans and soy, quite likely there will be deficiencies. The brain will not have enough of a supply to provide maximum functioning. It will be as weak as some muscle which does not get enough glucose. Such people will "lose it", "blow", "withdraw", etc., Having prayed for God to help them, and when He seemingly did not, they say "Forget it." to the things of the Spirit. Not all hot-tempered persons blow up only from poor nutrition, but a number of "withdrawing" persons are that way from inadequate vitamins or minerals.

There are some really fine people, who have grown cynical about the church, the Bible, and God, because they tried all the spiritual things, but failed to see the inter-connections between the body, mind and spirit.

They tried to be "spiritual" but did not make it a total commitment or a total involvement.

A recent client sat depressed for one year. My Life Stress and Coping Strength Inventory picked up "poor nutrition", "excessive alcohol consumption", and "excessive sugar consumption". She had been spiritually despondent as well. She corrected her nutritional intake, retained her mental health, and felt spiritually alive once more.

"DIGESTIVE AND MORAL INDISCIPLINE"

Paul Tournier, Swiss physician with interest in the whole man, speaks of lack of discipline which some patients exhibit. "Frequently, these (atherosclerosis patients) have behind them a long history of _digestive and moral indiscipline,_ with which they have the greatest difficulty in making a break. So long as they have not found the inner source of true renunciation, they continually contravene their doctor's orders, preferring to ask him for a medicine which will make it unnecessary for them to reform their lives, and are impatient when the medicine does not afford the desired relief. They are active people who have heaped on their shoulders responsibilities and cares from which they cannot now extricate themselves. From long habit they have come to enjoy the excess of diet their strong constitution has allowed them to indulge in. One cannot but point out how embarrassing to the doctor these patients are, with the endless little 'exceptions' they allow themselves, but rarely admit, compromising their health daily." (The Healing of Persons, N.Y., Harper and Row, 1957, p.29)

I rest my case for urging nutritional awareness and discipline in combating illness of the body, the mind, and the spirit.

DISCUSSION

1. Daniel, Shadrach, Meshach and Abednego knew more about nutrition than most of us. Where did that knowledge come from?

2. List the reasons why we know so little about what foods we need to eat to have balanced nutrition.

3. Nebuchadnezzar became ill with a mental disorder called lycanthropy. How justified are we in concluding that it was due, at least in part, to his diet?

4. Nebuchadnezzar regressed to behavior like that of an animal. Do you see or know of persons in your area whose emotional disturbance has made them begin to look somewhat savage?

5. Nebuchadnezzar had a dream which Daniel interpreted one year before Nebuchadnezzar's downfall. Do emotionally disturbed person's dreams have imagery which is helpful diagnostically? (Jungian analysts use dreams in therapy.) Was Daniel, therefore, a good psychoanalyst?

6. Do you think it is proper to discuss nutrition in the church, where we usually just discuss spiritual things?

7. Vitamin and mineral supplementation is still a debated issue. Are there Christian principles or ideas which would guide us to answer the vitamin and mineral supplementation issue?

8. This chapter focused a lot on the value of eating vegetables, but what other nutritional improprieties contribute to poor health? (excess salt, excess caffeine, excess sugar, excess alcohol, etc.)

9. Should the church get into the nutrition education business if the schools do not?

10. Would you be willing to get a coalition of concerned persons together to educate your school board about the value of making nutritional awareness as important for survival as reading, writing, and arithmetic?

Chapter 12

HEALING AFTER CONTROLLED

SUGAR CONSUMPTION

"Every alcoholic tested had hypoglycemia."

Abram Hoffer, M.D.

"Relative hypoglycemia . . . a drop in blood sugar levels in response to caffeine and a high carbohydrate intake, was a common cause of neuro-psychiatric illness."

Dr. Harry M. Salzer

Relative Hypoglycemia ———— "The fatigue disease"

Americans currently eat 125 pounds of sugar per year. Americans, 200 years ago, ate only 5 pounds of sugar/year.

Evaluate your Sugar Consumption. Do you have some problems with your health that are traceable to excessive sugar consumption? Fill out the Inventory on the following page.

183

STRESS FROM EXCESS SUGAR CONSUMPTION

(Relative Hypoglycemia Inventory)

Pick out the most appropriate response. Write the number of that response in the space provided by that statement.

0. Never 1. Rarely 2. ONCE A WEEK 3. TWO OR THREE TIMES A WEEK 4. FOUR OR FIVE TIMES A WEEK
5. DAILY

1. _____ I am excessively tired and feel fatigued.
2. _____ I get down-hearted and depressed.
3. _____ I do not sleep as well as I would like.
4. _____ I get anxious, uptight or nervous.
5. _____ I get irritable for no apparent reason.
6. _____ I have headaches.
7. _____ I get drowsy after meals or midway between meals.
8. _____ I get shakey, sweaty; after I eat I feel better.
9. _____ I have a pulse rate of 84 or more when relaxing.
10. _____ I worry and have fears.
11. _____ I cry easily, or feel like crying.
12. _____ I crave sweets or have a ravenous appetite.
13. _____ I am forgetful or indecisive.
14. _____ I have indigestion, heartburn, hiatal hernia or ulcers.
15. _____ I have a temper that gets out of control.
16. _____ I have cold hands and feet.
17. _____ I have a low sex drive.
18. _____ I am moody, or people tell me I am moody.
19. _____ I have difficulty getting started in the morning.
20. _____ I feel life is not worth living when I get depressed.
21. _____ I feel faint if I don't eat.
22. _____ I drink a lot of coffee with sugar in it.
23. _____ I eat doughnuts, sweet roll, pastries, cookies
24. _____ I drink sweetened carbonated drinks.
25. _____ I drink alcoholic beverages.
26. _____ I eat candy.
27. _____ I get muscle cramps.
28. _____ I get fearful in crowds; have fear of being closed in.
29. _____ I am agoraphobic; fearful of leaving my home.
30. _____ I have premenstral tension. (1. mild symptoms, 3. moderate symptoms 5. severe symptoms)

_______________ TOTAL (Range 0 - 150)

(Enter this score in the summary SCORING on Page 358)

INTERPRETATION

0 – 60   Your score on the RELATIVE HYPOGLYCEMIA inventory is low enough to suggest that you do not have this problem. "Relative Hypoglycemia" is a problem where excess sugar consumption triggers mood variations, temper outbursts, depression and other side effects.

60 – 80   Your score on the RELATIVE HYPOGLYCEMIA inventory is in the mid-range, indicating a possible problem with hypoglycemia, commonly called "low blood sugar" (opposite of diabetes). There may be a number of stressors in your life causing this score to be as high as it is. Excess sugar consumption may not be the main reason for this score, but it could be a contributing reason. Your physician should order a Glucose Tolerance Test (GTT) to determine whether or not you have a problem with low blood sugar (also called "hyperinsulinism").

Above 80   Your score on the RELATIVE HYPOGLYCEMIA inventory indicates a high probability that you are having problems with keeping your moods stable because you are overeating sugar-laden foods. Persons can have a problem because of an overactive pancreas which secretes more insulin than necessary. Insulin turns excess sugar into fat to store it, but in turn, lowers the blood sugar level excessively in the hypoglycemic. Low blood sugar causes mood variations, temper explosions, depression and other side effects. With your score, you should have a physician order a Glucose Tolerance Test (6 hour) to diagnose this blood sugar condition.

THE LOW BLOOD SUGAR PROBLEM

Excessive consumption of sugar and flour products, arouses the pancreas to secrete insulin, in order to bring the blood glucose back to normal. Some person's pancreas oversecretes insulin, thereby dropping the blood glucose below normal, and creating the low-blood-sugar situation called hypoglycemia.

Americans formerly ate only 5 pounds of sugar per year, but now they eat an average of 125 pounds of sugar per person per year. That means the pancreas (the Islets of Langerhans within the pancreas) has to work 25 times harder than 200 years ago. It can rise to meet the challenge, and it will do so for a long time, but then the pancreas will give out, and you have "adult onset diabetes". If you overwork the pancreas it simply will give out. The pancreas has been known to become the site of cancer as well. The direct link between excess sugar consumption and cancer has not been established. There is, however, much evidence that mood levels are highly affected by the sugar drop.

Seale Harris in 1924 first described the condition of low blood sugar which he called hyperinsulinism. The medical world did not pick it up strongly until the early 1970's. Then some physicians discounted the problem, and still do, believing that the condition is just an excuse for emotional problems. The condition is not a disease, but a malfunction. It can be diagnosed in a laboratory by a 5 or 6 hour Glucose Tolerance Test. (Do not waste your time with a 3 or 4 hour GTT.) There is a way to do this yourself. Simply ask your pharmacist for Chem-strip test tapes for evaluating blood glucose. When you feel fatigued, grouchy, irritable, etc., prick yourself for blood. Put the blood on a test tape. Compare the blood-tape color with the color on the box and you will know what your blood sugar level is. If it falls below 60 milligrams per 100 milliliters of blood then you are hypoglycemic at that moment. Try it several times, since you have to buy a box of 25 strips, and then you will prove to your self whether you are, or are not, a hypoglycemic.

SYMPTOMS OF LOW BLOOD SUGAR

Symptom lists are multiplying so that it is almost unnecessary to get a Glucose Tolerance Test, to determine whether you are a functional hypoglycemic. The Health Corps. P.O. Box 8218, Van Nuys, California 91409, have a very fine symptom list, but it is sold only to Medical Doctors. You may evaluate yourself with it, however, in the Dr. Atkins Nutrition Breakthrough book. It is very accurate.

Carlton Fredericks, in his book Eating Right For You (Grosset and Dunlap, 1972), gives us his list of the symptoms from which hypglycemics suffer.

SYMPTOMS OF LOW BLOOD SUGAR —HYPOGLYCEMIA

Percentages of patients complaining of these symptoms

Nervousness	94%
Irritability	89%
Exhaustion	87%
Faintness, tremor, cold sweats	86%
Depression	77%
Vertigo, dizziness	73%
Drowsiness	72%
Headaches	71%
Digestive disturbances	69%
Forgetfulness	67%
Insomnia (awakens, can't sleep)	62%
Constant worrying, anxieties	62%
Mental confusion	57%
Internal trembling	57%
Pounding heart, rapid pulse	54%
Muscle pains	53%
Numbness	51%
Unsocial, asocial, antisocial	47%
Indecisiveness	50%
Crying spells	46%
Lack of sex drive (females)	44%
Allergies	43%
Incoordination	43%
Leg cramps	43%
Lack of concentration	42%

Blurred vision	40%
Twitching, jerking of muscles	40%
Itching, crawling skin sensation	39%
Gasping for breath	37%
Smothering spells	34%
Staggering	34%
Sighing and yawning	30%
Impotence (males)	29%
Unconsciousness	27%
Night terrors, nightmares	27%
Rheumatoid arthritis	24%
Phobias, fears	23%
Neurodermatitis	21%
Suicidal intent	20%
Nervous breakdown	17%
Convulsions	2%

Persons may have a number of these symptoms, but they do not have to have all of these symptoms to be having mood problems due to swings in blood glucose levels.

ESAU IS IRRATIONAL WHEN HIS BLOOD SUGAR IS LOW

The mood swing of the hypoglycemic is very irrational. Below 60 (mg/ml) blood sugar is accompanied by a variety of fatalistic feelings; feelings of "I don't care". That appears to be the feeling or sentiment of Esau, in signing over his birthright to his brother Jacob. Observe the Biblical record.

"When the boys grew up, Esau was a skilful hunter, a man of the field, while Jacob was a quiet man, dwelling in tents. Isaac loved Esau, because he ate of his game; but Rebekah loved Jacob. Once when Jacob was boiling pottage, Esau came in from the field, and he was famished. And Esau said to Jacob, 'Let me eat some of that red pottage, for I am famished!' Jacob said, 'First sell me your birthright.' Esau said, 'I am about to die; of what use is a birthright to me?' Jacob said, 'Swear to me first'. So he swore to him, and sold his birthright to Jacob. Then Jacob gave

> Esau bread and pottage of lentils, and he ate
> and drank, and rose and went his way. Thus
> Esau despised his birthright." (Genesis 25:27-34)

Notice the symptoms of fatigue, depression (I don't
care attitude), irritability, faintness, anti-social behavior,
etc. Esau might have had more symptoms. We do not
know. It made no sense for Esau to give up his birthright at that point. Possibly they had not gotten along
well as brothers. The parents seemed to have played
some "favoritism" and that often incites anger. However,
such sibling rivalry would normally make brothers more
possessive of their territory. So the act of giving up
the birthright seems to be an irrational act.

That irrationality is apparent in hypoglycemics when
their blood sugar is low. They will be mean, vindictive,
pickey, insulent, crude, explosive, etc. Usually, such
persons will regret their behavior later. Hopefully,
such persons apologize when they are remorseful, even
though, at that moment, they do not understand their
loss of self-control.

NEBUCHADNEZZAR'S SUGAR INTAKE

Nebuchadnezzar ate "rich food" and drank "wine".
In the previous chapter, you saw how Daniel, Shadrach,
Meshach and Abednego got permission from King
Nebuchadnezzar to eat a diet of vegetables and water.
They apparently knew of the problems of excessive
consumption of alcoholic beverages.

> "Daniel (and Shadrach, Meshach, and Abednego)
> resolved that (they) would not defile (themselves)
> with the king's rich food, or with the wine which
> he drank."   (Daniel 1:8)

There is an enormous amount of sugar in wine. The
Nutrition Almanac says there are 329 calories in 1 cup
of sweet wine (18.8%) and 204 calories in 1 cup of dry
(12%) wine. Thus, a fifth of sweet wine (5 cups) is about
1645 calories; enough calories for a "diet", but with
so few vitamins and minerals that you would die of scurvy,
beriberi and pellagra in a short time if that was all you
consumed.

Think of meals of "rich food" and "wine". Since I have lived in the Middle East, and know what foods they probably ate, I suggest this as Nebuchadnezzar's "rich food and wine" diet for one day. (1000 years later the Muslims outlawed alcohol in the Middle East.)

BREAKFAST
Bagel (equivalent) 2 of them	330 Calories
Cheese	105 Calories
Olives (4) and butter (6 pats)	104 Calories
Bajilla beans	190 Calories
Milk	88 Calories

LUNCH
Bread (2 slices equivalent)	72 Calories
Minestone soup	105 Calories
Dried apricots (¼ cup)	80 Calories
Dried dates (¼ cup)	120 Calories
Wine (Nebuchadnezzar's 2 cups)	658 Calories

DINNER
Roast Leg of Lamb (6 oz.)	470 Calories
Rice (1 cup)	180 Calories
Cucumber (1)	1 Calorie
Dried dates (¼ cup)	120 Calories
Fig bar (1)	200 Calories
Olives (4)	60 Calories
Cashews (¼ cup)	196 Calories
Apple	125 Calories
Wine (Nebuchadnezzar's 3 cups)	987 Calories

EVENING ENTERTAINMENT
Wine (Nebuchaenezzar's 2 cups)	658 Calories
TOTAL	**4849 Calories**

A total of 4849 calories for one day is almost exactly double the Recommend Daily Allowance, set by the U.S. Department of Agriculture in the U.S.A., for a person 50 years of age. Now go back and add up the calories from the wine and you have 2303 calories. Nearly half of the calories in this kind of a diet come from the alcohol.

In a life-style of this kind the pancreas has to work, scrounge for minerals, beg for nutrients, holler for help, cry when it gets no rest, scream bloody murder when it is scolded for not doing its job, gripe at the boss, steal from other body systems —— all because it is required to make insulin and can not find enough raw materials to do so. If you were a cell inside the pancreas, would you not go crazy, mutiny (mutate), and run away, like a cancer cell driving every other cell around you crazy too, till all the crazy cells get removed by a surgeon or sprayed with high powered atomic rays to kill them all. (Forgive me for not being scientific at this moment.)

SUGAR PUTS STRESS ON THE PANCREAS

If Nebuchadnezzar actually consumed the foods in some proportion as I have hypothesized, he would have worked his pancreas to death.   Once the pancreas no longer secretes insulin, the person is a diabetic.   Why Nebuchadnezzar became mentally ill, rather than diabetic, could be the subject of research.   Taking the research that I do know, I would postulate that Nebuchadnezzar began to depend more and more on alcohol, and as a result he ate less food, became deficient in the B complex vitamins and amino-acids, and it affected his brain so he suffered from the mental illness called lycanthropy. If he would have simply balanced his "rich food" with his "wine", there would have been enough nutrients to keep his brain from becoming dysfunctional, but he would likely have become diabetic and died for lack of treatment. Sugar and white flour are refined carbohydrates. Fortunately, Nebuchadnezzar did not have white flour in his day, or it might not have taken one year for him to deteriorate, between the time Nebuchadnezzar had his first dream-nightmare and the time of his actual fall.   Refined carbohydrates carry no B complex vitamins with them.   Yet the refined carbohydrates require B complex vitamins to be metabolized.   Alcohol, sugar, and white non-enriched flour, not only do not add to the vitamin-mineral level in the body, but they drain essential nutrients from the slight reserves the body maintains.   Excess sugar consumption is a big stress on the body, the mind and the spirit.

AVAILABILITY OF SUGAR TO NEBUCHADNEZZAR

Essentially, cane sugar as we know it, was possibly not known at the time of Nebuchadnezzar. Nevertheless, he had plenty of honey and dried fruits available to him.

Sugar very likely existed since it is mentioned in records of Alexander the Great's conquests and travels. Alexander the Great encountered sugar along the Indus River in India about 325 B.C., which is about 2 centuries after Nebuchadnezzar. Scant records show it existed in Rome in Nero's day, for Dioscorides, a Greek physician, describes a substance which was crystalline and crunchy and sweet. The Moors brought sugar with them into Spain in about 1000, and grew it there. The Venician traders brought sugar to medieval Europe from the Tigris and Euphrates river basin and from Egypt. It has always been rare and expensive, being sold in London in 1742 for $2.75 per pound. Columbus brought sugar planting to the Carribean, and the first sugar mill was in Isabelle, Santa Domingo in 1508. Cortez established plantations for sugar cane in Central America in the 1600's. It was first planted in Louisiana just before the Louisiana purchase in 1803. Beet sugar technology came into being about 200 years ago. Depending on farm prices, sugar has been cheaper than wheat, oats, barley, rye, and vegetables. Is there any wonder we need a resurgence of mind-over-matter training, and a formal course in nutrition for all persons going through our school systems? For the purpose of survival, a person probably needs to know nutrition in the future, more than arithmetic.

TREATMENT FOR HYPOGLYCEMIA

The treatment for hypoglycemia (also called hyperinsulinism) is a high protein and high complex carbohydrate (whole grains, fruits and vegetables) diet. Hypoglycemics need to eat every two to three hours for months to tame the hyperactive pancreas. They need to refrain from all refined white sugars and flours during their treatment program. If the hypoglycemic is faithful and uses mind-over-matter he can reduce the hyperinsulinism.

SCHIZOPHRENIA HEALED BY HIGH PROTEIN DIET

Dr. Michael Lesser, M.D. tells a fascinating story of a schizophrenic healed through nutritional supplementation and alteration.

"While in the highlands of New Guinea, we met
a Methodist missionary. When the missionary
discovered I was a psychiatrist, she invited
us back to her mission, saying 'I have a patient
for you.' . . . The following day I met Parume,
a 35 year old woman so bedraggled and emaciated
she looked 50. Wearing Campbell's soup cans
as arm bracelets and bearing a bag of garbage
on her back, Parume greeted me with an
appealing but silly smile and laughed bizarrely.
The missionary said, 'She has been sick five
years. Her husband will not allow her to dig
in the family yam patch; her tribe has thrown
her out. She would have starved but for us.'"

"Wishing an interview, I requested an
interpreter and the mission lady and I retired
inside. Suddenly we heard a loud thud, followed
by shrieks and moaning from the porch. We
rushed out to find parume lying prone, blood
trickling from a gash on her scalp. A couple
of frightened native boys had stoned her, such
was the terror the mad woman held for her
tribe. Parume wasn't seriously injured, and
when the interpreter arrived the interview
commenced. She felt a divine calling to return
the natives to their ancestral Satan worship
and away from the colonizers' Christianity.
Parume spoke darkly of the skeletons of dead
men lying in the jungle and believed she
communicated with their spirits. Satan's demons
had thoroughly infested her with tormenting
aches and pains in her belly and joints. She
was indeed what Western doctors would call
a paranoid schizophrenic."

"What could I do for this madwoman whom
I saw for one hour and would never see again?
No talk therapy or social work could possibly
help because of the insurmountable language
and cultural barriers. Only a chemical therapy
could work; why not try the megavitamins?"

"I will give you foods which will slowly drive

the demons out of you,' I announced in my best witchdoctor fashion. She was pleased and grateful, and the missionary and I retreated inside. We wrote Dr. Ffeiffer, asking him to send niacin, vitamin C, and a B-complex which, along with a high protein diet, was my prescription. The native diet of yams is poor in protein, rich in carbohydrate, and contains a mild hallucinogen, the worst diet for most schizophrenics. The mission donated tins of fish, the only available protein."

"Five months later. . . . .A letter arrived from New Guinea, bringing a . . . surprise. Parume had recoverd completely and had been accepted back by her husband and tribe. A few months later, the missionaries sent a second letter. My patient had relapsed. When the missionary investigated, she found Parume's husband had been taking the tinned fish for himself. Restored to her high protein diet, Parume promptly recovered again." (Nutrition and Vitamin Therapy, Bantam, 1981)

How about you? Have you been suffering from some similar illness? Do you need to consider the possibility that your nutritional intake is contributing to your illness? In wholistic thinking the patient takes the initiative, and changes some life-styles to facilitate healing, in addition to doing a "poor me" genuflex in front of a professional care-giver and saying "Fix me".

PHOBIAS HEALED AFTER SUGAR REDUCTION

Here is how it works. The hypoglycemic, has a pancreas that overinsulinizes, and lowers blood sugar more than it should. If the pancreas takes too much sugar out of the blood, one would faint. The body protects itself. Adrenalin has the task of getting sugar in the blood. Thus, if blood sugar runs low, there will be an increase of adrenalin. That will make the heart and lungs go faster, producing a mild tachycardia or hyperventilation. Now, suppose that happens to you as you are driving. Two or three of those attacks will soon make you fearful of driving or going places, because your mind does not know what is happening.   If you see a psychiatrist about your phobia of driving and going places, he will label you an "agoraphobic" (agora in greek means market place).   Let the same thing happen to you a few times while shopping, and you may soon be fearful of shopping or going where crowds congregate.   Dr. Harvey M. Ross says,

> **"In my practice I do not treat the phobia. I treat the hypoglycemia."**

Dr. Harvey M. Ross is President of the Academy of Orthomolecular Psychiatry.   He has written about hypoglycemia in a book entitled, Hypoglycemia: The Disease Your Doctor Won't Treat (Pinnacle Books).   In an interview with Martin Zucker (Lets Live, April, 1983) Dr. Ross said that he believes about 15% of hypoglycemics have phobias of some kinds.

Try being your own psychiatrist, not replacing psycho-therapy, but supplementing your professional therapy with your personal nutritional therapy.   Swear off ("covenant with God" sounds better) all sugar, white flour, honey, dried fruits (especially raisens); all sugar-laden foods for at least three to six (3 to 6) months minimum.   Go with whole grains, vegetables, fruits, fish and poultry; a macrobiotic diet.   This is not as radical as the diet of Daniel, Shadrach, Meshach and Abednego, but let the diet show you what it can do.

MIGRAINES, PMS, ALCOHOLISM, ETC.....

Ailments of a mental and physical nature are counteracted by a macrobiotic diet.   The evidence is equally strong that a number of illness conditions like migraine headaches, PMS, and alcoholism, are being traced to the excessive consumption of sugar as one of the factors.   Far too long, we have simply worked for a singular diagnosis, and hoped we could cure it with a singular medicine.   We still use multiple medicines for multiple problems, but we do not yet think in terms of multiple treatment modes, which include sugar reduction, for one problem.

STRESS MANAGEMENT IS SUGAR MANAGEMENT TOO

Stress management is more than organizing your day so you can control yourself. Stress management is more than an aerobics course, or enforced jogging for executives. Stress management is a mind-over-matter approach to all that impinges on body, mind and spirit. Stress management is the control of a multi-factoral life-style which includes the management of refined carbohydrate intake.

DISCUSSION

1   Secular historical records of the existence of cane sugar date it at least as far back as 325 A.D. But in the Bible Jeremiah, a contemporary of Nebuchadnezzar (6th century B.C.), speaks of "sweet cane from a distant land" in Jeremiah 6:20. Are you impressed by Biblical information that corresponds to secular data?

2. Esau was depressed when he was hungry. His blood sugar was low. How responsible are we, or should we be, for actions and words said in times when we have low blood sugar? or if we are hypoglycemic?

3. Nebuchadnezzar became mentally disturbed. How justified are we to suggest that his mental condition was affected by excessive sugar intake?

4. Suppose you are ill with pancreatitis, or have cancer of the pancreas, will God hear your prayer for healing, if you have no intentions of cutting back on sugar intake, or alcohol intake?

5. Suppose you have an illness of the pancreas, and you go to a faith healer, what do you think will happen?

6. As you understand wholistic thinking, how much should you lean on professional care givers, and how much do you need to lean on the Biblical life-style?

7. How are we going to know the balance between eating an adequate amount of sugar, and eating too much sugar?

Chapter 13

HEALING AFTER

ALLERGY TREATMENT

"I have now seen a number of chronic schizophrenics whose hallucinations are directly related to certain foods to which they are allergic. When they were treated by a four-day water fast they were free of all their perceptual changes and when they consumed the food, milk or beef or corn or whatever they were allergic to, the hallucinations would return in a matter of hours." Abram Hoffer M.D. (Journal of Orthomolecular Psychiatry, Vol. 8, No. 3, 1979)

There are many "symptoms" for allergic reactions to foods and chemicals in the environment. Take the Allergy Symptom Inventory on the next page to analyze the stress overload from allergic reactions.

197

STRESS FROM ALLERGIC REACTIONS

TO FOOD AND CHEMICAL POLLUTANTS

Pick out the most appropriate response. Write the number
of that response in the space provided by that statement.

0. Never 1. Rarely 2. Occasionally 3. Sometimes 4. Frequently
5. Almost always

1. _____ I have a fast (racing) heart beat (above 84).
2. _____ I have headaches.
3. _____ I am restless, nervous or anxious.
4. _____ I have indigestion, heartburn, hiatal hernia or ulcers.
5. _____ I am tired to the extent that I am fatigued.
6. _____ I have diarrhea alternating with constipation.
7. _____ I have stomach pains, nausea or vomiting.
8. _____ I have an itchy, stuffy or runny nose.
9. _____ I have sinus drainage or sore throat.
10. _____ I have red, runny eyes or blurred vision.
11. _____ I get a rash or hives after eating certain foods.
12. _____ I have high blood pressure.
13. _____ I have chest pains.
14. _____ I have swollen or stiff fingers.
15. _____ I have a lot of gas in my stomach.
16. _____ I have shortness of breath, asthma or bronchitis.
17. _____ I have arthritis or aching joints.
18. _____ I have itching skin, anus, eyes.
19. _____ I have ringing in my ears, popping sounds (Meniere's)
20. _____ I am moody or depressed.
21. _____ I feel weak.
22. _____ I feel as if I have a hangover, even if I did not drink.
23. _____ I have numbness in my muscles.
24. _____ I have feelings of panic.
25. _____ I feel as if I am emotionally unstable.
26. _____ I am irritable.
27. _____ I have violent outbursts.
28. _____ I have foods that disagree with me.
29. _____ I have foods that I crave.
30. _____ I feel tired or irritable or uptight after I eat.

31. _____ I had colic when I was a baby.
32. _____ I was a hyperactive child.
33. _____ I sneeze or feel ill around fumes from

soap	waxes	fabrics
polishes	cleaners	deodorants
perfumes	ammonia	hair sprays
smoke	exhaust gas	factory fumes
magic marker	etc....................	

34. _____ I have colitis.
35. _____ I have gall bladder problems.
36. _____ I feel sick after drinking alcohol.
37. _____ I have urinary infections.
38. _____ I have back aches.
39. _____ I have acne.
40. _____ I have been diagnosed as schizophrenic .
41. _____ I have a fullness-in-the-head feeling.
42. _____ I have ear drainage or hearing loss.
43. _____ I have itching in one or both ears.
44. _____ I have hoarseness or a constant cough.
45. _____ I have canker sores.
46. _____ I have swollen glands.
47. _____ I have sores or polyps in my nose.
48. _____ I have times when my body feels bloated.
49. _____ I have a loss of interest in sex.
50. _____ I have recurrent infections.

_____________ TOTAL (Range 0 - 250)

(Enter this score in the summary SCORING on Page 358)

INTERPRETATION

0 – 70   Your STRESS FROM ALLERGIC REACTION score suggests that it is highly unlikely that you have allergic reactions to foods or pollutants in the environment. Many persons have mild reactions to pollens, perfumes or petrochemical smells, but do not become ill from such reactions.

71 – 100   Your STRESS FROM ALLERGIC REACTION score suggests you could possibly be allegic to some food or pollutant in your environment. Allergic reaction could be a stressor in you. It is difficult to be decisive about the conclusion from this score because your symptoms could be coming from some other stress or illness in your life. You are being asked only to consider the possibility of allergic reactions.

Above 100   Your STRESS FROM ALLERGIC REACTION score is elevated far above the average. Your body is apparently under some heavy stress and allergy problems could be the source of some of that stress. People can be allergic to foods. The four main food groups which produce allergic reactions are: milk products, wheat, legumes, and beef. Try eliminating them one by one for a few days and see whether you feel better. Eat them again, and, if your pulse increases 15–20 beats, you are probably allergic to them. Then try other foods like chocolate, caffeine, eggs, pork, sugar, etc. Allergic reactions to fumes in the environment are more difficult to discover, but heart beat rates do increase, most of the time, when a person is allergic to fumes from petro-chemical products. See a professional allergist to confirm or rule out such a possibility. Then use the "pulse test" to confirm his conclusions. The "pulse test" is still the most reliable test for allergic reactions to foods.

ALLERGIES AND ILLNESS

People can be allergic to pollens, molds, mildew, fungi, and generally airborn particles. That is one class of allergens and it involves mostly the respiratory system. A second class of allergens is certain chemicals found in foods. These allergens do most of their reacting in the digestive system. A third class of allergens is composed of the petro-chemical inhalents which are found in our cleaning products, solvents and exhausts. This third class of allergens primarily affects the brain and the neurological system. All of them can make certain persons very ill after long-term exposure, or when the stress levels are high and the immune system cannot handle the overload.

When the invading allergen makes contact within the body, the immune system responds to defend the body. Invading substances which are inert, lacking in active chemical properties, are not a threat to the immune system. Things like bacteria threaten the body, and they possess active chemical properties which affect living cells. The immune system perceives the allergens like bacteria. Therefore, the immune system will respond to overthrow them. The immune system mobilizes to retaliate and throws antibodies and white blood cells into the fight. The chemical warfare of the two sides is waged at some expense to the person's general health. The inflamation and pain of that inflamation are very real to the person.

ILLNESSES FROM ALLERGIES

Allergic reactions are problems of mild, moderate or severe proportions. Here are some of the illnesses which have responded to allergy diagnosis and treatment.

Alcoholism	Fatigue
Arthritis	Headache
Asthma	Hyperactivity
Colitis	Hypertension
Depression	Neuroses
Digestive disorders	Obesity
Ear, nose, throat disorders	Phobias
Enuresis (bed wetting)	Schizophrenia

Specialists like Theron Randolph, M.D., Marshall Mandell, M.D., Lawrence Dickey, M.D., Abram Hoffer, M.D., and others, treat people who have these illnesses from allergic reactions to a variety of airborn and foodborn allergens. People have these illnesses for reasons other than allergic reaction. Medical evaluation and treatment is of prime importance to differentiate whether the illness is from allergy or other sources.

GOD'S INSTRUCTIONS FOR ALLERGY RELIEF

God gave Moses and the Children of Israel a series of health enhancement principles. Among all the guidelines about fat reduction, about quarantine for identifying infectious disease, about sin offerings for the reduction of guilt, about prohibitions from eating disease-carrying animals, etc., there is a regulatory procedure to control or eliminate some allergic reactions. Observe for yourselves what was commanded.

> "The Lord said to Moses and Aaron, When you come into the land of Canaan, which I give you for a possession, and I put a leprous disease (a fungus, or mold, or mildew, or lichen) in a house in the land of your possession, then he who owns the house shall come and tell the priest. 'There seems to me to be some sort of disease in my house.' Then the priest shall command that they empty the house before the priest goes to examine the disease, lest all that is in the house be declared unclean; and afterward the priest shall go in to see the house. And he shall examine the disease; and if the disease is in the walls of the house with greenish or reddish spots, and if it appears to be deeper than the surface, then the priest shall go out of the house to the door of the house, and shut up the house seven days. And the priest shall come again on the seventh day, and look; and if the disease has spread in the walls of the house, then the priest shall command that they take the stones in which is the disease and throw them into an unclean place outside

the city; and he shall cause the inside of the house to be scraped round about, and the plaster that they scrape off they shall pour into an unclean place outside the city; then they shall take other stones and put them in the place of those stones, and he shall take other plaster and plaster the house."

"If the disease breaks out again in the house, after he has taken out the stones and scraped the house and plastered it, then the priest shall go and look; and if the disease has spread in the house it is a malignant leprosy in the house; it is unclean. And he shall break down the house, it stones and timber and all the plaster of the house; and he shall carry them forth out of the city to an unclean place." (Leviticus 14:33-45)

LEPROSY OR FUNGUS, OR MOLD, OR MILDEW

If you investigate the interpretation of "leprous disease" in the commentaries on Leviticus, you will see that almost every commentator suggests either the word "fungus", or "mold", or "mildew", or "lichen" (growth on the north side of trees) as the proper interpretation. They agree that the words "greenish or reddish spots" refers to some substance natural to rock-producing or wood-producing growth. The word "leprous", here, is used as an adjective describing the spreading nature of the disease, which is a characteristic of leprosy. Leprosy is known to be a communicable disease, transmitted by a bacillus through persons with discharge from active lesions, via the skin or open lesions in another person, or through the mucous membranes in the nose and throat of the recipient. For this reason contaminated furniture and clothing had to be washed in running water. The leprosy bacillus multiplies and stays alive in humans, but is not known to stay alive or grow in inorganic matter. For these reasons, people who know leprosy have difficulty interpreting the meaning as leprosy coming out of a rock. We live nearly 3500 years away from that happening. With current awareness, we find it more plausible to understand the substance in those contaminated houses to be a fungus, mold or mildew.

Current stress theory regards overload of almost any kind as detrimental to our health. If those rocks and timbers in the houses of the Israelites in Canaan were filled with a fungus, mold or mildew, the growth of a chemically active substance emitting spores to continue their life cycle, would be hazardous to the health of the occupants. The chemically active spores would be perceived by the human body as capable of altering chemical changes in the body by their presence. The immune system would be aroused. If someone slept beside a spore-spewing fungus or mold, that constant irritation or invasion by the spores would create allergic reactions. The overload would create many body responses resembling the symptoms of a variety of illnesses. Sufficient stressing from the spores of molds could eventually bring serious illness.

GOD'S PLAN — IDENTIFY THE ALLERGEN — REMOVE IT

The allergic effect of a mold in an Israelite house seems to have been known. The Israelites were alerted to a problem, to be sure, but now, 3500 or more years later, the problem seems to be amplified by science's ability to create many chemically active substances to which people can become allergic.

The reason the allergen has to be removed is that the constant bombardment of the allergen arouses the immune system, and eventually the immune system is overloaded. The immune system is stressed. It can become weakened to such an extent that bacterial and viral invasions can no longer be conquored. Thus illness sets in more quickly when persons are stressed.

Recall that Hans Selye, M.D. has established the proposition that stress from almost any source, if left impacting the body long enough, will produce disease. The task of discovering what a person is allergic to, has become so much larger because of the large influx of chemically active substances, like the spores of molds in the houses of the Israelites.

One of my clients had allergic reactions to a variety
of foods, molds and inhalents. She would be glad to
have you hear her story. Hers was a life filled with
periodic peaks of painful stress. She had ear, nose and
throat problems as a child and lived for years on
anti-biotics, which continually suppressed some of her
natural immune responses. As time went on the allergic
reactions to foods, molds and inhalents became worse
and her immune system was less and less able to fight
the battle. She was not ill enough to die, but not well
enough to live without misery.   In that miserable state
she heard about an ecology clinic in Dallas. It was costly,
but it gave her some answers and treatment ideas, hope
and victory.

TREATMENT FOR ALLERGIC REACTIONS

An ecology clinic places the patient in a room with
bed materials that are either iron or wood, no plastic
which gives off fumes. The bed linens are all cotton,
to rule out the "out-gasing" from fibers made from
petro-chemicals. There are no carpets, which have
formaldehyde "out-gasing". The heat comes from
electricity, steam or hot water; no gas furnaces which
might emit gas fumes. The air is all purified and filtered.
When you arrive you go on a 4-5 day fast, drinking only
spring water. Slowly, thereafter you are given singular
foods to check for allergic reaction. You are tested
for fumes of perfume, gas, plastics, exhausts. You are
tested for molds, mildew, pollens. The goal is to try
to see your sensitivity in relation to your environment.
Most persons are then put on a 4-day rotation diet, so
that the body can rest 3 days before eating any particular
food. Some foods are completely off limit. The goal
is to give you some awareness about what is making
you ill, so you can fight back.

In the 2 weeks or one month that you might be in
such a clinic, you are in group therapy and individual
therapy to help you eliminate stress. You are taught
stress management techniques of relaxation, meditation,
visualization, nutrition, exercise and whatever is needed
to lower inner psychic stress, so the healing of the immune
system can take place.

The fight against allergic reactions, that most of us know about, is those weekly injections for allergies. A good many of these allergies are traceable to genetic predispositions. We do not know why some people have allergies and some persons do not. Yet, if you ask a person with allergies, for which they get shots, they would probably be willing to acknowledge that their allergies flare up in time of stress. Thus, allergy reactions bear some connection to stress, but we may not always know what the stress is. Certainly, living in our society, where we have innumerable chemicals bombarding us in our foods, and living environment, it is surprising that more people do not have a deteriorating immune response.

A BIBLICAL ANALOGY REGARDING ALLERGY

In the Old Testament era, when the Children of the Covenant did not keep their half of the covenant, foreign nations invaded the Israelites, and created a lot of misery. During the time of the Judges, like Samuel, the Philistines were a plague to the Israelites. During the reign of Israel's kings and prophets, when the Israelites abandoned righteousness, the Syrians invaded and humbled them. Later the Assyrians invaded. Later yet, the Babylonians invaded. Each time the invasions came at a time when the Israelites had forsaken or slackened in their worship of God, and their pursuit of righteousness. The internal weakness of the Israelites, made them easy prey for the invaders. The Old Testament often teaches a lesson physically, geographically and chronologically, which is also true spiritually. Man is exceptionally vulnerable when he forsakes righteousness. That is the case with the body's vulnerability to the airborn and foodborn allergen. The body's immune response is strong when all the internal mechanisms are fueled, oiled, timed and strengthened. When there is inner harmony, a "right"-eousness of interaction between body, mind and spirit, then the system will be more able to handle invasive irritants. Stress results from systems being out of balance. When man is righteous his system is more in balance with the way it was intended to run. Then it will run smoother and longer. The immune system is like that.

Biologically, the body needs the proper fuel of nutrition, the proper strengthening of exercise, the proper tuning and timing with values that do not set up self-destructive vibrations. When that body hums smoothly, there is simply going to be less harm done by the invading airborn or foodborn allergen.

FACTORS CONTRIBUTING TO IMMUNE DEFICIENCY

People with chronic illness probably do not try to discover why they are sick so often. Religious people sometimes attribute illness to Divine intention or permission. Non-religious people chalk it off as "bad luck". There are a number of things that can influence immune systems. There are factors which affect our immune response to disease, such as malnutrition, infection, irradiation, prescription drugs, ingested and inhaled chemicals (fumes), genetic factors, etc. Most of these factors have been shown to have an effect on the thymus and lymph system which controls our immune capacity against disease.

Our behavior also affects our immune system. This may be harder for us to understand, but research is constantly working at showing how our emotions and our behavior affect our immune system's ability to keep us healthy. The Holmes and Rahe Stress Test, shows that an increase in stress from such factors as death of loved one, separation, divorce, moving, increased mortgage, etc., give people greater and greater probability of being ill. This proposition that elevated stress increases the risk of illness has been documented by others. (See Dohrenwend, B.S. and Dohrenwend, B.P. (Eds.) Stressful Life Events, N.Y.: Wiley, 1974) There is very little doubt among scientists about the immuno-suppressant effect of stress of all kinds, including the stress of airborn and foodborn chemicals; even the chemically active spores of fungi or molds. Therefore, some inappropriate, immature, inadequate attitudinal or behavioral response can allow that stressor to continue aggravating the immune system, giving us pain and illness.

PROPER BEHAVIOR INCREASES IMMUNE RESPONSE

If some lack of attitudinal or behavioral response

sets us up for illness by suppressing our immunity, then proper attitudinal response and behavior would logically contribute to health. Behavior, our behavior, contributes to health and longevity. We have that divine wisdom transmitted to us down through the ages by God.

"My son, do not forget my teachings, but let your heart keep my commandments, for length of days and years of life and abundant welfare will they give to you." (Proverbs 3:2)

"Wisdom has built her house. . . .The fear of the Lord is the beginning of wisdom. . . .for by me (wisdom) your days will be multiplied and years will be added to your life." (Proverbs 9:1,11)

God is promising a greater amount of immunity from pain, sickness and early death if we will practice some of God's principles of behavior that will foster our own health.

ARTHRITIS CASE STUDY

"Dr. Randolph had a case of rheumatoid arthritis in a 32 year old clergyman who had suffered intermittent cramps from the age of eleven to age 31. In all other respects, he had been in good health until one day he suddenly developed acute migratory arthritis involving his knees, feet, and sternum (breastbone). The arthritis was accompanied by progressively increasing fatigue and intermittent periods of mental depression. In 1967 he was hospitalized (under Dr. Randolph's care). . . .The patient fasted and was kept in a controlled environment. As expected, all of his symptoms got worse during the first few days in the hospsital; these were typical food-withdrawal symptoms. Then his arthritis began to fade away as the effects of the causastive food allergens disappeared." (Marshall Mandell, M.D., 5-Day Allergy Relief System, Denver: Nutri-books Corp, 1979, p. 73)

ASTHMA CASE STUDY

"M.S. is a 32 year old house wife with asthma, hay fever, gastrointestinal disturbances, urinary frequency, fatigue, depression and irritability. The clinical application of provocative food test data made it possible for this patient to be happy and comfortable after years of poor health. Her excellent response from the elimination of test-positive foods which were identified during the early phase of her investigation made further studies unnecessary." (Marshall Mandell, M.D., in A Physician's Handbook of Orthomolecular Medicine, edited by Roger J. Williams and Dwight K. Kalita; New Canaan, CT: Keats Pub., 1979, p. 132)

SEVERE EMOTIONAL PROBLEMS CASE STUDY

"Vivian R., the mother of three, often became sick while doing the daily chores in her home and while shopping downtown. Within a matter of minutes after she began housecleaning or when she was in moderately heavy traffic, she would suffer abdominal cramps and have to rush to the nearest bathroom because of severe rectal urgency. In addition, her throat would become parched and her eyes would burn and itch. Once this progression of symptoms began, she would usually become dizzy and disoriented. . . .Mrs. R. was highly susceptible to the chemical fumes from various cleansers and polishes; gasoline combustion products in automobile emissions also bothered her. . . . I had Vivian's husband remove the gas stove. . .she eliminated the odorous cleaning agents. . . . I did what every good psychiatrist someday will be able to do. I accurately identified the nature of her cerebro-visceral allergic disorder." (Marshall Mandell, M.D., 5-Day Allergy Relief System, Denver: Nutri-books Corp, 1979, p. 104-105)

FAILURE IN SCHOOL CASE STUDY

"Frederick Eccleson. . .was on the negative Dean's List for failing students. Although bright, he was flunking out of the scientific institution he had entered with such great expectations a year before. . .When he was tested in the office with scientific procedures, it was found that he was highly allergic to pork, milk, eggs, potato, beets and beet sugar, and peanuts. . .By avoiding these incriminated foods entirely, he underwent a transformation. His fatigue and headache went away quickly. One day he popped in to visit me and proudly handed me an official school certificate citing him for having completed the work of the past quarter with high honors'. He had obtained straight A's in all his courses. . .At the bottom of the photocopy he had handed me he had written simply. 'Thank you, Dr. Randolph'." (Theron G. Randolph, M.D., and Ralph W. Moss, Ph.D., An Alternative Approach to Allergies, N.Y.: Bantam, 1982, p. 166)

GROWTH IN AWARENESS REGARDING ALLERGY

The Israelites, with their possible allergic reactions to fungi and molds had potential health hazards, but the influx of chemicals into the current world has potentially alarming significance. Marhshall Mandell, M.D., estimates that "50 to 80 percent of the daily medical practice of many doctors" is because of allergic reactions to airborn and foodborn chemical agents which the body perceives as harmful, and reacts with illness symptoms. Arthur Coca, M.D., an immunologist of a previous generation, and originator of the "Pulse Test" for allergy diagnosis, estimated that as many as 90% of all Americans have one or more food allergies. (Familial Nonreaginic Food Allergy, Springfield, Ill.: Charles C. Thomas, 1945)

KNOWING THE TRUTH

Spiritually, knowledge of the truth of Jesus Christ, sets people free from their bondage to sin. Such knowledge enables the sinner to have faith in Christ and the atonement he made for sin. With that knowledge the Christian can go on to reconstruct his life in accord with the principles of the Word. Health, happiness and prosperity are then promised and obtained. Jesus said,

> **"If you continue in my word, you are truly my disciples, and you will know the truth and the truth will make you free." (John 8:32)**

You can apply the awareness-of-truth principle in almost every situation. You can apply it to awareness regarding allergic reactions to substances which the body perceives as foreign to its functioning. If, in fact, a person is chronically ill, and has not yet examined the possibility of allergic reactions, then that person ought to seek the truth. Once the truth is found, that person needs to translate that into behavior, which deals with the problem, whether it be sin or allergens.

DISCUSSION

1   There are allergic reactions to molds, fungus, mildew, pollen, dust, and animal hair. In what part or parts of the body will persons experience reactions to them? Foods and food additives also produce allergic reactions. In what part or parts of the body will the symptoms of allergic reactions to foods show up? Fumes from cleaning agents, solvents, plastics, aerosols,and exhausts, all produce allergic reactions for some persons. In what parts of the body does a person experience the reactions to petro-chemical fumes?

2.   The author is suggesting that it is quite possible the problem of "leprous disease" in the stones and plaster of the Israelites' houses, could have been spore-spewing fungi, to which people react allergically. Could those spores have lowered people's immunity to leprosy, so that leprosy was attributed to the molds or fungi in the rock and plaster of those houses?

3.   The Israelites were invaded, when they failed to worship God. What can happen to us spiritually, mentally, and physically if we do not worship God and live by His principles?

4.   Name the factors which contribute to immune deficiency. Can you describe how poor attitude and behavior, after the death of a loved one, creates an immune deficiency (is immuno-depressive)?

5.   What can one do to build up the immune system, or maintain its high level of efficiency?

6.   Prayer is an essential ingredient of Christian faith. For healing a weak immune system, in what proportion should one have faith, and in what proportion should that person pray? Is there some percentage of mind-over-matter that would help?

Chapter 14

OUT FROM UNDER THE STRESS

OF CARING

"Bear one another's burdens, and so fulfil the law of Christ."   (Galatians 6:2)

Child care can become a great burden. Sick care of a loved one can become an excessive burden. Religious care for a self-destructing sinner can begin to weigh down the human spirit. Professional caring in the role of counselor, pastor, social worker, elder, deacon, church school teacher, or public servant may begin to drain the human body-mind-soul complex.

If you are feeling fatigued, tied down, overwhelmed, more sullen than usual, and life is not as zestful, beautiful and joyful as you would like, examine the stress-of-caring syndrome and decide if you need to find a road to emotional freedom.

STRESS OF CARING

Pick out the most appropriate response. Write the number
of that response in the space provided by that statement.

0. Never 1. Rarely 2. Occasionally 3. Sometimes 4. Frequently
5. Almost always (For questions 2,4,6,8,10,12 use the number
of months appropriate to the question.)

1. _____ I feel stress in taking care of our young children.
2. _____ I have felt this way for months. How many?
3. _____ I feel stress in relationship to our teenager(s).
4. _____ I have felt this way for months. How many?
5. _____ I feel stress taking care of my spouse because of
his or her illness.
6. _____ I have felt this way for months. How many?
7. _____ I feel stress in taking care of one or both of my
parents.
8. _____ I have felt this for months. How many?
9. _____ I feel stress in taking care of a friend, neighbor,
foster child, foster adult, or other.
10. _____ I have felt this way for months. How many?
11. _____ In my job I am paid to care for people and their
problems. I have found this work stressful.
12. _____ I have felt this way for months. How many?
13. _____ I feel prevented from going to meetings, church,
shopping, gatherings because I take care of
someone.
14. _____ I feel uneasy when I go away because I have to let
someone else take care of this person.
15. _____ I feel as if I am in bondage or tied down by my
caring responsibilities.
16. _____ I feel I need to have someone to talk to other
than the person I care for.
17. _____ I have feelings of bitterness about all the care I
have to give.
18. _____ I have feelings that I would like to abandon the
caring respnsibilities I have.
19. _____ I regret that I got into these caring responsibilities.
20. _____ I feel some unfairness about my responsibility to
be caring, because someone else (or others)
could or should share my load.

______________ TOTAL (Range 0 – 200+) (Enter this Page 358)

INTERPRETATION

0 – 20   Your STRESS OF CARING score is in the lowest category. You know you have some responsibilities for someone else, and you seem to be able to handle it adequately, most of the time.

21 – 60   Your STRESS OF CARING score shows you have a moderately stressful task. At times you might even feel overwhelmed. Almost everyone can carry a burden for another person for a period of time. However, when the stress of this task continues for a longer-than-expected period of time, there is a potential for overload, and that could bring on illness. If your score is toward the higher level of this range, you need to reach out for help. Tell others of your feelings about the burden and let others help you. The Stress of Caring does not stand by itself as a problem. Usually, there are a number of stress factors which compound our situation. Eliminate as many negatives as you can, and use as many of the coping skills as you can, such as relaxation, exercise, good nutrition, socialization, meditation, and assertiveness.

61 – 100   Your STRESS OF CARING score is high.   If you do not have other stressors in your life, you may be able to handle your stress load without physical or emotional illness resulting from such long term stress. When multiple stress factors come in upon us, the load may become difficult to handle. Turn your responsibilities over to someone else for a time, if you can. Find periodic relief. Come to terms with your negative feelings. Reach out to others to talk about your stress load. Use all the coping skills you can, relaxation, exercise, good nutrition, socialization, meditation and assertiveness.

Above   Your STRESS OF CARING score is too high
100   for you to continue this way without becoming over – stressed. You should seek professional help to find ways to get relief from this amount of stress.

CARING MOTHERS WITH CHILDREN AGES 5,3, and 1

Mothers with children ages 5,3 and 1, are frequently counselor's clients. Their misery drives them to seek help, after exhausting a lot of time and money trying to determine why they are sick. Young mothers are God's angels, and most of them pour their loving hearts out for that precious bundle of joy, the newborn child. Subsequently, each child is perceived in a similar manner, and the flow of love and care siphons off increasing amounts of their coping capacity. Then they begin to get sick.

They have not read about stress overload. They do not know the pitfall of increasing isolation, in service of the growing children. Self-sacrificing instincts drive them to meet every possible human need of those dependency oriented bundles of joyful frustration. Their food gets heated before mother's. Their noses get wiped before mothers. Their wakefulness pre-empts mother's sleep. Their crying bars mother's finishing her tasks. Their playfulness cuts into her playfulness. All of this and more, until this beautiful young mother feels less and less capable of rising to one more need. She feels like a failure. She will cry herself to sleep. Her husband may try to console her, or even help her, but its "back to the doctor" tomorrow.

CARING FOR ANOTHER SICK PERSON

More than once, a healthy person got sick taking care of a sick person. We see this less and less, as nursing care facilities are doing professionally, what is sometimes difficult to do personally. The physical-mental-spiritual drain can be more than bearable.

Previously, we did not understand that not providing relief for one sick person, really, eventually created two sick persons. The oppressive burden of round-the-clock vigil and care weakened the care provider until a degenerative illness set in. Some of these sick persons did not have insurance to cover hospital costs. Some wanted to be at home, which forced someone to "care".

More recently, Home Health Care providers have filled the "caring" role, which hospitals and nursing care facilities could not justify. Why we did not think of this before, I do not know. Perhaps, the increase of medical cost demanded this new "caring", but also, we have become more aware of the devastating and debilitating role of an excessive "caring" load. People are speaking up. They do not want to have to carry a load which is stressful enough to make themselves sick.

CARING FOR A WAYWARD CHILD

Children involved with alcohol, mind-altering drugs, or rebelliously deviant behavior, elicit caring. The hurt, the anger, the conflict, the rejection drives the parent into endless self-examination questions, and waves of real and imaginary guilt. Every attempt at conciliation or influence comes out of untold amounts of caring.

The arousal of the emotions and the preoccupation of the mind burn up blood glucose, neuro-transmitters like norepinephrine and serotonin, send massive amounts of ACTH, producing both adrenaline for energy and corticosteroids to suppress thymus (immune) activity. Suddenly, the "caring" one is sick, and in need of someone else's "care". In this way, "caring" beomes a stress agent, when it is allowed to overload the body, mind and spirit.

PROFESSIONAL CARING

Public servants like school teachers, social workers, counselors, prosecutors, clergy, and others, are paid for their "caring". Some do it well, others not. Some go the second mile and go on caring long after others have quit. In their capacity they use the resources of their body, mind and soul, to take some pain out of another person's life. Frequently, we do not appreciate those who do the most caring. It is not uncommon for such persons to become so personally involved that they wear themselves out. If you are in an occupation of this nature, and you find that you are sick more days than most of your peers, it might be well for you to ask yourself a serious question about your involvement in a system that uses your blood glucose, your brain norepinephrine and serotonin, but does not give you endorphins (the chemical involved in happiness and thrills) in return.

HOOKED ON CARING UNTIL WE GET SICK

Why do we continue to stay in our "caring" role until it makes us sick?   Until stress research began to sound the siren about overload of stress, quite probably people did not see the connection between excessive distasteful stress and illness.   The reasons for being hooked into a self-destructive caring pattern are somewhat broad, deep and complex.

1.   DEPENDENCY: Dependency is an immature characteristic. Independence is more mature. Dependent persons care because they "need" the person. They are dependent on them. Spouses need their mate and that drives them into greater and greater self-sacrifice.   A more independent spouse may show as much care, but be more mature about breaking away to facilitate relief in their own system. The more independent spouse does not "care" less, just "cares" responsibly, with a fair balance between self and others.   The dependent person is less capable of self-saving decisions, and therefore is worn down more easily and becomes more susceptible to illness.

2.   POSSESSIVENESS: The mother who cannot get away from 3 small children long enough to preserve her sanity, is too possessive, too controlling. Let someone else run the show for a while.   The parent with the wayward child needs to look at some of the defiant aspects of the wayward behavior, as a reaction to feelings of bondage to parental control and possessiveness.   An inordinate compulsion to control violates the autonomy of the other person.   To be unhooked from your care for this child is not to be "uncaring", but to let God and others play a larger part in the influence of the behavior.

3.   SAVIOR COMPLEX: It is excellent to copy Jesus' behavior, but we are human and he was divine, so we cannot always be perfect.   Peter tried to copy Jesus behavior, when he walked on the waters of the Sea of Galilee, but Peter was not divine.   At times people feel they must be like Jesus, and care infinitely more than they have power to sustain. Pride prevents us from giving the reins of care to another.   Fear that no one will do things right prevents us from emancipation to the bondage of caring we imposed on ourselves.   The mother,

the spouse, the social worker, etc., all need to make sure they are not playing "savior" and hooked, so they feel what they do is a burden. If the fun is gone in the caring, get out for a while and let someone else enjoy it, or else you can become ill.

4. IGNORANCE: Sometimes "caring" persons do not know their own strength. They sometimes learn the hard way, by becoming sick. Mothers sometimes do not know that is is alright to "pawn off" a child or two so they can clear out the boredom, the bondage, and the overload. Professionals may know the problem of being hooked by their "caring", but not see it creep in and take such a hold, until they become physically weakened and sick.

5. NON-ASSERTIVE: Being poor, being shy, having some guilt feelings, feeling less educated, all may cut into the capacity to be assertive enough to speak up about one's own personal feelings. Your feelings inside will tell you about your overload if you will listen to them. If you feel more and more fatigued, irritable, angry, depressed, you are having some initial feelings which are telling you to find some relief. You are encouraged to speak up. Be assertive.

RECOGNIZING THE PRE-ILLNESS SYMPTOMS

Warning lights will be blinking or flashing long before an illness sets in. The ill patient may not have recognized them as warning signals, but in most cases, the alert signals were on. The Arizona Heart Test by Edward B. Diethrich, M.D., lists the following stress indicators.

Increased smoking	Coughing
Increased sweating	Excessive snacking
Headache, dizziness	Nagging
Dry mouth or throat	Unnecessary gesturing
Irritability or bad temper	Continuous talking
Lethargy, or inability to work	Nervous tic
Clammy, clenched hands	Stuttering
Sudden bursts of energy	Nausea,stomach/pain
Finger-tapping	Grinding teeth
Fatigue	Low-grade infections
Pacing	Rash or acne

Frowning	Constipation
Restlessness	Diarrhea
Rapid Walking	Frigidity
Rapid speech	Impotence
Muscular aches	High blood pressure
Increased appetite	Depression
Loss of appetite	Hives
Inability to sleep	Withdrawal
Nightmares	
Desire to cry, or crying	
Fear, panic, anxiety	

Little pains that come and go, are mother nature's way of alerting you to some stress. It is really rather simple to understand. If you overwork a muscle it will be sore the next day. Thus, if nervous tension is activating a muscle more than average, the net effect is going to be pain to the area in which your tension focused. The goal is not to tranquilize the pain, but to remove it by finding the cause and making a decision not to allow stress factors to have control.

Another simple test is, "Are you happy doing what you do?" In Transactional Analysis, the word "strokes" is used extensively to describe the flow of positive and negative input into your life. "Positive strokes" are all the things that make you happy, content, and feeling satisfied —— like AAAHHHhhhaaa! "Negative strokes" are those things in life that put the scowl on our face and the anger in your emotions. Listen, if the "Negative strokes" are far exceeding the "Positive strokes", then its time to scram, at least for a while.

JESUS — MASTER CARER WHO COULD ESCAPE

The bondage of the stress of caring seems to be the major problem. It may be a bondage due to almost any set of reasons, but the lack of freedom to choose is a major ingredient. Jesus was in that bondage. God created His son for the purpose of the salvation of sinners. Jesus was destined to go to the cross. Jesus played a voluntary role in his humanity, but played a predetermined role in his divinity. His life was to be given as an infinite ransom for the infinite amount of sin in this world. With the sacrifice of his life, Jesus was to set men free from bondage to temporal and eternal damnation. Jesus was sent forth to care and to serve. His mission was inscribed in a human heart. Jesus human heart struggled with that mission. He knew he had to serve, yet, in the garden of Gethsemane, he verbalized an inner struggle between caring for self or others. His spiritual mission was transparent, but his bodily mission was only translucent, inhibited and bound to its humanity. That is sometimes the feelings of persons under the stress of caring. There is so much clarity of vision about the service to be performed, but there is a lack of total support from the flesh.

In Jesus case he had some things going for him to enable him to transcend the burden, which most people do not have. His spirit was willing, but his flesh was weak. For a lot of us, both the spirit and the flesh are insufficient to enable us to fully transcend the problem and meet everyone's expectations, including our own. Mothers literally want to run away. Professionals really want to find another job. Spouses can get so overwhelmed with the illness or infirmity of the other that they begin to feel life is not worth living.

JESUS RETREATED TO HILLS, DESERT AND SEA

Jesus got away. Jesus frequently found time to break away from his ministry of caring for sinful humanity, and relax, meditate, and be renewed. His first retreat happened immediately after his baptism.

> **"And Jesus, full of the Holy Spirit,
> returned from the Jordan and was
> led by the Spirit in the wilderness
> for forty days." (Luke 4:1,2)**

After Jesus had selected his first four disciples in Capernaum, on the Sea of Galilee, healed Peter's mother-in-law, and many others. Then

> **"In the morning, a great while before
> day, he rose and went out to a lonely
> place, and there he prayed." (Mk 1:35)**

Jesus made a trip to Jerusalem for the passover. Upon his return he had spent a long day teaching and healing multitudes beside the Sea of Galilee. Then

> "In those days he went out into the
> hills to pray; and all night he continued
> in prayer to God. And when it was
> day, he called his disciples, and chose
> from them 12. . ." (Luke 6:12)

John the Baptist was beheaded by Herod, and the news was brought to Jesus. Whereupon

> "He said to them, Come away by
> yourselves to a lonely place, and rest
> a while." (Mark 6:33)

Again, Jesus lectured beside the Sea of Galilee, and delivered many of his ideas in the form of parables.

> "And on that day, when evening had
> come he said to them, Let us go across
> to the other side. And leaving the
> crowd, they took him with them,
> just as he was, in the boat." (Mark
> 5:35)

Jesus sent forth his 12 disciples two by two. They taught, preached, cast out demons and healed people. They had a very good time, and yet it was probably stressful. Whereupon Jesus says,

> "Come away by yourselves to a lonely
> place, and rest a while, for many
> were coming and going, and they had
> no leisure even to eat." (Mark 6:30)

Jesus was on his way to another desert retreat, when, having traveled across Galilee, he found 5000 people waiting for him. He performed the miracle of feeding 5000 people with 5 loaves and 2 fish. The people wanted to make Jesus their king. But

> "Jesus therefore perceiving that they
> were about to come and take him
> by force to make him king, withdrew
> again to the hills by himself." (John
> 6:15)

At midpoint in his ministry Jesus took a trip outside of Galilee to the Mediterranean seaport towns of Tyre and Sidon. When he returned to Galilee

> **"He went into the mountain and sat there." (Matthew 15:29)**

Finally, Jesus set his face toward Jerusalem for the final few weeks. He made a little excursion through Samaria, which had split from Judea about 1000 years before, under Rehoboam, son of Solomon. The bitterness never stopped. Jesus was miffed, and Peter wanted Jesus to call fire down on the Samarians. Jesus refused. (Luke 9:51-56) Jesus engaged the Jewish leaders at the Feast of The Tabernacles in Jerusalem. That night

> **"And they went every man unto his own house; but Jesus went unto the Mount of Olives." (John 7:53)**

I marvel at the frequency of Jesus' escapes from his task of caring for hurting humanity. We have a number of his escapes recorded. How many others were not recorded in the gospels?

THE GREATER THE CARING LOAD, THE LARGER THE NEED FOR RETREAT AND ESCAPE

Tell this to your elders, you boss, your supervisor, yourself. They may not be willing to support the number and duration of the retreat escapes you might feel is appropriate. You might have to use some of your own free time, or vacation time. Cutting through the red-tape, the bondages of time, money and family schedules can be a bigger problem than adopting the idea in the first place.

Jethro saw Moses "judging" the people from morning to night, and viewed that as self-destructive. Jethro, Moses father-in-law, suggested that Moses organize the people and place a leader over groups. Martha felt she was overburdened by her household duties, and cheated when she could not just sit and listen to Jesus. Jesus said to Martha that her cares were getting in her way. Jesus felt she ought to cool it a little on the food preparation, and join in the fun. I suspect Martha felt that such an arrangement was irresponsible. It may have been irresponsible, but that is still the antidote for the stress of caring. Let someone else care. Do something different. You may be so concerned to "Reach out and touch someone." that you cannot let them "Reach out and touch you", or help you.

MANAGING THE STRESS OF CARING

You have to get to stress before stress gets to you. Preventive maintenance requires a willingness to buy the concept of human limitations, and confess that you need some help. You probably have been taught to be strong, have faith, be responsible, pray in time of need and to trust God. Well, those are all fine Christian virtues, but if you are hurting and not crying out for relief, then it just may be that your next illness will be your surest sign of need for help. That should not have to happen.

Getting out from under the stress of caring is not easy. Sometimes there is no place to go, or no money to get there. In the following chapters you will be introduced to a number of stress relief skills. None is magic, and few things happen without some human effort. If you will use socialization, exercise, relaxation, medtiation, and become more assertive, you will be managing some of your stress of caring, and preventing illness.

STEPHEN MINISTRIES —
MOBILIZED CARING FOR YOUR CHURCH

The church inspires persons to be care givers. Just as Jesus was sensitive to human need, so, with the Holy Spirit enlightening us, we will be sensing human need. That is the spirit of caring, a hallmark of being born-again.

Jesus spoke of His Kingdom, as one in which people become servants and slaves, caring for others, rather than receiving glory, power, and prestige which was not even earned.

"Whoever would be great among you must be your servant, and whoever would be first among

you, must be your slave; even as the Son of
man came not to be served but to serve."
(Matthew 20:26-28)

The apostle Paul commends the caring style of living
to us with equal clarity. Paul cites the "fruits of the
spirit" which includes most of the characteristics which
a person needs to "care". They are, "love, joy, peace,
patience, kindness, goodness, faithfulness, gentleness
and self-control." Almost immediately after that Paul
says

**"Bear ye one another's burdens, and so fulfil
the law of Christ."** (Galatians 6:2)

The Stephen Ministries program organizes persons
in the church to perform caring functions. The program
is for Christian congregations who "are looking for ways
to become more meaningfully involved in ministry".
It is for "Pastors (who) are seeking new ways to multiply
their ministry, to share the challenges and the joys of
ministering to and with others."

**"The Stephen Series is built solidly on Biblical
testimony and draws from the best tools of
the health and psychological sciences. It is
a response to the challenge of Christ to each
Christian and to church leaders through the
scriptures."**

**"The Stephen Series believes that Christians
have a unique opportunity to reach out to others
— the lonely, the depressed, the inactive, the
bereaved, new people in town, those hospitalized
and convalescing, the divorced, the aged, and
many more."**

Obviously, this is not for the person who is currently
under a depressing load of caring-stress. Yet, once
you have been able to get out from under your stress
of caring, perhaps you have time and energy to become
part of a Stephen Ministry in your own church. For
information, write, Stephen Ministries, 1325 Boland,
Saint Louis, Missouri 63117 Phone 314-645-5511.

DISCUSSION

1. Let us discuss the stress of caring for young children. What was your biggest frustration with caring for your young children? What enabled you to cope?

2. Caring for a teen-ager who has been lead astray into alcohol, mood-altering drugs or immoral values can be devastating. How does one continue to care without letting the caring become a burden and create illness?

3. Are nursing care facilities and home health care programs a necessity or a convenience so we do not have to spend time doing as much caring?

4. What is happening to the caring that previous generations did for their parents? for society?

5. If you are caring for someone and owe many bills, but you need to escape for a while, what do you do for money?

6. Jesus was the master care-giver. He also knew his limits for his work of caring. How does one know what the limits are to his or her emotional caring resources?

7. What role does exercise play in relieving the stress of caring? What good would relaxation and meditation do? What value would come out of more prayer?

8. Is there someone in our community, who needs us to help them care for someone?

9. Hospice is a community based program for helping to care for the terminally ill person. Is there a Hospice organization in your community? Should you organize one?

10. Stephen Ministries is a church based program for meeting human need. Does your church have such a program for its members and your community? Should your church get involved in this program?

SECTION 3

§§§§§§§§§§§§§§§§§§§§§§§§§§§§§§§§§§§§§§§

HEALING

RESULTING FROM

MIND-OVER-MATTER

COPING SKILLS

§§§§§§§§§§§§§§§§§§§§§§§§§§§§§§§§§§§§§§§

INTRODUCTION

TO SECTION 3

BEHAVIORAL IMMUNOLOGY

Stress is not bad. Coping is just better. The effect of stress on the immune system is counteracted by behaviors that resist the immuno-suppressant effect of stress. That is behavioral immunology, a study of how life-style affects the immune system. This is hard for us to comprehend and then believe. The germ theory of illness has so completely dominated our thinking that to consider behavior as a cause of illness sounds preposterous. Yet, by now you should be somewhat more convinced than you might have been before you joined me in this book.

Germs are really not a very big threat to our biological systems any more. We can either immunize the body against most germ causing diseases, or we can medicate them. The larger looming problem is with the **dis-eases** of the body, mind and spirit. A dis-ease is what happens when something we eat, do, or think upsets the equilibrium and unbalances the homeostasis of the person. When dis-ease affects the human biological, mental, or spiritual system, then a process of degeneration can be set in motion, which can be much worse than a what we get from a germ-induced disease. One's life-style can create that dis-ease. Too many changes (Chapter 1), too much hysteria (Chapter 2), too much anxiety or depression (Chapter 3), too much stress in marriage (Chapter 4), too much suppression of negative feelings (Chapter 5), too much stress at work (Chapter 6), too much financial stress (Chapter 7), too much alcohol, smoking, overweightness, sugar consumption, (Chapters 8,9,10,12,

14), poor nutrition (Chapter 11) and allergic reactions (Chapter 13), — all are life-style behaviors which affect a person's health. A study of changing behaviors in a positive direction would be behavioral immunology.

Changing a life-style to maintain or regain one's health requires some new awareness, some guidelines and some motivation. Behavioral immunology, therefore, requires the disciplines of psychology, philosophy, and religion, to work in close harmony with the biological and medical sciences. When you see illness resulting from behavior, you enter the world of the social sciences for some guidelines about normative healthy behavior.

CHRIST'S ROLE IN BEHAVIORAL IMMUNOLOGY

The exceptionally documented historical development of the Judeo-Christian tradition gives Christianity a strong place in history. It deserves that position, without being disrespectful of the devout religious practices of others. For centuries, magistrates, kings, princes, judges, counselors, social workers, religious entrepreneurs, political theorists, economists, etc., etc., have been immersed in its value system and life-style.

Critics will claim this has stagnated progress, but that is hardly the case in light of the course of history. Any respected philosopher has to take Christianity seriously, either in support or in attack. The church is intertwined with the world view. The church contributes toward a world view, and is updated by the world view. Life-styles of people come out of that world view, its economics and its politics. When the world view, the zeitgeist, suddenly turns conservative, after world crude oil prices soar, that affects the life-styles of people. Conversely, when a Martin Luther, a Ghandi, or a Martin Luther King take their stand and "can do nothing else", the world view of man is affected. The indwelling presence of Christ can change our zeitgeist, our world view, our life-style.

On the personal level, healing through stress management can work better in Christianity, through Christianity and because of Christianity. Jesus, the Son of God, had to have been the healthiest person who ever lived.

He did not live without stress. He lived with stress and used every coping skill he had to keep from going under into physical, mental, or spiritual illness. Jesus had all the lessons of 2000 years of Jewish history to draw from. He had inside information on what was important for health and happiness. He communed with his Father in heaven, to draw deeply from heavenly sources. He fasted, prayed, retreated into the desert, to meditate and draw from the deepest inner resources. His divine nature was ever present, yet he did not use it to turn stones into bread. He was human, like us, with a divine counterpart, hard for us to understand. Jesus, his predecessors and his followers, had their collective wisdom pooled by scholars and councils. If you avoid that body of knowledge for gaining health and happiness, "You gotta be stupid".

MIND-OVER-MATTER

In this section you will see healing as an end product of the cooperative efforts of the patient and God. This is, in essence, the theme of this book. Sections 1 and 2 dealt with cleaning up problems. Section 3 emphasizes more mind-over-matter skills. The chapters in this section will cover the following skills and their effects.

     -- Socialization
     -- Values
     -- Physical fitness
     -- Relaxation, meditation, visualization
     -- Assertiveness
     -- Prayer, laying on of hands, touch

When Jesus practiced these things, he did them so naturally. His commission from the Father, and his communion with the Father, God, put him in touch with an ultimate source of healing. I see this in my clinical practice as a counselor. The person who gets a glimpse of putting it all together through Jesus Christ finds healing, mentally, physically, spiritually, maritally, financially, etc. But let a person try to get by with minimal changes, when more important life-style behaviors hang back, the desired healing will not take place as certainly or as quickly.

HEALING WHEN YOU HAVE IT ALL TOGETHER

You will never really "get it all together", since you
are a human being, but when you slow down and calm
down (Section 1), and moderate your indulgences (Section
2), and add some positive steps, like those to be discussed
here in Section 3, then you have a healing package that
can be trusted.

The story of M.J. in Chapter 4 underscores this
principle of increased chances of healing when obstacles
are removed and positive mind-over-matter effort is
expended. M.J. is only one story of thousands, which
are told by "behavioral immunolgists" such as counselors,
psychogists, pastors, etc.   These persons deal with
people's feelings and values, and the behavior that comes
out of them.   When truth can replace immature and
and unrealistic behavior, lives function smoother, and
health is better.

Jesus is the way, the truth, and the light. In him
is distilled all that it takes to find health, healing,
happiness and heaven. Fortunately, for the non-Christian
world, the social sciences have mounted an extensive
campaign over the last 2 or 3 generations, to research
and find whatever norms there may be, which contribute
to health. Without their efforts there might be a number
of persons who would be cheated out of health. Christians
accept the proposition that Jesus had it all together,
so from the point of view of behavorial immunology,
Jesus becomes the supreme example of a life-style which
resists and counteracts illness.

COPING SKILLS AND THE WILL

The major part of getting it all together is mobilizing
the will. Sick persons are sometimes too sick to activate
their will. Some are too medicated, with good reason,
to have their will activated. Yet, when persons live
with degenerative diseases like arthritis, gout, undiagnosed
pains, cancers, generalized poor health, they still have
a functioning will which can be integrated with Coping
Skills.

Wholistic health principles suggest that the patient become more involved in the treatment. The patient may use multiple and simultaneous treatment programs. The patient sees himself/herself as having some control over the outscome, by altering life-style factors such as nutrition, exercise, assertiveness, and all the others.

In the chapter on Socialization, the fundamental proposition is that sick people habitually retreat from involvement with friends, but there is healing in socialization.

In the chapter on Values, we see how Spiritual Values of a higher order promote a life-style which makes health and healing more easily attainable.

In the chapter on Physical fitness, health is seen as the result of fitness efforts; small at first, but increasing until health is once again reestablished.

In the chapter on Relaxation with Biofeedback, the health of people is gained by a variety of relaxation exercises, meditation skills, and self-affirming processes.

In the chapter on Assertiveness, the fundamental need for Conversion is seen as part of the process in a total package of healing.

There is a final chapter on Prayer, Laying-on-of-hands, and Spiritual healing.

In attempting to put it all together, patient effort must be expended, the mind informed, the will activated, and the heart filled with faith in the cooperative efforts of self, medical assistance, support from friends, and the blessing of God.

Chapter 15

HEALING AND SOCIALIZATION

"Come, listen to me, my sons,
      I will teach you true religion.
Tis your disire to live,
      to live long and be happy?
Then keep your tongue from evil,
      keep your lips from deceit,
      shun evil and do good,
      seek to be <u>friendly</u> — aim at that."

(Psalm 34:11-14, Moffat)

"If tens of thousands in our institutions today had developed such Scriptural attitudes, they would not be kicking out their last tantrums in asylums and nursing homes." (S.I. McMillen, M.D., in None of These Diseases)

How social and friendly are you? Are you sufficiently active with friends to ward off some illness or disease? Take the following Socialization Inventory to analyze your social health-giving strengths.

SOCIALIZATION

Pick out the most appropriate response. Write the number
of that response in the space provided by that statement.

0. Never 1. Rarely 2. Occasionally 3. Sometimes 4. Frequently
5. Almost always

1. _______ I enjoy social gatherings.
2. _______ I enjoy making new friends.
3. _______ I enjoy belonging to clubs or social groups.
4. _______ I go to parties.
5. _______ I like being with people who joke with each other.
6. _______ I talk to strangers.
7. _______ I like to entertain friends or guests.
8. _______ I participate in a wide variety of interests.
9. _______ I visit my relatives.
10. _______ I socialize with my co-workers.
11. _______ I enjoy competition.
12. _______ I like to explore new places.
13. _______ I am warm hearted.
14. _______ I am friendly.
15. _______ I am a talkative person.
16. _______ I compliment people.
17. _______ I send cards or make phone calls on birthdays.
18. _______ I share my feelings.
19. _______ I apologize if I hurt someone.
20. _______ I help my neighbors or friends.
21. _______ I spend more time with people than reading.
22. _______ I speak in groups.
23. _______ I like how I look.
24. _______ I trust people.
25. _______ I make up my mind fairly easily.
26. _______ I express sympathy to persons in need.
27. _______ I share personal problems with a friend or two.
28. _______ I feel comfortable with the opposite sex.
29. _______ I laugh at myself when I make a mistake.
30. _______ I talk with friends rather than watch TV.
31. _______ I am more talkative than I am silent.
32. _______ I feel people look up to me.
33. _______ I feel I am intelligent enough.
34. _______ I spend more time with people than daydreaming.
35. _______ I am a good listener.

_______ TOTAL (Range 0 – 175)

(Enter this score in the summary SCORING on Page 358)

INTERPRETATION

0 - 90   Your score on the SOCIALIZATION inventory was lower than average. People who have lower scores will have more difficulty coping with their stress because of their limited desire to be involved with others. People can be caring and helpful if they know of the stress in our lives, but, if we isolate ourselves from others, they may not be able to be helpful to us in time of stress. It would be adviseable for you to work at social relationships. Cultivate your relationships with people by inviting them to go places and do things with you.

91 - 125   The score you have for SOCIALIZATION is in the safe range. You seem to have enough contact with people so that if stressful emergencies should arise, people would probably know and be helpful to you. You apparently need and enjoy being with people. This is a healthier style of life. Research is showing that people cope better with stress when they have an adequate circle of friends.

Above 125   Your appetite for SOCIALIZATION is above average. You are to be congratulated. You will, in general, be more able to cope with stress because of the social support you are building in your friendships. There are many stressors in life, and some strong coping skills. Socialization is one of the coping skills. This does not mean that you will have less stress, but that the strain on your body and emotions will be alleviated more quickly and thoroughly through your sharing and others' caring.

SOCIAL ISOLATION AND ILLNESS

Perhaps I do not need to try to overwhelm you with evidence that social isolation is bad for your health. Your instincts could tell you that, and it would be unkind to tell someone that social isolation makes him/her die at an earlier age. Every shy and withdrawing person should know that such behavior is a stress factor, contributing to physical, mental or spiritual illness. The evidence for this is strong enough to catapult the reclusive and the home-bound solitare into the closest church, Bible study group, or bowling league. The following facts should root out the snug, engage the aloof, warm up the inhospitable, and awaken the non-social recluses of mankind. The facts probably won't motivate the intractable, but here they are.

Bachelors become patients in mental hospitals 23 times more frequently than married men.

Unmarried women enter mental hospitals 10 times more often than married women.

Persons over age 17, who live alone spend an average of 13.5 days in a hospital, while the average married person only spends 8.5 days in the hospital for similar diseases.

Widowed women have a 50% greater chance of dying from heart disease or stroke, and twice the risk of dying from cancer of the cervix and four times the risk of dying in an auto accident, than married women.

(James J. Lynch. The Broken Heart: The Medical Consequences of Loneliness, Basic Bk, 1977)

Social isolation is one of multiple causes, which encompass the entire life-style. As such, a person cannot single out a factor and point to it as "the" cause, not unless the social isolation is severe. People have compensating behaviors, skills and outlets. They have places to get their "strokes" and "warm fuzzies", even though they spend a large amount of time in isolation. Therefore, so long as the illnesses from isolation are counterbalanced by other coping skills, the detrimental powers of isolation are nullified.

EXTROVERTS HAVE LESS COLDS

In England, 52 men and women were used in an experiment to see the connection between psychological make-up and the severity of a common "cold". They were all innoculated with the cold virus. In a hospsital, the amount of virus present in their mucus, the number of coughs, sneezes, and nose-blowings was calculated. At the conclusion there was "clear evidence of a psychosomatic component in colds." The more out-going persons, the extroverts, definetly had milder colds, than the introverts. (Journal of Psychosomatic Research, Vol.24, 1980) There may have to be a few more repetitions of this research to make introverts sit up and listen, but it is simply one more piece of evidence to motivate us away from that bitter-sweet snugness of social ineptitude.

JESUS WAS AN EXTROVERT

Jesus' encounter with the priests in the temple, at age 12, demonstated the combination of a good mind and good emotions in a good body. Jesus was no intellecually slithering misfit. He demonstrates the kind of ego strength we would all like to have. Such an ego could only have come from a proper balance of love and discipline. The negative "strokes" he likely received for childish behavior, simply had to have been counterbalanced with a surplus of positive "strokes" and affirmations. Positives make extraverts. Negatives make introverts.

In Jesus ministry we see him as a social being. He dines with Zaccheus, after the encounter in the sycamore tree. He worked his first miracle at a wedding feast. He broke bread for multitudes. He visited people in their homes and healed the paralytic, lowered through the roof. He had a personal friendship with Lazarus, Mary and Martha. He was really so sociable that they called him a "glutton" and a "winebibber". (Matthew 11:19) All this social involvement was tempered and balanced by his escapes into the desert, the mountains, on the Sea of Galilee, to find the appropriate solitude for body, mind, and spirit.

Jesus was not a natural extrovert. True, he was divine as well as human, so it might be easy to argue that Jesus was a born extrovert. Yet, Jesus' humanity was like ours. He was "in every respect tempted as we are, yet without sinning". (Hebrews 4:15) That indicates that his ego strength had to grow like ours. He had to deal with his "Superego" (conscience) and his "Id" (impulses). He needed the emotional "strokes" from his parents, family, and friends, for his sense of well-being, his ego strength. If he would have gotten yelled at, more than loved, hit more than hugged, axed more than affirmed, Jesus' ego strength would have become weaker rather than stronger, and Jesus would have retreated, emotionally, rather than blossomed. You cannot go on knocking someone down, and expect them to stand up. Jesus knew how to stand up majestically, princely, lovingly, and out of him flowed truth and grace.

JESUS HAD FAMILY SUPPORT FOR STRESS RESISTANCE

Jesus had brothers, possibly sisters too. In Jesus early ministry in Galilee his "mother" and "brothers" came to see him. (Mark 3:31-35) The gospel writers only record that Jesus used this ocassion to say that anyone who "did the will of God" was his brother. How Jesus related to them, we do not know. I cannot imagine anything but good will, love and family support, being in their minds. That may not always have been the case as the children grew up. I suspect that whimpering, manipulating, sibling rivalry, and parent-child power struggles existed there like in most homes. These are not bad. Under good parental tutelage children learn more about justice, equality, negotiation, and all the skills that are necessary for good interpersonal relations. Jesus would need to know this as he had to deal with the rich and the poor, the young and the old, the intellectual and the rebel. He needed a good base of social interaction for his humanness to weather the storms of the three years of his ministry.

Research has validated the stress-reducing benefits

of social interaction. Morton Lieberman began a Transitions Study in 1974, conducting interviews with 2300 adult persons representative of the Chicago population. The study aimed at discovering the range of hardships, the identification of resources and responses to them, and thirdly, the symptoms of emotional stress, and psychological disturbance. This has become a longetudinal study, and includes life-cycle transitions and experienced crises. There are many conclusions from the study, which are reported in the Handbook of Stress, by Leo Goldberger and Schlomo Breznitz, N.Y.: Free Press, 1982, p. 779) The following conclusion is relevant to highlight the health value of social support.

> **"There is some evidence that good levels of social resources and highly interactive social networks will buffer individuals from day-to-day occupational and economic stresses and will dimish the person's perception of stress in the event of high levels of role strain."**

Jesus may not have needed the "buffer" for his "occupational stresses" and "role strain" as we do. We know we need a buffer, and it is good to see that the time and energy we invest in generating good relationships is an aid to our health and healing.

Exactly how well do you function socially? Jesus made at least 2 or three trips to Nazareth during his three years. That would be about a 2 day walking trip from Galilee to Nazareth. How much energy do you expend to maintain the ties with your family and friends?

JESUS SURROUNDED SELF WITH FRIENDS TO COPE

Jesus body, mind and spirit were not phoney containers for a divine spirit. The blood was real. The mental anguish over pharisaical hypocrisy was real. The emotional turmoil of setting himself up to get killed was real. A human needs a support system to go through that.

What will each of us have to go through? Will we face alienation, torture, painful illness? Will we have the courage to marshal our resources and fight with every ounce of our will, or will we wind up feeling a sense of hopelessness? Jesus had his disciples with him in the Garden of Gethsemane, and he asked them to stay awake while he prayed. He wanted their support. (Mark 14:32-42) Unfortunately, Jesus had to go it alone, and his Heavenly Father pitched in and supported. All of us have that easy access to the Father. We do not practice close communication, and when the chips are down we do not have our hoping machinery very well trained. But even if it were trained it needs human support. William F. Lynch writes in Images of Hope (N.Y.: Mento-Omega, 1965),

> **"Hope cannot be achieved alone. It must in some way or other be an act or community, whether the community be a church or a nation or just two people struggling together to produce liberation in each other. People develop hope in each other, hope that they will receive help from each other."**

My Chaplain Internship at the M. D. Anderson cancer research hospital, in Houston, Texas, gave me opportunity to treat the "hopelessness" feelings in persons. I've seen persons die in 3 days who had no hope and refused to look for anything that gave hope. I've seen people revive their hoping machinery, through my human care, and other person's human care, and go on to conquer an equally dismal prospect. William F. Lynch is right. "Hope cannot be achieved alone." It needs to be mediated through a friend, and that is reason enough to be a social person. It brings healing and could save your life. True, God is merciful, when friends are incapacitated by their human weakness, as was the case of Jesus and the disciples. God's mercy may sustain your hope in time of trouble, but you'll be a lot happier if you have layed a good groundwork for friendships. Jesus surrounded himself with 12 friends, partly to enable himself to maintain his hope, and partly to enable himself to cope.

LOVE CALLS FORTH HEALING FROM WITHIN

I have witnessed human interaction having healing
power. My chaplaincy calling program brought me to
a patient who was in a coma. I visited him one day.
The next day I came, there was a young girl there. I
asked if she was his girl friend. She said she was not,
but only a friend through their mothers who lived 500
miles apart and had not seen each other in years. But
due to another accident the mother of the patient could
not get to her son, so asked if the other woman could.
She sent her daughter. Two days later, this girl, who
had not known this man before, was allowing this now
delerious young man to paw all over her in his
semi-conscious state. I was surprised, but she came
day after day, and sat hour after hour. After some
time the young man regained his consciousness, got well,
and went home. If William Lynch is right, this young
girl probably saved this man's life by letting herself be
the object of hope in those dreary weeks of
semi-consciousness. Karl Menninger has said that "Hope
is an activating force of the ego's integrative function".
(Am. Jrnl. of Psychiatry, Dec.,1959) Hope is a spark.
Hope has a way of motivating, calling forth reserves,
rejuvenating and shifting from reverse to forward. That
hope, that love, that healing, can only be mediated in
the context of human interaction. Without adequate
social exchange there is a higher probability of lingering
illness and early death.

BEING CONVERTED AND BEING SOCIAL

Jesus was the most converted man who ever existed.
He was the most turned-around person we know. He
was not shackled to sin; he served God. He was not
stuck on himself; he was stuck on loving others. He
was not narcissistically fixated on self-satisfaction but
on the needs of the poor, the oppressed, and the sick.
How truely, he took up the cross, denied himself and
followed God, his Father. That is like a 180° switch
from the way sinners operate. You might say that Jesus
was psychologically converted from self to others, from
sin to salvation.

That psychological direction is part of the total mental, physical, and spiritual life-style which made Jesus the extrovert that he was -- the healthy person that he was. You cannot be converted and stay in your shell. The good news which comes in to convert us has to come back out in words and action. "Every good tree bringeth forth good fruit, but a corrupt tree bringeth forth corrupt fruit." (Matthew 7:17) If after years of acting like a Christian, a person is still more withdrawing than outgoing, that raises some serious questions, whether the "conversion" was really a turning-around conversion, or a "for show" conversion.

If you are non-social, and you claim to be a Christian, don't cheat yourself out of health or embarrass God any longer. Conversion changes people's lives. Don't be satisfied with a conversion that left you passive, mousy, shy, and uninteresting. Get mobilized. Go out and find something to do to serve in the church or world. Enroll in some classes in community education. Spend some money traveling, and practice talking to strangers. Ask them questions. Find out what is important to them. Make yourself interesting by expanding your awareness, your world, your vision.

CASE STUDY

James J. Lynch M.D., treated a 54 year old man, but watched him slowly die. He had a heart problem. In the 14 day hospitalization, he went into a coma. At one point a nurse went in to comfort him. She held his hand. The monitors on the heart recorded a more normal heartbeat, with lingering effect, even though he was in a coma.

> "He also had no visitors during the 14 days that he struggled in the hospital and in a real sense this man was alone in the world surrounded by strangers and a strange technology. . . .But were his joys and his sorrows related to his ruptured heart valve? Was his life filled with love, or was it one of loneliness? Did he, like so many alcoholics, eventually end up all alone and totally isolated? And were his loneliness

and anxiety related to his ruptured heart valve?
Somehow all these questions seemed inappropriate, strangely out of place on the battlefield
of the intensive care unit. How could one
ever hope to repair the damage created by
a lifetime of loneliness and constant drinking?"
(p. 93)

In his book, The Broken Heart: The Medical
Consequences of Loneliness, (N.Y., Basic Books, 1977)
Dr. James Lynch cites other scientific validation for
the proposition that social contact, to the point of
touching, has powerful therapeutic effects. All patients
need the support of family and/or friends, but cardiac
patients, who now need to have as much stress eliminated
as possible, need to have the assurance of their family
and friends even more. Within the context of cardiac
problems, Dr. Lynch says,

"In the macroscopic, statistical overview, the
lack of human contact seemed to be the crucial
force leading to premature death." (p. 121)

Dr. James J. Lynch has powerfully forced us to look
at the effects of social interaction on health and healing.
Skeptics should let him bend their ears and minds. They
will see the connection between socialization and health
or healing.

REPLACE SOME PSYCHOTHERAPY AND MEDICINE

Freud lead us to the realization that problematic
interpersonal relations produced mental illness. He
brought in the couch and free-association talking to
enable persons to ventilate their repressed anger from
traumatic experiences of hostile interpersonal relations.
Psychoanalysis traced most mental aberations to traumatic
conflict in early life. Some of the talking helped some
of the anger in some of the patients. We have learned
from Freudian retrospective psychoanalysis that conflict
which stifles socialization is detrimental to one's emotions.

Hans Selye lead us to the realization that stressful
phenomena of all kinds, in sufficient quantity, could
produce physical illness. If that stress is a constant

warfare between two people, and one of them gets sick after some time, then the healing of that relationship will allow the immune system to go back to work, now that the stressful fight-flight emergency is gone. That will facilitate healing, since, if the stress is removed, the immune system can go back to work. Thus, conflict which stifles socialization is detrimental to one's physical health.

Jesus lead us to the realization that anger has to be resolved and replaced with love. Jesus said, "Being angry, do not let the sun go down on your wrath, (lest) you give opportunity to the devil." (Ephesians 4:26) Thus, conflict which stifles socialization is detrimental to one's spiritual health.

If conflict is so detrimental to our general health, it might be good if we replaced, or supplemented, some of our current medical and psychiatric treatments with "Social Skills Training". That is how strongly Richard M. Eisler, of the Virginia Polytechnic Institute and State University feels about proper treatments.

> **"I am advocating teaching distressed individuals social coping skills as an alternative to treating the symptoms that result from excessive stress, (especially for those with) inability to deal effectively with others in their social environments." (In Behavorial Health, (ed.), Joseph Matarazzo, N.Y.: John Wiley and Sons, 1984, p. 354)**

Dr. Eisler also points out that this is, in fact, happening in a variety of ways. Communication is taught. Assertiveness is taught. Emotive skills are taught. We, however, have not adequately been teaching these to our youth. It may take time, but eventually interpersonal relations courses will be taught at many levels. It is as important as some of the survival courses (reading, writing, and arithmetic) now being taught.

THE SIN OF NON-SOCIAL BEHAVIOR

I want you to take this information, and let it be

a catalyst to get you to be a social person. Sin is composite term for behavior that leads to hell. If non-social behavior is one of the factors that prevents healing then it is a sin, because it will lead us to the hell of illness. In this context, every stressor is then, in fact, a sin, because stressors do drain us until we become ill. We fight stress with coping strengths. Socialization is in that category of a coping strength. It can counteract the effect of some of the other stressors in life. Let your socialization be a positive force in sustaining or regaining health.

RELATIONSHIP IS NUMBER ONE

Adam and Eve had a good relationship with God in the Garden of Eden. One day, they decided to compromise that relationship. They ate fruit of the Tree of Knowledge of Good and Evil. They chose the object in preference to relationship. They hurt their relationship with God, and paid the price. They were thrown out of the Garden, and experienced pain thereafter. There is a fundamental lesson in this story. Whenever you take your mind off the primary need for relationship, and think you can get by just as well, getting happiness from objects, you are on the road to trouble. If you spend money freely on houses, cars and objects, but do not spend money to cultivate relationship with persons around you, you can wind up with few friends and die (statistically) earlier. If you can spend all your spare time manicuring the yard, but do not have time for fun with your children, then you have majored in objects and not in relationship. You will pay some price for that. If you grind out production objects from your employees, but have no concern for relationship, people, and feelings, your chances of progress will be reduced. You cannot violate a fundamental principle, like the importance of relationship, without paying some price. God does not ask for perfection. He simply asks us to focus properly and grow in that direction. Go for relationships. Make them a priority item. In chronic mental, emotional, phycical and spiritual illness, put your faith in God's fundamental principles that socialization contributes to health and healing.

DISCUSSION

1. Do you think Jesus was ill with colds, flu, digestion problems, neurological problems, etc.?

2. How does socializing with friends help prevent illness? How does socializing contribute to healing?

3. If you were ill with cancer, would it be better for you to join a community education class or stay at home?

4. And the Lord God said, "It is not good for man to be alone. I will make a companion for him." (Genesis 2:18). What do you think God had in mind when he said, "It is not good for man to live alone"?

5. The author indicates that Jesus surrounded himself with disciples to sustain his "coping" strength. While that may not be the only reason for having disciples, is it a valid one? What can we learn from that? How do we go about surrounding ourselves with people we like, and who like us, so that we will have a support system to help us face life's problems?

6. If conversion can make someone into an extrovert, why do so many church-going people remain shy, withdrawing, non-assertive , and weak?

7. What makes the difference between a "turned-around" conversion and a "for-show" conversion?

8. If you violate any of God's principles is that sin? If you violate God's command to be shining examples of His indwelling presence, is that sin? Is violating God's principle of being social a sin?

9. Let us list what we can do to break out of our shell.

10. Some critics say that the church sometimes gets too involved in socializing. Others use social time/s in the church to win people over to Christ. What should your church do about promoting more social times together?

Chapter 16

HEALING AND HIGHER VALUES

"Whatever is true, whatever is honorable, whatever is just, whatever is pure, whatever is lovely, whatever is gracious, if there is any excellence, if there is anything worthy of praise, <u>think on these things</u> . . . and the God of peace will be with you."   (Philippians 4:8)

"The tongue of the wise brings healing."   (Proverbs 12:18)

"Pleasant words are like a honeycomb, sweetness to the soul and health to the body."   (Proverbs 16:24)

"A cheerful heart is good medicine."   (Proverbs 17:22)

People with higher values are generally healthier. Fill out the Values Inventory on the next page to analyze the health-giving contribution of your values.

HEALTH GIVING VALUES

Pick out the most appropriate response. Write the number
of that response in the space provided by that statement.

0. Never 1. Rarely 2. Occasionally 3. Sometimes 4. Frequently
5. Almost always

1. ____ I try to be loving to others.
2. ____ I am helpful to people in need.
3. ____ I practice self control.
4. ____ I cooperate with people to keep peace.
5. ____ I try to be humble, gentle, modest.
6. ____ I have a lot of respect for God and people.
7. ____ I am a friendly person.
8. ____ I treat people fairly, justly, and equally.
9. ____ I am clean in body, mind, and spirit.
10. ____ I am honest, truthful, not double tongued.
11. ____ I am obedient and respectful of authority.
12. ____ I am an ambitious and hard working person.
13. ____ I work at task and goals with determination.
14. ____ I have inner harmony; I am genuinely contented.
15. ____ I am tolerant and forgiving of people who hurt me.
16. ____ I have the courage to do things others don't do.
17. ____ I have faith and hope that make me optimistic.
18. ____ I am polite and courteous in my relations with others.
19. ____ I am wise and sensible in decision making.
20. ____ I am cheerful at work and at home.
21. ____ I am responsible and trustworth. People rely on me.
22. ____ I am loyal and faithful to friends, spouse, family
23. ____ I have regrets and apologize when I have done wrong.
24. ____ I have sympathy for people and am a good listener.
25. ____ I have an imagination and like to be creative with it.
26. ____ I am accepting, broadminded, and tolerant.
27. ____ I believe in free choice, so I do not dominate people.
28. ____ I respect myself and have self confidence.
29. ____ I maintain exclusive sexual relations with my spouse.
       (You may use a 6 for "Always")
30. ____ I keep my drinking of alcoholic beverages under
       control.
31. ____ I am conservative in my spending.
    __________ TOTAL (Range 0 – 156)

(Enter this score in the summary SCORING on Page 358)

INTERPRETATION

0 - 60   Your VALUES score was extremely low. Very few persons have scores this low. This low-level score would indicate some emotional disturbance or an extreme amount of unhappiness with your life. No one should have to live with a low level of values, unless the person chooses this style of life.

61 - 110   Your VALUES score is much lower than average. You seem to have lost hope, courage, or faith. Could you be depressed and have lost some of your interest in life? Some persons with this score hate someone or hate the world and have withdrawn from people. Talk with someone about your feelings and find a way to live with more zest and optimism.

111-135   Your VALUES score is average. The inner computer which runs your life has strong enough guidelines to keep you functioning, but you are not committed strongly enough to the higher values which are advocated by specialists in human behavior. Commit yourself to being loving, serving others, maintaining self-control, being a peace-maker, being gentle, etc.

136-145   Your VALUES score is excellent. You live by good principles. Living by a high-level value system contributes to health. You are to be commended for your values. You can go forth in considerable confidence that the world will treat you with respect for the values you hold. Try not to compromise the principles you hold for your life.

Above 145   You have a superior score in the area of your VALUES. You are to be congratulated for living by some of the universal standards taught by the major philosophers, psychologists, poets, and religions of the world. Living by these values will keep you healthier and happier, unless you abuse your body with substance abuse, poor nutrition, etc.

VALUES — COPING STRENGTH — WELLNESS

The research hypothesis behind this test was that persons with a higher Value system would have less stress, more coping, and be healthier. That is true. Those whose totals for Stress in Chapters 1-14 were high (i.e. problematic), generally had lower (problematic) Values, and those whose totals for Coping in Chapters 15-19 were high (good), had higher values (good). This leads to the conclusion that our Values contribute to our health, and lack of effort put into our Value systems parallels or causes high stress, which, in turn contributes to illness.

There were 15 persons who had very low scores out of the 165 persons who took this test at the early stages. Fourteen of the 15 persons had low total coping strength scores, which indicates that not only did they have poor values, but they did poorly in socialization. They exercised very little. They did not have relaxation skills, and they were not very assertive. Of those same 15 low-scorers on values, 13 of them had above average stress scores, which means their total points for tests in Chapters 1-14 were higher than average. That indicates an extraordinarily high connection between a poor value system and health problems. With this, one can predict fairly accurately who will be having the high stress and increased illness, by simply looking at their low "value" score.

Analysis was also made of the top 32 persons who had 135 points or more on the values inventory. There were 29 who had above average total coping strength, which means they socialized well, did some exercising, knew how to manage, both to relax and to assert themselves appropriately (Chapters 15-19). Also, 27 of the 32 had below average stress symptoms, so they generally functioned better in all of the tests of the first 14 chapters. These 29 (and 27) validate the proposition that good values and lower stress go together. These statistics substantiate what educators, prophets, evangelists, and mind-over-matter people have been saying for years. It pays off in health benefits to be dedicated to a value system which is congruent with the Divine order of things.

Even though persons with scores of 127 or more were considered to be functioning at a higher level, some with scores higher than 127 were still sick or had other problems. We need to remember, that illness is usually not caused by one thing, unless the illness is a contagious disease. Illness results from both singular causes, and multiple-compounding causes. Low "values" can be either "cause" or "contributing factor".

EVALUATION OF SPIRITUALITY

Granger Westberg, author of Good Grief, pioneer in Wholistic Health concepts, friend, and former professor, inspired me to pursue the instinctual awareness some of us have, that persons with Christian values live longer. Sitting late into the night, we asked, "Can you measure spirituality?". Abraham Maslow understood people in terms of lists of "B"-eing values and "D"-eficiency values, coupled with concepts of "self-actualization". Was there not something similar in the Bible? We believe there are many concepts which are actually "value" concepts and they are known to Christians as "spiritual values". You see them in lists like

FRUITS OF THE SPIRIT (Gal 5:22)	BEATITUDES (Matthew 5:3-11)	SINS OF THE FLESH (Galatians 5:19-21)
Love	Poor in spirit	Immorality
Joy	Mourn	Impurity
Peace	Meek	Licentious
Patience	Righteousness	Idolatry
Kindness	Merciful	Sorcery
Goodness	Pure in heart	Enmity
Faithfulness	Peacemaker	Strife
Gentleness	Persecuted	Jealousy
Self-control		Anger

ARMOR OF GOD (Ephesians 6:14-18)

Truth	Salvation	Selfishness
Righteousness	Spirit	Dissension
Peace	Word of God	Party Spirit
Faith		Envy
		Drunkenness
		Carousing

Add to this the list of "values" in the 10 commandments, and the lists of virtues which are required for
elders and deacons. The lists begin to overlap values,
but soon you have a composite picture of what it means
to be spiritual. You gain insight, through these lists,
about what it means to be a Christian.

THE SEARCH FOR A LIST OF SPIRITUAL VALUES

My earliest encounter with "values" was with reading
Abraham Maslow. I once plotted a very detailed
single-page outline of his "value" system, and from time
to time I use it for relating cognitive information in
helping a client, or when making a speech. The subject
of "values" was sufficiently intriguing to motivate me
to accumulate various research papers and books on
the subject.

I have believed in truth for years. I could get extremely fascinated that some of the fundamental propositions
of psychology ran in such a parallel with Christian principles. I saw truth as truth, whereever it came from.
It always pleased me that there seemed to be no conflict
between what I knew psychologically and religiously.
I believed that time telescoped into eternity, and eternity
telescoped into time. There was temporal truth, and
transcendent truth. Not all of the transcendent truth
reached down into time, or could be seen in time, and
not all earthly or temporal truth could stand the test
of eternal truth, but there was a great body of truth
in between, which bore the stamp of temporal and eternal
credibility. That area in the middle was filled with "value"
concepts which appeared to be spiritual and measurable.

Values and lists of values have been constructed by
early theorists (Allport and Vernon, 1931; Allport, Vernon,
and Lindzey, revision, 1951). Hunt (1935) established
76 "ideals", and grouped them into 17 categories. Subsequently, Morris (1956), Gorlow and Noll (1967),
Woodruff (1948) and Catton (1954) developed values
classification systems. Scott (1959) developed 18 "moral
values". Rokeach (1969, 1970) developed a concept
of values in which there were 18 "instrumental values",
and 18 "terminal (end product) values". Rokeach (1969,

built his list on the work of Hunt (1935) and Scott (1959) and others. Bales (1970) and Kilmann (1972,1975) have also done work in the area of values research.

The 31 "Values" of the Inventory are the result of tabulations made from these 14 published research articles, and from another 7 major religious and secular organizations or authorities: Rotary, Boy Scouts, Tae Kwon Do, Alcoholics Anonymous, Abraham Maslow, Christianity and Islam. Each "value" which is found in the documents of these organizations was placed in a matching category, until all "values" had been included. The tabulation was made on the basis of frequency of appearance. The list is numbered in order of the frequency of their appearance in all of these 21 sources. No.1 is cited most frequently and No. 31 is cited least frequently. There were additional "values" listed by the scholars and the 7 other sources, but lack of support and consensus prevented such "values" from making the list. Here is the list of "values" along with the synonyms from the various sources.

1. Loving – caring – compassionate – tender
2. Helpful – charitable – generous – serving
3. Self-controled – self-disciplined – patient
4. Peaceful – compromising – cooperative
5. Humble – gentle – modest – unostentatious
6. Reverent – respectful – obliging – thankful
7. Friendly – hospitable – neighborly – brotherly
8. Equalitarian – just – impartial – democratic
9. Clean – above reproach – blameless
10. Honest – truthful – candid – frank – open
11. Obedient – compliant – respectful of authority
12. Ambitious – hard working – assertive – eager
13. Perseverant – persistent – determined – dedicated
14. Harmonious (inner) – genuine – tranquil
15. Forgiving – merciful – tolerant – conciliatory
16. Courageous – brave – fearless – bold – daring
17. Believing – hoping – expectant – optimistic – (faith)
18. Polite – kind – courteous – civil – mannerly
19. Wise – sensible – discrete – discriminative
20. Cheerful – joyous – happy – smiling – buoyant

21. Responsible - dependable - reliable
22. Loyal - faithful - committed - covenanted
23. Regretful - remorseful - repentant - contrite
24. Empathetic - sympathetic - listening - inclusive
25. Imaginative - creative - inventive - ingenious
26. Accepting - broad minded - tolerant
27. Free - autonomous - independent - unshackled
28. Self assured - confident - trustful - non-jealous
29. Faithful (sexually too) - loyal - honorable
30. Sober - moderate (in relation to stimulants too)
31. Thrifty (in spending)

This sounds like a list from the Bible. You can find passages of scripture to substantiate every one of these. Yet, each of these values is listed, not primarily because it comes from the Bible, but primarily because of universal consensus to fundamental truth. I would not claim that this is the final list for all of the future. I simply want you to realize that the Bible is so universally applicable that the social scientists are often only spending their time validating its significance.

SPIRITUALITY IS VALUES AND MORE

Spirituality is more than the pursuit of a higher and more normative set of values. Spirituality suggests an instinct and skill to be in touch with the inner self, and to deal with the larger forces that impinge upon the inner self. The spiritual life-style is a transcendent life-style, where persons get on top of problems through spiritual focusing. Spirituality is people's attempt to understand their uniqueness, allow their systems the freedom to be creative, so they can be emancipated from some of the stress of life.

Christian spirituality incorporates and embraces these qualities. Yet, Christian spirituality is a step up, even from this. Christian spirituality transforms you. It turns you around. Much spirituality is inner-directed, and a great deal of the process of meditation focuses inward. In Christian spirituality, if you do not get beyond the contemplation of your self, or some inocuous and meaningless brain-mesmerizing phrase, you missed what Christian conversion is all about. The kind of spirituality that is available to Christians is one which transforms not only the person, but the environment around the person. Christians do not stop with a spirituality that simply transforms the self. Changes within are valuable, but change in a converted person mandates an outflowing of love and service that affects others.

The end product of the Christian spiritual process is a better world. That must start with inner contemplation, confession, forgiveness, and not just a psychic imagery trip into the intestines, eyeballs, arteries, or into a green fawn-filled meadow. Christian spirituality is achieved by meditating on truth, revealed wisdom, divine understanding, and by fellowshipping with others who are seeking after norms, givens, certainties, principles and absolutes. With these strong assurances the converted-one begins to mend his own ways. He shares his life-style with others. He witnesses to some new-found joys. The end product is not just a more spiritual person, but a more spiritual world; a world that lives by a higher set of values. That person who shows his life-style is having an impact on others, we call "spiritual".

VALUES AFFECT LONGEVITY IN U.S.S.R.

French demographer Jean-Claude Chesnais recently supervised a study of life expectancies in 35 countries. Men in the USSR have the lowest age life expectancy of any country in Europe. Their life expectancy has dropped from 66.2 years in 1965 to 61.9 years today. This unprecedented phenomenon "has no historic parallel in time of peace" says Chesnais. There are several factors. More hard liquor is consumed in the USSR than in any other nation. Health services are free, but money spent on them often takes second place to defense spending.

Perhaps we ought to have more concern than pride. Yet, history is casting a verdict, not us. We know that their value system is not the same as ours. They claim allegiance to a system which has not stood the test of time as has the system of Judeo-Christian tradition. Without values to uphold one, or a savior to transform us, we could sink to the same low age for life expectancy. Values do affect longevity.

VALUES AFFECT LONGEVITY IN U.S.A.

The Seventh-day Adventists have been studied because of their low incidence of heart disease and cancer. Adventist men had only 53% of the risk of cancer as other men, and only 18% of the overall risk for lung cancer. (Am. Jrn. of Epidemiology, Aug, 1980) Adventists are known to advocate a diet high in vegetables, fruits and whole grains. About 44% of the Adventists are vegetarian. They have lower blood pressure, lower cholesterol, and weighed less. (Medical Journal of Austrailia, May 19,1979) The values of the Adventists, are obviously affecting their life-style, which in turn affects their health and longevity.

Members of the Church of Jesus Christ of the Latter-Day Saints (Mormons) have also been studied to determine the connection between their values regarding food, and their longevity. Mormon men, ranging in age from 35-64 have only 38% of the deaths per thousand, of men in the USA. Mormon men in California and Utah have about half the risk of developing cancer as other U.S. white males." (Cancer, October, 1978) Mormons do not have a ban on meat as do the Adventists. About 70% of them use vitamin supplements. They generally refrain from caffeine, nicotine and artificial stimulants, much like the Adventists. Their values are producing good health statistics in relation to cancer and heart disease. It is quite likely that "various social and psychological aspects" of their religion (namely the close social ties) produce good effects in their health. (Am. Jrn. of Clinical Nutrition, July 1977)

Some of our conservative forefathers were converted from abuses to the body, mind and spirit as a result of value systems which influenced them. They threw off liberal theology and indulgent life-styles in Europe, fled for their lives, and began anew. The current generations may yet have to see the effects of a liberal indulgent value system, before they become turned-around or converted to a life-style which adheres to a higher values.

HEALING FROM CONVERSION TO HIGHER VALUES

Samuel B. was told that he had 6 months to live. Cancer was present in the pancreas, and was spreading. The shock of being sick was now overlayed with the shock of being snuffed out so quickly. Samuel reviewed his 46 years. The pleasures and pains swirled in and out, raising devastating questions about the sense of life. He had six months time to either supersaturate his life with pleasure, or attack healing with the same gusto he had attacked pleasure.

Instinct told him what books and friends cannot. Conscience told him that if he turned things around he might be able to have a second go-around with life. No one preached at Samuel. He had never let them preach to him before either. He had seen people jog for health reasons. He heard people say that junk food contributed to poor health. He knew from somewhere, that people who relaxed more were healthier. Stimulants had always been enjoyable, but his gut feelings told him that cutting back on those would certainly give odds makers a better chance on their bets on his survival. Subconscious communication was now getting through to the conscious. Trauma had knocked off the lid he hammered down on so tightly.

Instinctual messages, advocating a mind-over-matter life-style got through to Sam's conscious awareness, but sheer terror drove those messages a step further into the area of behavior. Sam was converted, not by any altar-calling preacher, but by the greatest motivator of all, love for life. The chips were down, and the instinct for self preservation was activated. Sam went to the greatest "self preserver" there is, Jesus Christ, who stands waiting for us to invite him in to help us.

Sam's conversion created a new life-style which placed higher values at the top of his psychic priority list. If you could have looked inside Sam you might have seen his new found values stirring different emotions like this,

   1. "Love" -- If I am going to die, I better love while
      I can.

2. "Helpful" -- Why not be helpful, since making
   lot of money isn't important anymore.
3. "Self-controlled" -- Get going on jogging, and
   cut out poor food habits. Give yourself a chance
   to be fit, healthy, and heal.
4. "Peaceful" -- Since death seems close; don't
   get upset over trivial behaviors of people.
5. "Humble" -- You got it. You can't be more humble
   than when you are slated to die.
6. "Reverent" -- When you want to live, you go
   for broke, and even solicit the help of a former
   enemy.
7. "Friendly" -- Gosh, I should be nice to people.
   Wouldn't it be embarrassing if only a few persons
   came to my funeral.
8. "Equalitarian" -- Death is the great leveler. Now,
   is not the time to use power to get my way.
9. "Clean - above reproach - blameless" -- When
   a person is going to die, he better get his life
   in order and clean up his act.
10. "Honest - frank - open" -- I never used to want
    people to know me. Now I am hurting and
    I am scared. Somebody, talk to me.
11. "Obedient - compliant - respectful of authority"
    Sorry God, I still have a little problem with
    this one, but I'm working on it.
12. "Ambitious - hard working - assertive - eager"
    Yes, I'm converted here too, from working hard
    at my job, to working hard on family fun.
13. "Perseverant - persistent" -- I find this hard,
    because I need faith, faith in physical healing,
    to motivate me to be perseverant.
14. "Harmonious - genuine - tranquil" -- Life is too
    short to let disharmony mar an hour. I will
    resolve problems, not bottle my anger.
15. "Forgiving" -- Facing death really changed my
    attitude toward people. They are frail, fragil,
    and possibly hurting like me. I will be forgiving
    rather than vindictive.
16. "Courageous -- fearless" -- No way can I do
    this by myself. Only faith in healing, or faith
    in God, can calm my inner terror.

17. "Believing - hoping - faith" -- "I believe, help
me O Lord with my disbelief." (You may finish
the remainder of the list of value changes that
result from conversion.)

Terror of death, and love for life, motivated Sam
to get his life turned around. Sam was converted. His
whole life-style was converted. Sam is living today,
years after the verdict of death goaded him into finding
a health and healing life-style that makes the tour of
duty on earth, a pleasant tour. Healing comes naturally
to a life where all systems are under control, and directed
toward higher values.

VALUES AFFECT HEALTH, HAPPINESS, AND SEX

Values determine destiny, much like stars and compass
determine destination. Redbook magazine evaluated
65,000 responses to a survey made in 1977, of Redbook
readers, and determined that

**"The more religious a woman is, the happier
she is."**

**"Health is another blessing for the very religious
woman. She suffers less from headaches and
stomach upsets than do women who are less
sure of their beliefs. . .the symptoms of poor
health increase as the firmness of faith
diminshes."**

**"The very religious woman is least likely to
report a loss of sexual interest or plseasure
during the past year, and is most likely to say
that her faith enhances her marriage and her
sex life." (Redbook, April, 1977)**

Lest I beat the drums so long, that I cause loss of
psychological and spiritual hearing, I will rest my case.
I am continually impressed by correlation, connection,
correspondence, and congruence between secular and
religious truth. I wish the church would claim more
credibility for itself. I wish the secular person would
not be so resistant to letting the church teach him/her
some fundamental values.

DISCUSSION

1. How much do people live by values and how much by simple need, impulse or economic determinism?

2. What values does your church stand for most strongly? in the area of morals? -- in the area of economics? in the area of missions? -- in the area of education? in the area of social justice? -- in the area of poverty? --in the area of exercise, nutrition, smoking, alcohol, or other life-style factors that influence health?

3. In the book of Proverbs, we are prompted to seek out the values; wisdom, understanding, discretion, knowledge, instruction, insight, etc. How much more than a 30 minute sermon on Sunday do we need to give us enough of these?

4. If you could flash each of the 31 higher values of this chapter on your television screen, at random, for a year, do you think you would become more like these values?

5. How does conversion work to turn us around so that we become people who want to pursue higher value?

6. How do you communicate your values to your children when they are pre-school? -- when they are in grade school? -- when they are in high school?

7. What are some good value-enrichment programs?

8. Do you believe that Christians should have less illness than non-Christians?

9. Suppose a Christian becomes ill, do we conclude that such a person is not living up to higher values?

10. How do you feel about paying health insurance premiums that, it appears, pay for larger medical costs of persons who do less mind-over-matter controlling of their life-style, out of the money saved by persons who function with a good life-style and save the company money?

Chapter 17

HEALING AND PHYSICAL FITNESS

Patient: "Doctor, I,m calling you by phone, because I have a pain in my head, neck, shoulders and back."

Doctor: "O.K., Take two miles of brisk walking and call me in the morning."

§§

"Do you not know that in a race all the runners compete, but only one receives the prize? So run that you may obtain it. Every athlete exercises self-control in all things. They do it to receive a perishable wreath, but we an imperishable. Well, I do not run aimlessly, I do not box as one beating the air; but I pommel my body and subdue it, lest after preaching to others I myself should be disqualfied." Yours truly, Walker—Jogger—Aerobic boxer, Apostle Paul, (I Corinthians 9:24-27, Ephesus, 57 A.D.)

Analyze your Physical Fitness level with the questions on the following pages. Let them motivate a life-style change.

PHYSICAL FITNESS

Pick out the most appropriate response.   Write the number of that response in the space provided by that statement.

0. Never 1. Rarely 2. Occasionally 3. Sometimes 4. Frequently 5. Almost always

1. ____ I exercise for at least 15 minutes three times a week. (Multiply your 1 or 2 or 3 or 4 or 5 by 10 and place that number in the space.)
2. ____ I walk at least a mile a day. (Multiply your 1 or 2 or 3 or 4 or 5 by 10 and place that number in the space.)
3. ____ I work out on an exercise bicycle, trampoline, rowing machine or weight bench.
4. ____ I get plenty of exercise doing my home duties.
5. ____ I walk up and down stairs at home, work or school.
6. ____ I participate in the following sports activity.

dancing	skating	hiking
bowling	karate	swimming
bicycling	hunting	horseback riding
aerobics	softball	weight lifting
baseball	basketball	golf
tennis	racketball	track
Other _________________________		

(Add up the number and put that in space 6.)

7. ____ I have a garden that I work in during the summer.
8. ____ I rake leaves in the fall and shovel snow in the winter.
9. ____ I have a job that requires physical activity on Monday.
10. ____ I have a job that requires physical activity on Tuesday. (This question is repeated to give additional points to persons doing physical labor.)
11. ____ I have a job that requires physical activity on Wed. (This question is repeated to give additional points to persons doing physical labor.)
12. ____ I have a job that requires physical activity on Thurs. (This question is repeated to give additional points to persons doing physical labor.)
13. ____ I have a job that requires physical activity on Friday. (This question is repeated to give additional points to persons doing physical labor.)

14. ______ If you were asked to do chin-ups, how many do you
think you could do? (0 means none, 1 means one,
2 means two, etc...)

15. ______ If you were asked to do push-ups, how many do you
think you could do? (0 means none, 1 means one,
2 means two, etc...)

16. ______ Check your pulse rate for 1 minute. Score it
according to the following guidelines:

Put a 5 in the space if your pulse is under 60.
Put a 4 in the space if your pulse is between 60 & 70.
Put a 3 in the space if your pulse is between 70 & 80.
Put a 2 in the space if your pulse is between 80 & 90.
Put a 1 in the space if your pulse is between 90 & 100.
Put a 0 in the space if you pulse is over 100.

17. ______ Hold your breath as long as you can; count the seconds.
(Count 1 and 2 and 3 and 4 and 5 and 6 and 7, etc.)

Use 5 if you can hold your breath longer than 85 sec.
Use 4 if you can hold your breath 70 to 85 seconds.
Use 3 if you can hold your breath 55 to 70 seconds.
Use 2 if you can hold your breath 40 to 55 seconds.
Use 1 if you can hold your breath 25 to 40 seconds.
Use 0 if you can hold your breath 10 to 25 seconds.

(You may guess your point level.)

18. _____ Do some running-in-place, making sure that your
feet are lifted at least 8 inches off the floor. Count
only the step of your right foot. How many steps can
you do before you are tired enough to quit or sit down?

Put a 5 in the space if went over 175.
Put a 4 in the space if you reached 150.
Put a 3 in the space if you reached 125.
Put a 2 in the space if you reached 100.
Put a 1 in the space if you reached 75.
Put a 0 in the space if you reached 50.

(You may guess your point level.)

19. ____ The "step test" raises your heart beat rate. Find a
stairway and use one step. Place your right foot on
the   step and then your left foot beside it. Then
step down with your right foot, and follow it with
your left foot. Do this twenty times and take your
pulse immediately after you have finished.

Put a 5 in the space if your pulse is below 90.
Put a 4 in the space if your pulse is between 90-100.
Put a 3 in the space if your pulse is between 100-110.
Put a 2 in the space if your pulse is between 110-120.
Put a 1 in the space if your pulse is between 120-130.
Put a 0 in the space if your pulse is above 130.
    (You may guess your point level.)

20. ____ Repeat the "step test", doing the 20 steps in less
than one minute.   Then rest for one minute and
immediately count your pulse. (Count pulse before
and after.)
Put a 5 in the space if the final pulse rate was less
than 10 beats faster than when you started.

Put an 0 in the space if the final pulse rate is 10 or
more beats faster than the pulse taken before the
repeat test.   (You may guess your point level.)

__________TOTAL (Range 0 - 200)

(Enter this score in the summary SCORING on Page 358)

INTERPRETATION

0 – 65 Your PHYSICAL FITNESS score is low. You are not active enough. The average resting pulse rate is 74 for men and 77 for women. Pulse rates above this suggest possible anxiety, allergic reactions, poor physical fitness, etc. Find some type of exercise that is appropriate for you and do that exercise at least every other day to bring your pulse rate into the average range.

66 – 90 You are engaged in enough physical activity to put you in the average range of PHYSICAL FITNESS. While this may be adequate exercise for you to sustain the flexibility of your physical body, in time of stress you may not be sufficiently physically fit to withstand increased stress. Exercise alone will not be the only factor determining your ability to cope. You need to understand that physical fitness through exercise simply increases the total coping capacity. It is one of several factors.

91 – 150 Congratulations on your efforts to maintain or regain your PHYSICAL FITNESS. You are either a person whose job requires physical activity, or you must be having enough physical exercise through conscious mind-over-matter involvement. You are definitely decreasing your risk of illness through your exercise. Keep up your activity, while also eating properly, getting enough sleep, practicing relaxation and/or meditation, and living a life which is guided by the principle of moderation.

Above 150 You are to be praised for your excellent PHYSICAL FITNESS efforts. Persons in your Physical Fitness category are working diligently to regain or sustain Physical Fitness. The efforts you are making will reward you with increased health, unless there is an undetermined bodily ailment which is preventing you from having a healthy system. Continue to use exercise as a supplementary therapeutic treatment.

FREE MEDICINE FOR YOUR ILLNESS

Healing benefits result from three exercise sessions a week, when the exercise is sufficiently energetic to raise the pulse rate to the required level. Aerobic exercising is any activity which "aireates" or "oxygenates" the blood and body tissues, at the right pulse level, for at least 15 minutes, three times a week. The goal is to give the heart muscles a work-out, strengthing the heart to meet some possible emergency. There are many good side effects, in addition to heart-strengthening, which come out of aerobic exercising. An enormous amount of research has suggested the following conclusions.

1. Aerobic exercise increases norepinephrine, a neuro-transmitter, by 4½ times, and therefore helps emotionally disturbed persons.

2. Anxiety can be alleviated by aerobic exercising on a regular basis.

3. Exercise is a muscle relaxant, and is helpful in alleviating pain, if managed properly.

4. Depression is alleviated by aerobic exercising on a regular basis.

5. Aerobic exercise counteracts stress, because there are less adreno-cortical reactions in an exercising person.

6. Exercise reduces lactate, a muscle acid that has been found to play a role in anxiety.

7. Chronic fatigue is alleviated by aerobic exercising on a regular basis, for some persons.

8. Aerobic exercise increases slow-wave sleep (which is deeper sleep).

9. Decision making and manual dexterity (hand coordination) were improved 60% after 6 months of treadmill walking, bicycling, step-bench exercising, sprinting and running.

10. Exercise elevates body temperature like a fever and counteracts illness-producing bacteria.

11. Running improves physical health, appearance and body image, which creates corresponding changes in self-acceptance and self-esteem.

(The references for these research conclusions are found in another book by the same author, entitled, Health through Stress Reduction.)

JESUS WALKED — HE HAD A HEALTH ADVANTAGE

The walking which Jesus did gave him a health advantage. We hardly know of that, and really do not want to hear that. Without automotive transportation, he either had to travel by horse, camel, donkey or foot. People in Jesus day lived in a psychologically smaller world. Relatives probably did not live far away. What could not be grown locally, was brought in by others. Merchants did the traveling, but they usually reserved camel space, or donkey space, for the load that needed to be transported.

Walking was the primary locomotive transportation system. Jesus was from Nazareth, about 1 day walking time (20 miles) from the Sea of Galilee, and about 4 days walking time (80 miles) from Jerusalem. In Jesus' ministry he started in Galilee, went to Jerusalem and back to Galilee a couple of times. During his ministry Jesus made one trip to the Mediterranean Sea cities of Tyre and Sidon, a round-trip of at least 150 miles. Walking at a pace of 3.5 miles per hour, that would be about 41 hours of walking time. Chicago people will take that much time driving to California, but not get the exercise. Jesus also made a trip into Phonecia, northeast of Galilee, and then south, avoiding the territory of Herod Antipas, and going into the Decapolis, which is the west bank of the Jordan River. That trip must have been at least 50-70 miles long, like driving down to the Gulf Coast, from Chicago, and without the exercise. If you calculate 3 round trips to Jerusalem, of about 200 miles each, add the trips to Tyre, Sidon, Phonecia, you have 800 to 1000 miles of walking. At 3.3 miles per hour, that is 300 hours, or about 40 eight-hour days in three years. We know there are health benefits from walking. Jesus was probably healthy, in part, from walking.

APOSTLE PAUL — ON MIND-OVER-MATTER

Paul believed in self-control (Galatians 5:23). Paul believed in mastery of self (I Corinthians 9:25). And Paul believed in conquering (Romans 8:37). Paul's Christo-centric understanding puts Christ's life-style at the core of mind-over-matter thinking. Therefore, for countless thousands, the transcendent life-style is possible with their conversion. Without being born again, some may never know victory over much of anything. They live by impulse, satisfying basic human need, but do not get their eyes off survival. Conversion takes a person's eyes off self, survival, and surfeiting. Conversion fixes the mind on God, Christ, forgivenness, release, freedom, hope -- everything outside the self. Forgiven sinners focus externally, instead of internally. They challenge obstacles and blockages, with their new-found allies, the Church, God, and the Holy Spirit. Their new confidence gives them a mind-over-matter perspective.

THE HEBREW WRITER — ON MIND-OVER-MATTER

The writer to the Hebrews seems to be recommending a jogging program in Chapter 12, verse 12,13. Closer reading makes us see metaphorical language, driving home a spiritual truth.

> **"Therefore lift your drooping hands and strengthen your weak knees, and make straight paths for your feet, so that what is lame may not be put out of joint, but rather healed." (Hebrews 12:12-13)**

The writer is telling people to "Brace up!", "Straighten up.". The verses form an admonition to the healthier portion of the church to make no deviation from the straight course set before them by the example of Christ. It is like he is saying, "Get control. Get psyched up. Don't stand there like a bunch of whimps. You are making a poor example for people walking this life-style. Go forward on the Christian path of life demonstrated by Jesus Christ; don't go back to Judaism. If you don't do something, conditions will deteriorate. If there is weakness and drooping limbs, that may turn into lameness, and then you won't make it to where you are going. If you do not straighten out, you will twist your psychological ankle on the rough road of life. You can prevent spiritual lameness and dislocation, but you must get your back up. Your defeatism is going to destroy you. You need to replace your spiritual wilting with spiritual resolution. You need to get with the program."

The Hebrew writer says there is "healing" from a mind-set of assertiveness. Sinners still like to play "poor me", getting others to wait on them. That is spiritually backwards, and no healing can come from spiritual regression. You need to put yourselves in synchronization with the divine order of things to benefit from participation in it. If aerobic exercising facilitates the body's return to health, the Hebrew writer might say, "Lift **your drooping hands, and strengthen your weak knees. Do some aerobic exercising.   Do some preventive maintenance.   There is healing in it.**"

GLORIFY GOD IN YOUR BODY

I was really turned-off by this idea as a teen-ager. Those were the days of the Women's Christian Temperance Union's battle-cries against a variety of things no one had then proved were very harmful for people. Stress researchers have vindicated most of the "aged women's" instinctually derived fears. I still have a bit of a hard time recording Paul on this subject, but here is what he said.

> **"Do you not know that your body is a temple of the Holy Spirit, within you, which you have from God? You are not your own; you were bought with a price. So glorify God in your body." (I Corinthians 6:15,19-20)**

Aerobic exercising is good for you; body, mind, spirit. The evidence is convincing. You do not need to die younger than necessary from a coronary heart attack or stroke, when you exercise properly. Let your body be infused with healing from exercising before the deteriorative processes become a disease.

WALKING — A SPORT

Walking is now an American sport. It is done for fun, for competition, for fund-raising, and for health. According to a national fitness study entitled, Fitness in America, walking is now the most popular exercise in America. There are 34 million persons walking. Some have revived the "walk to work" practice. People walk to rebuild their system after a heart attack. People walk to prevent one. Competitive walking is for the high steppers. More sedentary persons in the upper eshelons of age brackets, seek out the Civic Centers or local tracks. Others use swimming pool tracks and lanes to "oxygenate" their systems and strengthen their hearts. Fund raisers see a gold mine in getting others to pay for their walking. It is a wave of health, inspired by the instinct for self preservation.

Walking can change the fitness level of a person by 10-20 years. Once people thought age and decrepitude went together. Mostly, the decrepit person is the non-exercising person. Fitness helps preserve health and life. Fitness is important for enabling persons to obtain the fullest enjoyment from their years. Fit persons go places and do things that others do not. Zest for living goes with fitness. Fitness also helps preserve health and life. With fitness through exercise, the body is more able to meet emergencies and survive them. Sudden stress or strain does not raise blood pressure and pulse rate as much in a fit person.

Walking is free. You cannot usually overdo it. You can carry on some of your social life while walking. You can lose weight through walking. Brisk walking burns about 300 calories an hour. That is 3000 calories in 10 days, which is a loss of one (1) pound of fat. Restrict sugar intake during those 10 days to a minimum, eat more vegetables, drink double the amount of fluid, and you can lose 2-5 pounds in the same 10 days. Walking removes grunts, sighs, moans, and poor-me's. Friends will like you more. Enemies will have more difficulty finding you. Walking energizes the fatigued, tranquilizes the hyper. It gives muscles to the young, increasing their maturity, and rejuvenates the aged. Walking expands the world of the mind, and reduces its skittish escapes into fantasy. Walking is work and fun.

HEALING POWER IN EXERCISE

During exericise 70 percent of your body energy turns to heat. That heat can build up to 7 degrees above normal. That would be equivalent to a fever in the body, building up to fight off bacteria. That is nature's way of defending the body and bringing healing. A fever in your body kills off germs. This can be proven by manipulating the heat on a throat culture. When a doctor suspects a streptococcal infection, he or she swabs your throat and then rubs the swab on a culture dish. The dish is placed in an incubator which is set at 98.6° degrees F. This is your body's normal temperature. If the strep is there, it will be seen growing. If you turned the heat up to 101°, either before or during the test, the culture of the strep would not grow. Bacteria cannot grow in elevated heat. Elevated heat in the body from exercise will act in a natural way to destroy germs and facilitate healing. Joseph G. Cannon, Ph. D., and Matthew J. Kluger Ph. D., of the University of Michigan reconfirmed these findings and they were reported in several publications in 1983

This is how it works. When the body, or a part of it, is inflammed by germ or exercise, the white blood cells release an agent (endogenous pyrogen = EP) into the blood which absorbs some of the circulating nutrients, namely zinc and iron. "Decreases in iron and zinc concentrations occur during bacterial and viral infections, and exercise. While this may not sound beneficial at first glance, studies have shown that many bacteria cannot flourish in iron-poor environments. . . .Studies by Drs. Matthew J. Kluger and Barbara A. Rothenburg at the University of Michigan Medical School showed the potency of combined elevated body heat and reduced iron in the blood. . . .Professional athletes are frequent victims of 'sport's anemia' or 'runners anemia' (iron deficiency). . . .Studies at the University of Copenhagen indicated iron deficiency in 56% of the 113 joggers and competition runners surveyed. After taking supplements daily (200 mg per day), some of the distance runners achieved new personal, and even national records." (Alan Donald)

"Fever and exercise share the ability to stimulate the immune system. The cells of the immune system include two distinct types of white blood cells called T and B lymphocytes, and a number of other cells which seek out and destroy invading bacteria and viruses. T cells provide protection from cancer and viral and fungal infections. B cells produce antibodies which are released into the bloodstream and eliminate bacteria and chemical toxins."

"Fever and exercise activate the body's defenses. This was born out by recent studies performed with laboratory-cultured cells. Drs. Gordon Duff and Scott Duram at Yale University found that production of T cells and disease-fighting antibodies increased 20 fold when the temperature of the culture medium was raised only two degrees above normal." Professors in Stockholm, Sweden have also seen positive effects of exercise on the cells of the immune system. (Alan Donald, Bestways, January, 1985) (See also, RN, July, 1983)

So, you are sick. Are you just going to let it put an end to you? How about trying some mind-over-matter exercising to get your body temperature up? Obviously, this will not be practical, possible or therapeutically helpful for every illness. Nevertheless, be serious about activating or stimulating your immune system with exercise, instead of suppressing it with stress or chemical agents.

EXERCISE — SUPPLEMENTAL PSYCHOTHERAPY

A young lady waited on me as a clerk. She knew I was a counselor. She grinned a little and said, "I was going to go to you for counseling, but I got started jogging, and I found I didn't need you. My fatigue and depression lifted when I began to run. It changed my eating and my outlook." I wish we could solve all counseling cases with some aerobic exercising, and I know that an exercise program would be good supplementation to any therapy program.

Exercise releases a neuro-transmitter called norepinephrine. That chemical is measureable in the urine up to 4½ times more, after 30 minutes on a treadmill at 80% capacity (Howley, 1976). Endorphins, the body's natural tranquilizers, are generated in larger amount during strenuous exercise and in thrills. Besides this, the lymph system drains off more of the waste-material toxins during exercise. People are often benefited too, by the socialization taking place around aerobic exercising.

Mental hospitals provide opportunity for patients to exercise. That is currently seen as recreational therapy. For many it was more of a joke, and a relief from all the psychotherapy, but recently strides have been made in seeing the therapeutic effect of an exercise program as part of therapy.

It is doubtful that any exercise, by itself, would change the course of the emotional troubles of a psychotic. Yet, as an adjunct therapeutic intervention, it produces that percentage of difference that enables people to transcend illness.

FROM FITNESS TO SMARTNESS

Your instincts tell you it is true, that mental processes are affected by lack of fitness. That has been proven to be true. The interconnections between the mind and the body are abundant enough to allow either to pull the other down. Everyone I have ever listened to about the virtues of exercise, point out how much clearer their heads are.

> **"In a four month study of 48 middle aged men, professor A. H. Ismail, of Purdue U., found that the mental processes controlled by the brain's left hemisphere are heightened by strenuous physical activity."**

There were 30 persons in the study, who participated in a 1½ hour physical education program 3 times a week. Eighteen served as the control group. "The cognitive skills of the exercisers improved significantly, while the control group did not improve at all.", says Ismail. That is encouraging, and the needy ones can find hope and encouragement in the therapeutic benefits of exercise.

Combine exercise with good nutrition and the combined synergistic effect will be even better for your health. Sugar has no vitamins or minerals in it. White flour has had 22 vitamins and minerals removed, and 4 artifically synthesized ones put back in. Both sugar-laden and white flour products make up a large part of the ordinary diet. Replace the sugar and white flour with whole grains, vegetables, and fruits. Consume protein and complex carbohydrates in a good balance, and you will be eating a winning diet. The winning Japanese Baseball team in 1984 attributes its success to such a macrobiotic diet. Combine this with exercise.

PULSE AS AN INDICATOR OF FITNESS

Your pulse rate is a vital indicator of fitness. If you answered Question 16 with a "5" that is a strong indicator that your heart beat is within the range of fitness. Forrest H. Blanding, a former analyst from Exxon, collaborated in a study of 200 pieces of research on cardiovascular problems and established a correlation between pulse rate and fitness. Here is their formula.

HEART PERFORMANCE INDEX (HPI) FROM LOW RESTING HEART RATES IN BEATS PER MINUTE. (Condensed form)

Heart Beats per minute	Heart Performance Index (HPI) Men	Women	
100	74	77	Sedentary Condition
95	78	81	" "
90	82	86	" "
85	87	91	" "
80	93	96	" "
75	99	106	" "
70	106	110	Fair Condition
65	114	119	Good Condition
60	124	129	Fine Condition
55	135	140	Excellent Condition
50	148	154	Extremely Fine Con.
45	165	171	Top Athletic Condit.
41	181	188	" "

The lower the pulse rate you have, the higher level of fitness.   Forest H. Blanding also reported, "Roger Bannister had a resting heart rate above 70 beats per minute before he started training.   After hard training and just before he broke the record for the mile run, his resting heart rate was a remarkably low 35. One of the astronauts acquired, after serious conditioning, a fine resting heart rate of 43, which suggests an athletic level of HPI of 173.   After six weeks of confinement in a small chamber, he had a resting heart rate that had increased to 68, showing that his HPI had declined to 109." (Blanding, 1982, p. 83)

Substantiating this connection between high pulse rate and coronary problems, Dr. Kenneth Cooper cites a 10 year study by Jeremiah Stamler. Stamler studied 1,329 men and found that men with resting heart rates above 90 died from coronary disease at a rate 2½ times greater than men with resting heart rates below 70. At the Cooper Clinic, he says, "We list the resting heart rate on the Coronary Risk Profile." (Cooper, 1977, p. 37)   Pulse rate becomes one of the diagnostic guidelines for the need of exercise.

THE ONE MUNUTE LIFE SAVING TEST

People with high pulse rates should take that as the body's signal of a possible heart problem, as well as an indication of lack of fitness, allergic reaction and anxiety. The heart is not able to endure excessive overwork any more than animals or machines can endure overload. The on-going study of the population of Framingham, Massachusetts, has given a large amount of information about heart problems and death from heart disease. It has shown that "men with resting heart rates over 85 had three times the coronary risk, or an estimated fifteen-year lower coronary age than those with resting heart rates below 67. (Blanding, 1982, p. 83)   Thus, a one minute pulse count can give you a clue as to whether you need to consider exercising. Get an exercise program from your physician.

GETTING STARTED WITH EXERCISE

1. KNOW YOUR HEARTBEAT RATE: Do not go out and get your heart rate to speed up too fast or too quickly. There is an ideal "minimum" and "maximum" pulse rate for aerobic exercising. Kenneth Cooper M.D., author of THE AEROBICS WAY and THE AEROBICS PROGRAM FOR TOTAL WELL-BEING has developed standard guidelines for the training rate of the heart. Here is the formula that is used. Take the number 220; subtract your age; then multiply that by 75%. That gives you the maximum heart rate for aerobic exercising. (220 minus age 50 is 170; times .75 equals 127) This figure of 127 should be your pulse rate per minute if you are age 50. The minimum heart beat for aerobic exercising is 66% of 170 (220 minus age 50). Thus, the optimum aerobic exercise range for a person about age 50 is from 113-127 beats per minute.

AGE RANGE	MINIMUM	MAXIMUM
Age 20	133	150
Age 30	127	143
Age 40	120	135
Age 50	113	127
Age 60	107	120
Age 70	100	113
Age 80	93	105

2. IN THE HOME EXERCISING: Remember your calisthenics in high school or college? You see them repeated in various exercise programs on TV. That is what you can do without cost to you. If you have some interest in exercising and can afford a record or a cassette tape, you can probably find an exercise program in your supermarket or local drug store. The music on these tapes is set to a tempo that is quite helpful for you. Most of the in-home exercising you will probably do will be "flexibility" exercises. If you begin to work at it hard enough, there may be some "aerobic" quality to them. After two or three minutes check your pulse rate to make sure you are not exceeding the maximum training heart rate.

3. USING A JOGGING TRAMPOLINE: The small round trampolines that you can have in your home are excellent for aerobic exercising. Do not expect to lose weight using a trampoline because the primary usefulness of a trampoline is for cardio-vascular (heart) exercise. Your physical activity on a trampoline will raise your heart beat, and you can regulate the speed of your heart by lifting your legs higher when you jump. Start out with 1 minute a day for the first week. The second week jump for 2 minutes a day. The 3rd week jump for 3 minutes a day. The 4th week jump for 4 minutes a day. Increase this until you get to 15 minutes a day on the 15th week. By the time you get to the 15th week you can cut back to 3-4 times a week, but then increase the time to 20 minutes. This is considered a maintenance level for good circulation and a healthier heart. Trampoline advocates are claiming that,

TWENTY MINUTES OF REBOUND EXERCISE EQUALS:
- **Jogging 3½ miles in 32 minutes**
- **Playing handball for 40 minutes**
- **Playing racquetball for 40 minutes**
- **Swimming 800 yards in 16 minutes**
- **Bicycling 5 miles in 18 minutes**
- **Jumping rope for 15 minutes**
- **Walking 2½ miles in 34 minutes**

4. STATIONARY RUNNING: This in-home exercise is also good for the heart, and for the entire arterial system. It will also aid relaxation, metabolism of food and speed up the elimination processes. There must be a gradual increase in the length of time doing "stationary running", and you can take your pulse from time to time to keep yourself within the minimum-maximum limits. Kenneth Cooper's guidelines for stationary running are detailed for every age group and are found in his two latest books.

5. GETTING STARTED WITH WALKING: Check out your heart/pulse rate before you start. Count your pulse for one minute and then proceed to go for a walk. After you have walked for 5 minutes, stop and immediately

check your pulse rate again. Keep walking and checking your pulse to assure yourself that your are not overdoing exercise.

In the next 5 minutes increase your pace to be more vigorous in your walking. Then stop and count your pulse for the next minute (or count for 15 seconds and multiply by 4). Your goal is to walk at whatever pace brings your heartbeat/pulse rate into the "aerobic" range as described on a previous page. Take your time. Be cautious and slow at first. You do not need to do this more than every other day to maintain cardio-vascular fitness.   Dr. Cooper says that if you are 60 years of age, you should walk a mile in 20 minutes. At the 5th week the goal is set at 1.5 miles in 28 minutes. At the 10th week the goal is 2.5 miles in 42 minutes. By the 18th week the goal is 3.5 miles in 55 minutes. When you have arrived at this stage you can maintain fitness by keeping up the pace set for the 18th week.

Persons younger in age than Age 60 are programed to use slightly longer distances and cover them in less time. All the exercise programs developed by the Cooper Clinic in Dallas have point values and the ideal is set at about 30 points per week. Thus, one can interchange running, cycling, walking, swimming, so that the final total for the week is 30 points.

6. JOGGING — RUNNING: If you are under the age of 35 you are young enough to begin a gradual program of walking — jogging — running. Medical clearance from your physician is recommended for everyone, but especially for persons over age 35.

Warm up by walking progressively faster for 5 minutes. Check your pulse rate. Next, jog slowly until you start to feel heavy breathing. Check your pulse again. You want to make sure that the pulse rate is within the training range described earlier. Resume jogging at a moderate pace until you feel your heart rate increasing again. Slow down to a walk and/or stop. Check your pulse again.

You are exercising your heart and cardio-vascular system so you do not need to excel in speed, endurance or become sweaty. Alternate your walking -- jogging -- running to maintain the heart rate at the proper training level.

THE 12 MINUTE FITNESS TEST

Kenneth Cooper offers us a fitness level test which enables us to evaluate our physical fitness level. Most of us know how "unfit" we are, but we can become aware of the process of evaluation.

See how much distance you can cover in 12 minutes by any combination of walking, jogging or running. Then take your automobile and check that distance on the odometer. Obviously, you should be dressed properly and not overdo exercise. The younger you are, the more distance you will probably cover. Also the more physically fit your are the more distance you will cover.

THE 12 MINUTE WALKING/RUNNING TEST

(Miles covered in 12 minutes)

FITNESS	0 Mi.	1 Mi.	1.25	1.50	1.75	2.0

Very Poor
Men ————————— <1.14 Mi.
Women ————————— <.88 Mi.

Poor
Men —————————————1.19 Mi.
Women ———————————.93 Mi.

Fair
Men ———————————————1.32 Mi.
Women —————————————1.05 Mi.

Good
Men —————————————————1.37 Mi.
Women ———————————————1.18 Mi.

Excellent
Men —————————————————————1.60 Mi.
Women —————————————————1.30 Mi.

Superior

Men	————————————————————> 1.66
Women	————————————————>1.35

This is based on an average for men and women ages 40–49 adapted from "The New Aerobics", 1970, Kenneth Cooper. See his book for guidelines for other age categories.

A DO IT YOURSELF JOGGING PROGRAM

1. Find a quarter mile track at your high school, or take your car and measure 1 mile.
2. Walk — Jog — Run without elevating your pulse rate above the maximum described earlier.
3. If you are between age 30 and 40 use this guideline.
   1 mile in 11 miniutes indicates <u>poor</u> condition.
   1 mile in 8.5 minutes indicates good condition.
   1 mile in 6.6 minutes indicates <u>superior</u> condition.
4. Younger persons, take ½ minute off for each decade younger.
5. Older persons, add ½ minute for each decade older.
6. Women, add two minutes to the above scores.
7. Start out by setting your goal at walking – jogging – running for three times a week for 12 weeks.

```
Week  1 — 1 mile in 12 minutes
Week  2 — 1 mile in 12 minutes
Week  3 — 1 mile in 11 minutes
Week  4 — 1 mile in 11 minutes
Week  5   1 mile in 10 minutes
Week  6 — 1 mile in 10 minutes
Week  7 — 1 mile in  9 minutes
Week  8 — 1 mile in  9 minutes
Week  9 — 1 mile in  8 minutes
Week 10 — 1 mile in  8 minutes
Week 11 — 1 mile in  7 minutes
Week 12 — 1 mile in  7 minutes
```

8. If you do not lower your time as much as you wanted,
but you keep your heart beat/pulse rate within
the desired training (aerobic) range, you
have fulfilled your major purpose in strengthening your heart, facilitating metabolism, im-
proving circulation, increasing peristalsis of
the colon, and relieving tension.

EXERCISE AND WEIGHT LOSS

It takes about 3000 – 3500 calories to make up 1 pound
of human body fat. Reduction in caloric intake enables
many persons to lose weight. However, there are some
persons who have great difficulty losing weight even
if they cut back on caloric intake.

The reason exercise is so important is that when
a person goes on a diet, s/he frequently eats insufficient
amounts of essential vitamins and minerals. After a
period of dieting s/he begins to feel weak or gets sick.
This is due to inadequate nutritional intake.

Weight control programs that do not include exercise
are self—defeating. Exercise enables a person to
continue with some reduced intake of food, but the
unwanted fat is burned off with exercise. Instead of
becoming weak and letting the muscle tissue shrink due
to inactivity, the person increases muscle tissue by
exercise. With the increase in muscle tissue there is
increased burning up of the remaining fatty substance.
Simple! Muscle burns fat. More muscle means less fat.

There are many activities which burn off those extra
calories and pounds. According to Robert E. Johnson,
M.D., Ph.D., of the University of Illinois College of
Medicine, a 150 pound person will burn the following
number of calories per hour (cph) while participating
in these activities.

ACTIVITY	CALORIES PER HOUR
Sleeping	80
Sitting	100
Driving a car	120
Standing	140
Domestic work	180
Walking 2.5 MPH	210
Bicycling 5.5 MPH	210
Gardening	220
Golfing	250
Mowing lawn	250
Bowling	270
Walking 3.75 MPH	300
Swimming ¼ mile	300
Square dancing	350
Volleyball playing	350
Roller skating	350
Chopping or sawing wood	400
Tennis	420
Cross country skiing	600
Squash playing	600
Handball playing	600
Bicycling 13 MPH	660
Running 10 MPH	900

WALKING IS RECOMMENDED

Brisk walking at 3 miles per hour or more, four days a week for at least 40 minutes should keep you in good cardiovascular shape. Jogging is fine, but it does not actually burn off that many more calories. Brigham Young University researchers compared a walking 12 minute mile with a jogging 8½ minute mile, and found only 26 fewer calories burned by the walker. (These Times, Dec, 1983) "Running is not for everyone," says Charles T. Kuntzleman, a runner for years and consultant to the YMCA. Dr. Michael Pollock, coauthor of Health and Fitness Through Physical Activity, found that men who walked briskly for 40 minutes, four days a week, over 20 weeks, had measureable improvement equal to that of similarly aged men jogging 30 minutes for three days a week.

Walking is No. 5 on Kenneth Cooper's list of aerobic exercises. No. 1 is cross country skiing. No. 2 is swimming. No. 3 is jogging or running. No. 4 is cycling. No. 5 is walking. Kenneth Cooper, a former colonel in the Air Force Medical Corp, coined the word "aerobics" (in its noun form) in the 1960's. His clinic in Dallas, Texas has treated thousands of cardiac cases. In view of the relative difficulty of finding snow, No. 1 is out for most of us, even though it would do us the most good. No. 2 limits a sizeable population for lack of facilities. No. 3 and 4, jogging and cycling, are good for the robust. No. 5, walking, has almost no objectionable dimensions. It wins the vote of most exercise advocates.

In a conversation with Ralph Blodgett in These Times (Nov, 1983) Kenneth Cooper was asked;

> **"As a devout Christian doctor, do you find anything in the Bible that talks about health?"**

Dr. Cooper's reply

> **"Without question, yes. We are commanded in the Bible to glorify God in our body as well as our spirit, and the body is identified as the temple of God. Yet we abuse our temple tremendously. Our bodies are designed to last 120 years. The reason that they don't is not because of any design deficiency; it's the way we treat our bodies -- especially our lack of exercise."**

DISCUSSION

1. Exercise contributes to health and happiness. Why is so little said about exercise in the Bible?

2. In I Corinthians 9:24-27 Paul refers to boxing. Do you think Paul worked out on a punching bag from time to time?

3. The Apostle Paul believed in self-control. How much did he practice self-control? Is total self-control a good thing?

4. Psychotherapy for mentally disturbed persons in a hospital sometimes includes recreational exercise. What is the difference between recreational exercise and aerobic exercise?

5. What are some of the benefits of exercise? How can we get more self-control to keep up exercising?

6. What can we do to make it easier for people to be self-disciplined?

7. Can you think of other Bible passages which promote exercising?

8. Some people have never gone to church and have more self-control than Christians. How did the secular person get his self-control?

9. Is exercise Christian? Is not exercising a sin?

10. What should your church do, if anything, to foster more exercise?

Chapter 18

HEALING WITH RELAXATION

MEDITATION, VISUALIZATION

"Oh, how I love thy law! It is my <u>meditation</u> day and night."   (Psalm 119:97)

"I <u>meditate</u> on all that thou hast done."   (Psalm 143:5)

"Let the words of my mouth and the <u>meditation</u> of my heart be acceptable in thy sight, O Lord, my rock and my redeemer."   (Psalm 19:14)

"<u>Meditate</u> upon these things; give thyself wholly to them."
(I Timothy 4:15)

Before trying to understand the therapeutic values of relaxation, meditation, and visualization, simply fill out the Inventory on the next page, and evaluate your level of these coping skills.

RELAXATION SKILLS

Pick out the most appropriate response. Write the number of that response in the space provided by that statement.

0. Never 1. Rarely 2. Occasionally 3. Sometimes 4. Frequently 5. Almost always

1. _____ I enjoy relaxing at mealtime.
2. _____ I have time alone to relax.
3. _____ I stand by a window and stare into space to relax.
4. _____ I have my day planned so that I feel in control.
5. _____ I go out for coffee or lunch to get away.
6. _____ I work hard and then treat myself with relaxation.
7. _____ I get involved in a sport. It is refreshing , relaxing.
8. _____ I turn to a hobby like sewing, hunting, reading, etc.
9. _____ I go for a walk or a ride when I need to relax.
10. _____ I wear comfortable clothing.
11. _____ I watch light and humorous television to relax.
12. _____ I do some meditation.
13. _____ I spend time in prayer.
14. _____ I have fun socializing.
15. _____ I sit and dream about future plans, goals, activities.
16. _____ I make sure I go somewhere for vacation.
17. _____ I stand up, stretch and breath deeply to relax.
18. _____ I do physical work, so I sit to relax.
19. _____ I do some exercises to help me relax.
20. _____ I can unwind and go to sleep easily.
21. _____ I change and vary my activities to keep stress down.
22. _____ I do things spontaneously for a change of pace.
23. _____ I put my worries aside and do something else to
            divert my mind.
24. _____ I look for humorous things to make me feel good
            or laugh.
25. _____ I practice mind-over-matter (or faith) to
            eliminate fears.
26. _____ I go to concerts, plays, civic events, movies or
            travelogues to relax and feel good.
27. _____ I spend time relaxing in the sun.
28. _____ I play games or play cards with friends.
29. _____ I check my pulse or blood pressure to determine
            the degree of my relaxation.
30. _____ I practice relaxation when I sense that my hands
            or feet are cold.

_____________ TOTAL (Range 0 - 150) (Enter this on Page 358)

INTERPRETATION

0 – 30 Your RELAXATION SCORE is extremely low. You should learn and use relaxation techniques.

31 – 60 Your RELAXATION score is very low. It is quite likely that there is some problem in your life making it difficult to relax. Problems need to be discussed and resolved. Some problems are very difficult to resolve, but keep working at them. If you have tried to resolve your problems, but cannot, you can be benefited by the use of relaxation skills. Meditation, religious and/or secular, can bring relief and prevent illness which results from long periods of stress.

61 – 90 Your RELAXATION score is within a relatively safe zone. Most persons are in this general area of scoring. If you are in the lower part of this zone, you need to remind yourself that your body and mind require a variety of relaxing diversions. You cannot stay with one activity a long time without stress building up. If you have been having some particular problem, forget the problem for a time and do something to divert your attention. Join an aerobics class. Sign up for a Community Education class. Find a sports league of bowling, softball, etc. Go out with a friend to some community event. If you are at the upper end of the scoring zone, you are probably already doing these things.

90–120 Your RELAXATION score is excellent. You seem to know that it is not healthy to dwell on problems. People like you are mostly outgoing persons — kind, helpful, thoughtful of others. etc. Keep it up. This score may also represent your strong effort to combat some problem. Congratulations.

Above 120 Your RELAXATION score is superior. You are one of very few persons who knows the value of stress-reduction, and also practices the art.

HEALING WITH DIVINE—HUMAN COOPERATION

Marilyn Ludolf becamed plagued with acne at the age of 32. It appeared suddenly. It made her appearance so unsightly that even a child in her classroom asked what was wrong. She tried medicine, allergy shots, rotation dieting, gels, creams and consultation after consultation with a never ending stream of specialists. For 16 years she ached emotionally, yet kept her faith and taught Sunday School.

One day she heard Cheryl Prewitt, Miss America 1980 say, "God healed me. I prepared myself to be healed, and God healed me." That day Marilyn vowed to use every ounce of faith necessary to bring healing into her life. On May 1 she began to prepare herself for healing by looking up every verse of scripture on healing she could find. She wrote them down on paper. For the next 10 weeks she muttered those verses over and over again, at stop signs, between classrom instructions, walking here, sitting there.

On July 12, the day circled on the calendar for the healing to be complete, she was glad that so much of the acne was gone, but she was not completely healed. The day wore on, and it was a challenge, but she and God came through with healing before sundown.

We will never know how much of the healing came from mind-over-matter and how much from God. Let us not take credit away from either God or from Marilyn Ludolf. (See the complete story and verses in the Appendix.)

That is the theme of this chapter and the essence of this book. When a person puts his body, mind, and spirit in synchronization with divinely ordained processes, there will be unlimited potential for healing. The contemporary ideas on relaxation, meditation, visualization, etc., are not new ideas. People have used them for their healing from the time of creation. Some of those ideas have been lost in the secularization of society and the church.

YOU CAN HAVE HEALING, AND.....

You can participate in the kind of healing Marilyn Ludolf experienced. It will require determination, guts, will-power, mind-over-matter thinking. "Poor me. I need help." attidudes need to be traded in for assertive behaviors. You simply must get your back up and begin to think in terms of "fight" (II Timothy 4:7), "overcoming" (Romans 7 and 8), and "wrestling" (Ephesians 6:12). I never advocate abandoning medical treatment. I favor the resolution of all problems, and the activation of faith and will, so that healing can take place. If you pray for healing, resolve the problems that brought on the degenerative disease or illness in the first place. God is very merciful, and He wants us to change the behavior that brought on the digestive disorder or the neurological disorder in the first place. Likewise, if a person's indulgent behavior brought on an illness, would it not be helpful, for healing, if that person pledged to change that behavior. God is so merciful that He does not need to wait for our "pledge" or our "change", but He wants it.

HEALING WITH RELAXATION

Two of the most acclaimed experts on the subject of relaxation tell us that they see therapeutic value in the skill of relaxation. Barbara B. Brown cites the following list of ailments, for which relaxation, monitored by Electro-Myographic Response (EMG Biofeedback), is a recognized treatment.

PRIMARILY EMOTIONAL PROBLEMS

1. Anxiety
2. Phobias
3. Tension headache
4. Chronic headache
5. Social problems
6. Learning problems, hyperactivity
7. Stage fright
8. Subvocalization
9. Insomnia
10. Alcoholism

11. Drug abuse
12. Depression with anxiety

PRIMARILY PSYCHOSOMATIC PROBLEMS

1. Asthma
2. Essential hypertension
3. Bruxism
4. Intestinal disorders (ulcer, colitis, spasms of intestinal sphincters)
5. Menstrual distress

PRIMARILY PHYSICAL PROBLEMS

1. Muscle spasms with pain
2. Nerve-muscle injuries .. stroke, paralysis
3. Hyperkinesias, dyskinesias
4. Spasticity
5. Cerebral palsy
6. Spasmodic torticollis
7. Tinnitus with anxiety
8. Migraine headache
9. Dystonias
10. Dysphonia

(Stress and the Art of Biofeedback, N.Y., McGraw - Hill, 1977, p. 54-55)

The other expert is Herbert Benson, M.D., author of the No. 1 best selling, The Relaxation Response, and Harvard University cardiology professor-researcher, has concluded that if a person adds his "belief system" to his "relaxation response", there is a "Faith Factor". Dr. Benson says, "My research and that of others has disclosed that those who develop and use the Faith Factor effectively can

-- Relieve headaches
— Reduce angina pectoris pains (heart) and and perhaps even eliminate the need for bypass surgery (an estimated 80 percent of angina pain can be relieved by positive belief!)
— Reduce blood pressure and help control hypertension problems
— Enhance creativity, especially when

experiencing some "mental block"
— Overcome insomnia
— Prevent hyperventilation attacks
— Help alleviate backaches
— Enhance the therapy of cancer
— Control panic attacks
— Lower cholesterol levels
— Alleviate the symptoms of anxiety that
    include nausea, vomiting, diarrhea,
    constipation, short temper, and
    inability to get along with others
—Reduce overall stress and achieve greater
    inner peace and emotional balance
(Beyond the Relaxation Response, N.Y.:
Times Books, 1984, p. 6-7)

Benson gives credit to "relaxation" and "belief system", though not exclusively, for the above therapeutic benefits. The safest approach would be to follow a multiple-impact approach, where all possible stress factors are dealt with, and every possible healing skill employed.

BIOFEEDBACK — FACILITATES RELAXATION

If you count your pulse, that is biofeedback. When you take your temperature or your blood pressure, that is also biofeedback. An electro-cardiogram is biofeedback. These are fairly common practices, and we think of them as necessary to diagnose physical problems. In the past two decades other biofeedback devices have been produced to diagnose mental and physical conditions coming out of stress.

Currently we have electronic technology to measure a variety of responses the body has to stress. Our body's bio-chemical processes can be electronically monitored. The **Electroencephalogram (EEG)** measures brain wave activity and the EEG can detect varying levels. The patterns of brain wave activity are divided into four categories.

DELTA — This is the slowest frequency, 0.5 to 3 Hz (cycles per second). These occur at the deepest stage of sleep, or deliberate relaxation.

THETA — This frequency of 3.5 to 6.5 Hz (or
to 8 cycles per second) occurs during light sleep,
and also at moments of sudden insight or
recognition of events in one's memory.

ALPHA — This rythmic frequency starts at
8 or 9 and goes up to 12 or 13 Hz (cycles per
second). It is a state of relaxed wakefulness.

BETA — Above 13 Hz and up to as high as
40 Hz (cycles per second), is the range, both
for solving problems in mathmatics and life,
and is also associated with anxiety and
apprehension. (Source: Barbara B. Brown)

EEG is not used in very many clinical practices. While
it is important much of the desired results can be found
in other ways, like through an **Electromyogram (EMG).**
This electronic monitor senses the electrical stimulation
of the muscles, and magnifies the sound to be registered
by a meter or heard as sound. The sensors of the EMG
are attached to the forehead, and give a reading of the
electrical stimulation which may be coming from stress
in the body. A very relaxed person may have only 1
to 2 microvolts of electrical energy showing on the meter.
When the monitor registers 5, 10, or even 15 microvolts,
we can be faily assured that the person is not relaxed.
When repeated measurements show high EMG readings,
the clinical therapist knows that relaxation therapy is
essential. Individual muscles can be monitored, or
a larger group of muscles such as the entire upper half
of the torso, can be measured. Deviations from the
norm determine the need for relaxation therapy. Therapy
uses the same EMG equipment, and the patient is taught
relaxation exercises. As the patient practices relaxation,
the monitor will show the success. This gives the person
"feedback" and "rewards" the behavior. People learn
very quickly.

Galvanic Skin Response (GSR) is monitoring equipment
which detects moisture in the finger-tips as a result
of stress or arousal. This monitoring device serves the
same purpose, to enable persons to detect a high state
of anxiety, and then to use relaxation skills to reduce
the levels, thus reducing the effects of stress on the

body.   The GSR sends out a variable tone buzz, so that under high anxiety the buzzer is high-pitched. Then as you relax, the tone of the buzzer descends to a relaxed clicking sound, and then finally, no sound when you are as relaxed as you want to be. A GSR monitoring device costs only about $50.00 and is very effective in enabling someone to learn how to relax.

Dermal monitoring is a measurement of the skin temperature, usually of the finger-tips, but also of the toes.   The reason that finger-tip temperature indicates the degree of anxiety or arousal, is that under stress the emergency reactions demand all the blood leave the stomach and skin area, and go to the leg and arm muscles (the striated muscle system) for fight or flight. Thus, under stress, with the smooth muscles constricting and driving blood out of the small capillaries, the skin becomes colder.   Finger tip temperature can go from 96 degrees to 76 degrees in a matter of seconds when stress happens.   My relaxing finger-tip temperature is 94 degrees.   My speaking-to-a-small-group finger-tip temperature is 84 degrees.   My preaching finger-tip temperature is 76 degrees. There are variables which make exceptions, but usually, the colder the finger-tips, the more anxiety is in the system at that moment.

Some person's stress shows up better on one instrument than on another.   EMG, GSR, and DERMAL readings become helpful, because they tell us when we need to make some helpful changes in our life-style to combat stress-induced illnesses.

RELAXATION — CONTROL OF THE ANS

Since the advent of biofeedback-monitored relaxation, no one believes anymore that the **"Autonomic Nervous System"** is automatic.   Science now recognizes that the mind has power over what was believed "automatic". Biofeedback monitoring devices recorded what relaxation, coupled with meditation, and visualization could do. This opens up the whole world of mind-over-matter.

Control of the Autonomic Nervous System reduces activity along many fronts, preventing the deterioration

which results from bombardment by stress factors. With
less stress, there will be less illness, as well as a greater
chance of healing.

You need to remember and/or recall that Hans Selye
M.D., pioneered a movement demonstrating that excess
stress induced illness. He "stressed" a wide variety
of animals, with an equally illustrious array of stressors
until the animals died. Postmortem examination showed
1. The adrenal cortex was enlarged, meaning it had been
overworked and was exhausted. 2. The thymus gland
was shrunken in size from suppressive bombardment
by the adrenal cortex. 3. The animals had ulcers. The
conclusion was always that excessive stress caused the
varying illnesses from which the stressed animals died.

Under stress, the body responds with two systems;
1. hormonal 2. neurological. First, hormonally, when
the brain (hypothalmus) perceives a fight-flight
emergency, it sends a message to the pituitary, which
energize the adrenals with an adrenocorticotropic hormone
(ACTH). The adrenals activate the body with adrenaline,
but suppress the thymus with corticosteroids, because
in an emergency, there is no time to fight infections
or allergens. That explains why the thymus (the immune
system) is shrunken in size after a never-ending flow
of stress, and therefore, cannot fight off illness.

Simultaneous to the activation of the hormonal system
by stress, the autonomic nervous system (ANS), which
is the neurological system, is likewise activated by the
hypothalmus. This autonomic nervous system (ANS)
produces a variety of body responses.

1. Constriction of blood vessels
2. Elevation of blood pressure
3. Increased pulse (heart beat) rate
4. Increased perspiration
5. Pupils of the eyes dialate
6. Senses improve -- eyesight is keener
7. More red corpuscles are released
    by the spleen
8. Fats are released into the blood
    stream for energy

9.   Adrenal glands convert glycogen to glucose.
10.   Chemical released into the blood to speed coagulation of blood
11.   Salavation and musous secretions slow down
12.   Digestion shuts down
13.   Sexual arousal is inhibited

The sympathetic nervous system branch of the ANS is responsible for Nos. 1-11, and the parasympathetic nervous system is responsible for Nos. 12 – 13. The ANS also has an indirect effect on the activity of the stomach. Under stress the digestive processes shut down and food can easily be left in the stomach. The acids of digestion soon prove to be too powerful for the stomach lining and the irritations eventually cause inflamation and

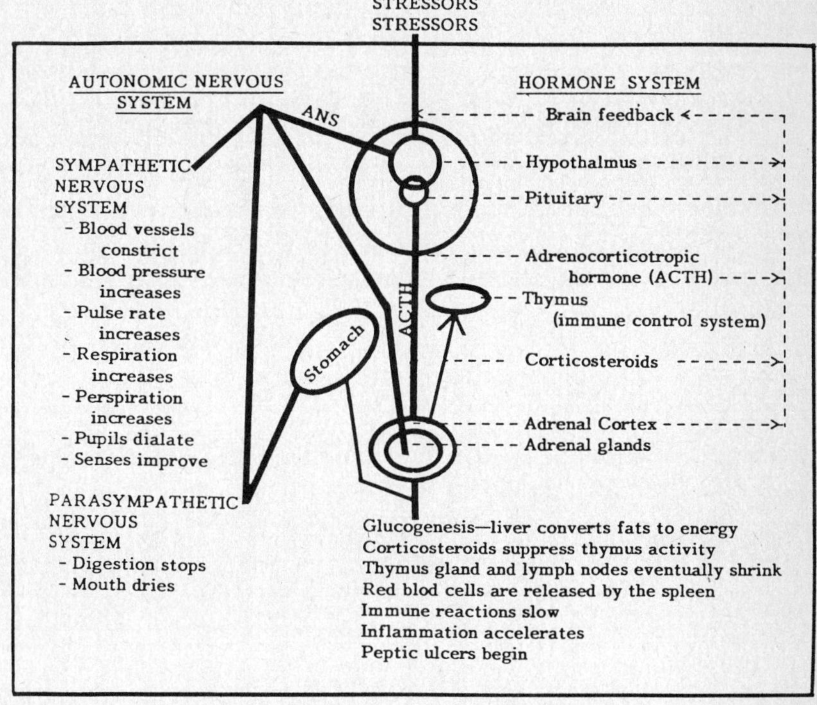

breakdown of the tissues into ulcers. Nausea and vomiting are often the result of a sudden surge of stress. All of this takes place as the body attempts to cope with stress. All of these hormonal and neurological (electrical) reactions are good in order to meet temporary stress, but not good under long term stress.

So, therefore, if you can control the body reactions, even though you cannot put out all the fire of the stress, you have some mastery which is going to prevent illness and create the conditions of healing.

RELAXATION EXERCISES — JACOBSON

Almost 50 years ago Dr. Edmond Jacobson devoped tensing and relaxing exercises to produce a relaxation response. He was the first one to make Luigi Galvani's discovery of electrical impulses to body muscles, useful to psychologists. He was the first to measure these muscle impulses with an electromyographic device. The tensing and relaxing exercises have been modified by different persons, but the original ones are still the most helpful. You may make your own tape of the Jacobson Relaxation Exercises, and use the tape to practice relax-ation. The words are found in the Appendix.

There are several variations of this Jacobson Relaxation Exercise. I apply them clinically to persons for whom relaxation seems like a relevant adjunctive therapeutic treatment. About half of the persons to whom I teach this exercise, fall asleep about three-quarters of the way through the 15 minute tape. That is not the intent of the use of the tape, but that is evidence of the power of this treatment. When these persons are monitored through Dermal (skin) temperature, you always see a rise in finger-tip temperature, if it starts out low (low indicates anxiety's power to constrict the smooth muscles of the arterial system and make the skin turn cold). EMG readings show increased relaxation too, through Jacobson Relaxation Exerrcises.

Christians can use this relaxation process. These processes were created by God. God gave them for stress-management. We can pray, and ask God to heal us, simultaneously, while we are doing the very thing God created for us to do when we are overly anxious. Sometimes we ask God to do for us, what we might be able to do for ourselves. Why not do praying and relaxing at the same time. Let prayer and relaxation work together synergistically, to quadruple quintuple, or compound the effect by 10 or 100 fold.

AUTOGENIC TRAINING

"Auto" means self, and "genic" means to create, so Autogenic Training has become the phrase to indicate that persons can be trained to have control over their Autonomic Nervous System. In the 1890's Oskar Vogt taught some of his experienced hypnotic subjects to put themselves into a trance that reduced fatigue, tension and headaches. Johannes H. Schultz, a Berlin psychiatrist, found that he could produce the same results without the hypnosis and wrote of this in a book entitled AUTOGENIC TRAINING in 1932. The exercises he developed and used effectively are aimed at reversing the fight-flight arousal from stress, when it does not subside automatically.

Use a thermometer. Place it between your thumb and forefinger. Then say each of the following phrases to yourself three times. Go through the routine for a minimum of 10 minutes two times a day.

> **My right arm is heavy and warm.**
> **My left arm is heavy and warm.**
> **Both of my arms are heavy and warm**
> **My right leg is warm and heavy.**
> **My left leg is warm and heavy.**
> **Both of my legs are warm and heavy.**
> **My arms and legs are heavy and warm.**
> **My stomach is warm and calm.**
> **My breathing is calm and regular.**
> **My forehead is cool.**

Persons who often have cold fingers as a result of slight stress constantly running in their lives, will experience a warming. Warm fingers indicate a state of relaxation. Obviously, if there is arterial constriction due to hardening of the arteries, or are on tranquilizers, etc., this exercise may not be helpful. Usually, exercises are helpful to the persons who need it, but are considered worthless by others, who do not need the treatment, or are not putting their whole self into it. Electromyographic (EMG) recordings also lower during Autogenic Training. Finger-tip temperature elevates. Experts suggest that persons practice these Autogenic phrases two times a day for a month, for maximum skill at reducing problems related to excess arousal from stress.

The exercises have been around longer than the biofeedback to measure their effectiveness. The knowledge of mind-over-matter did not come out of biofeedback research, but the marriage of biofeedback and mind-over-matter thinking has been producing results, both in the area of prevention as well as healing.

Christians, generally, spend time thinking about principles that control their behavior. So does everyone, to some degree or another. No one spends much time telling toes and fingers to warm up. Yet, if a person can control the biological processes, we can also control psychological process, and even spiritual processes. If you tell them what you want them to do, often enough, they will perform within their divinely ordained patterns.

Apply Autogenic Training to any behavior you want from your body, mind and spirit. In effect, we do that. We say, "I will have faith". "I will have faith." "I do not know why it happened, but I will have faith." Our brain, which remembers the promises of God, drills that into our emotions, our heart, to keep it from deteriorating in time of stress. Christians have been some of the strongest practicioners of Autogenic Training. They may not have warmed finger-tips, but they have stabilized emotions, thoughts and behavior. There are more ways that this skill can be utilized by Christians.

Marilyn Ludolf was probably combining some Autogenic training (the repetition of healing scripture verses) with faith and prayer, as she used those verses and found healing. Marilyn did not ask God to do it all. She "prepared" herself, and "God healed", she said. Don't try it. Just do it.

MEDITATION

Let us review meditation in general, before describing Biblical meditation. Persons practicing meditation differ widely in their desired goals, how they achieve those goals, and what happens to them as a result of their meditating.

Some common characteristics of meditative processes.

1. Meditation is associated with relaxation.
2. Meditative techniques require concentration.
3. Meditation leads to some form of possitively altered state of consciousness.
4. A word or phrase is used (mantra, to some) which centers the mind and emotions.

Some reasons or goals for using meditation.

1. Relaxation
2. Discover inner direction
3. Find inner peace
4. Integrate painful experiences
5. Change personal behavior
6. Find meaning to life

Experiences people have in meditation

1. An awakening of a level of existence not known before, such as the world of feelings
2. Relaxation
3. Getting in touch with deep emotions
4. Transcending time and space, euphoria
5. Feelings of deep inner peace

Results from meditative practices

1. Lowered metabolic rate
2. Decreased muscle tension
3. Decreased oxygen consumption
4. Decreased blood pressure, heart rate, respiration rate
5. Increased Alpha waves, skin temperature and skin galvanometric resistance
6. Decrease in lactate ion (which accounts for pain, fatigue, and anxiety)

Types of meditation

1. Reflective — thinking about some desireable

quality such as joy, faith, courage, serenity,
or some "seed thought" for stimulation
2. Receptive -- beginning with silence and
blankness, and allowing awareness and
truth to break in
3. Creative — using meditation to renew the
self, modify the self, transform the self,
train the self, etc.

(Source: Garfield, Pelletier, Pahnke, Richards, Assagioli, in Stress Power, by Robert A. Anderson, M.D., N.Y.: Human Sciences Press, 1978)

This outline of meditative practices and results shows us the broad range of applicability. That is encouraging to some, but a threat to others. The Christian church has been justly proud of its heritage and uniqueness in the place of history. Since meditation has historically been thought of as something from the Eastern cultures and religions, Western culture and religion has not wanted to acknowledge any validity in the practice of meditation.

The debate continues regarding the uniqueness of Transcendental Meditation (TM), Yoga, The Relaxation Response, and any other form of mind-over-matter technique which produces the physiological changes mentioned above. Dr. Herbert Benson, cardiologist at the Harvard Medical School, author of Beyond the Relaxation Response, obliterates some of the distinctions that have been held in the past, demonstrating that the phrases of Jews, Christians or others, are reference points for fusing the religious and the not - particularly - religious practices of meditation.

RELIGIOUS MEDITATION

Marilyn Ludolf, in bringing healing to her acne, practiced a form of religious meditation. It was a "reflective" meditative process, using the power of the Word of God, and faith in the Healing power of Jesus Christ. She used no relaxation exercises and no biofeedback that I know of, but everything she did was geared to anxiety reduction. She meditated, using many passages from the Bible. Dr. Herbert Benson put his professional reputation and world-wide fame on the line, when he said that phrases from the Bible have the same power as anything someone else would say when meditating. Benson does not go on to say that the religious phrases have any "more" power. No, he may not be able to say that, either personally or publically, but Christians take the position that when a person claims the promises of God in the passages of scripture, that is faith. Faith brings healing. So a meditating Christian, not only reduces stress through his meditation, but he adds the power of God. That is a winning combination, where the entire emotional make-up of the person is mobilized in faith, for God to bless. Far too often, people just do a "poor me" before God, but never activate their will (or faith?).

To meditate is to "mutter", or to "mumble". Marilyn Ludolf "muttered" and "mumbled" those verses which were used in the Psalms, and by Jesus to those he healed, and by the Apostle Paul. The Hebrew word for meditate is "hagah" or "haguth" and Young's Analytical Concordance says that means "mutter". Joshua told the Children of Israel to "mutter" "on the law day and night" (Joshua 1:8). He was suggesting that these people repeat and repeat and repeat the law, until it was indelibly inscribed on their unconscious psychic systems. There are several references to "meditating" on the law of God in the Psalms (1:2, 19:14, 63:6, 77:12, 104:34, 119:15,23, 48, 78, 148). There is a picture in these verses of a person repetitiously reciting the important requirements of God, and drilling his mind, heart, and soul, until his entire makeup takes on the qualities which are being learned. The Apostle Paul said to Timothy, "Meditate upon these things" (King James). Paul wanted Timothy to drill (his responsibilities) into his unconscious so that any behavior in the future would be based on them. Meditation is a memorization process for the unconscious. It can include relaxation and Autogenic Training. Marilyn Ludolf put these all together.

That meditation is a drilling-memorizing-muttering-mumbling process, in which the subconscious learns, is further substantiated by a reference Jesus makes.

Jesus is telling his disciples about what they will face in the future. Jesus does not want them to become worried about what they will say when they meet persecution. He tells them not to plan ahead, not to drill answers into their minds, but to wait for the leading of the spirit.

> **"Settle it therefore in your minds, not to <u>meditate</u> beforehand how to answer." (Luke 21:14)**

Jesus saw no value in trying to get totally prepared for speeches, when the content of those speeches would be coming automatically out of their heart. Meditation is not for witnessing, but meditation is for healing. Meditation is for planting, watering and cultivating faith into behavior.

My grandmother used to meditate. I often heard her attending her housewife chores and either citing a verse of scripture, or singing a familiar hymn. Sometimes she "mumbled" and sometimes she "muttered", and sometimes she sang. She was as fine a Christian as possible. She kept her mind clear, and her mood stable with her Christian meditating. Whether she used that meditating activity to bring healing, or just prevent illness, I do not know. I only remember her remaining remarkably stable in the presence of her grandchildren's antics. I never heard her "mutter" anything that was not truly spiritual.

VISUALIZATION — IMAGERY

Marilyn Ludolf did this too. She began to visualize what she wanted to accomplish. She used mental imagery to foster positive faith and expectant hope. Here are her words

> **"Then I added another exercise. I began to visualize my complexion as pink and clear as a newborn baby's and my sinus passages free and well. I imprinted it on my mind day and night. This exercise became rather a strenuous one, because the mirror was such a contrast from my image.**

> **But after a while the image, like the Scriptures, began to sink into the deep believing places of my life."**

Marilyn did, instinctually, what was helpful. She did what Bruce Jenner did to win the Decathalon, and what thousands of athletes do to become a winner. She did what O. Carl Simonton, M.D. suggests and teaches in his book Getting Well Again, (Bantam, 1978). Cancer patients find hope, meaning, and the will to live in being able to participate in their own healing processes. And when they can be mobilized to relax, meditate, visualize, eat macrobiotically, pray, serve, and stay psychologically fit as well as physically fit, these cancer patients are in a better position to transcend their illness and prolong their lives.

There is a visualization lesson in literature. Ernest is a young boy, in Nathaniel Hawthorne's short story, The Great Stone Face. Ernest is mesmerized by a great stone face peering out from a granit cliff high above his village. Everyone marvels at this Great Stone Face and travelers come from afar to see it. Ernest is fascinated with the granite face. He looks. He stares. He meditates. In between errands, after school, any spare time he has he gazes. Days turned into weeks, and weeks into years. Ernest grows in wisdom. One day, while dispensing some wisdom to a crowd younger than himself, the people are amazed. Ernest has come to resemble the Great Stone Face. His intense gazing has transformed his face into the likeness of the rock. This reminds us of what the Apostle Paul said

> **"And we all, with unveiled face, beholding the glory of the Lord, are being changed into his likeness from one degree of glory to another; for this comes from the Lord who is the Spirit."**
>
> **(II Corinthians 3:18)**

The Word of God and fictional literature agree with the concept of "image rehearsal" to transform the person into becoming what s/he wants to be. A human being is capable of fixing the mind, heart, and soul on a goal, which in turn magnetizes and empowers the person to arrive at that goal. The goal can sometimes be quite unrealistic, and still act as an empowering agent. It cannot be irrational or incongruent with functional principles, without aborting along the way. Yet, hunching and pursuing the hunch is like sensing some truth within, and being carried along on the thrill of seeing the hunch validated.

Norman Vincent Peale tells about the day his Guideposts magazine had 40,000 subscribers, but had many financial struggles. They believed they needed 100,000 subscribers to make the magazine financially solvent. One of his board members, Tessie Durlack, challenged the entire board to "visualize" those 100,000 subscribers. They did. They began to get fired up with enough new ideas, so that they surpassed the 100,000 subscribers and went to 3,600,000 subscribers and 12 million readers. Tessie quoted from the Bible when she challenged that board to "visualization".

> **"Therefore, I tell you, whatever you ask in prayer, believe that you receive it and you will."** (Mark 11:24)

You do not sit back when you pray a prayer like that. You set your back. You set your jaw. You ruffle your psychological fur. You aim your spiritual self. You fire and fire and fire and fire. You challenge God, in a friendly way, to activate himself, and blend with your energy in a synergistically powerful way, with strength that exceeds human proportions.

JESUS — PRAYER — PUTTING IT ALL TOGETHER

Jesus was the great "relaxer", "meditator", and "visualizer", who put it all together in **"Prayer"**. Having grown up a Jew, Jesus knew what it meant to meditate or "mutter" in a repetitive form, the "law" of God. From the frequent references of Jesus going "into a mountain", "into the desert", "across Galilee", etc., to "pray", we know that Jesus had some awareness of the effect of stress on his life. He knew that "relaxation" was essential for his ministry. At some point he knew he would die on the cross, and one day he "set his face to Jerusalem" to make that come true. For many years he "visualized" that final sacrifice for the sins of the world. He finally achieved his goal, and finished his mission.

Prayer, for the Christian can put it all together. In prayer people relax when they turn their problems over to divine help. That is meditative prayer. In meditative prayer you transport your psychic self to a safe and nurturing position, away from the cares of the world. In prayer Christians repeat and repeat their requests and commend themselves to the protective sanctuary provided by God. In prayer Christians place their psyche within that sanctuary. They focus their attention on all the imagery of the Christ who healed people, did miracles, and showed saints the way to ultimate bliss in heaven.

There are prayers of thanksgiving, prayers of intercession, and prayers of supplication. Jesus took time to find a relaxing place to pray. Jesus wept a prayer over Jerusalem. Jesus sweat a prayer in the garden. Prayer can keep you awake like it kept Jesus awake in the Garden of Gethsemane, but prayer is a good sleep-inducer, and it put the disciples to sleep! Jesus prayed aloud and he prayed silently. Jesus recommended "prayer and fasting" to the disciples to bring speedier healing. Jesus prayed verbally when he taught his disciples to pray.   When Jesus was called to the tomb of Lazarus, "he lifted up his eyes (both meditators and praying Christian do this) and said, Father, I thank thee that thou hast heard me." (John 11:41) In effect, we have evidence that Jesus, in all his humanity, used prayer as a survival skill. He used prayer, rather like relaxation, to control the Autonomic Nervous System, which constantly faced the stress of critical Pharaisees and demanding peasants. He fought off indecision in the Garden through a prayerful meditative process, which helped him "center" or be in touch with his true inner mission. Jesus put it all together in prayer.

If you are ill, with some degenerative disease, (not

contagious disease), and you haven't known the kind of prayer that "relaxes", or repeats in a self-affirming (meditative) way (like, "I am being healed."), then start now.   If you have never prayed like Marilyn Ludolf, read her story again, and drill your psychic conscious and subconscious so incessantly with the promises of God, that God will be embarrassed not to get with the program.   If this sounds a bit sacrilegious, I don't mean it to be. It is just that passive praying, when you need the "big needle", isn't where its at. You need to take God so seriously that your faith and prayer almost sounds defiant.

MIND-OVER-MATTER

After Jesus' round-three-temptation by Satan, we read that Jesus had some mind-over-matter thoughts which he shared.

> **"Get thee behind me Satan."**
> **"Begone, Satan.**
> **Get out of my life. I don't need you.**
> **(Matthew 4:10)**

Firmness counts when fighting tempting behavior. Counselors see numerous problems, where innocent and pleasurable behavior got out of hand. Sexual deviations seem to be the worst. People play with a fascinating experience, think about it some more, allow themselves to be drawn into it more, and find themselves hooked on the behavior. There are behaviors, that, "If you don't get to it, it will get to you." Alcoholism, drug addiction, anorexia, bulimia, etc., result from some early failure of mind-over-matter.

The human spirit, coupled with faith, has unlimited power to muscle into Satanic intervention.   There is an urgency about learning to snuff out what may grow up to consume you later.

"Get out of my life" can be said to bad habits, addictive patterns, obscessive patterns, almost anything. It is somewhat on the order of a self-hypnosis program, without the sleep. I am no longer skeptical of self-hypnosis programs. If I want to drill an attitude into my unconscious system, and it is a good attitude, by relaxing and meditating I can make it sink in faster and more permanently. Self-hypnosis is simply drilling, drilling, drilling into the mind, what you want it to think, and how it should perform. I do not want someone else to hypnotize me, and tell me what attitudes and behavior to have. I do not want someone to tamper with another person. We memorize facts, because we want to store those for future reference. We memorize for special reasons. We train our minds, hearts, and souls so they will act or react for our benefit and God's glory. It is mind-over-matter. We need to learn mind-over-matter for healing benefits as well.

TAKE UP THY BED AND WALK

At some point during the healing process you need to decide that healing is actually taking place. That is faith, and a person needs to act on that faith. Friends brought a paralyzed man to Jesus for healing. They had to break a hole in the roof of the house to get to Jesus, but never mind the house. Jesus said,

"Rise, take up your pallet and walk."
(John 5:8)

Something made the paralyzed man decide to see what his legs would do. Whether skepticism or faith drove him to make that first move, the man did get activated. There are degenerative illnesses which require an activated inner psychic response. Hospitalizations are not conducive to this model. Hospitalization requires confinement, passive restraint if you are too energetic, knuckle under to hospital rules, be waited on so you lose all your muscle power, eat fairly high calorie meals because most physicians believe fasting for any reason would be inappropriate. Despite cynicism regarding some hospital practices, we need the hospital, and are glad we have them. The paralyzed man whom Jesus treated recuperated a bit faster than most of us, yet the lesson is one of self-motivation and self-mobilization which engages divine involvement.

A RELAXATION HYMN

The hymns of the Christian church have many of the qualities of relaxation, meditation, and visualization. Most Christians believe their hymns, along with liturgy and symbols, are highly therapeutic. There is Wellness in them. There is illness prevention in their use. There is a wealth of theology in hymns. Hymns lift spirits, and calm nerves. Relaxing hymns relax us. Marching hymns arouse us. Sanguine hymns call forth emotions and loyalty. Hymns are very ingenious stress-reduction tools. Says Benson

> **To get the maximum benefit out of the Relaxation Response, you should tailor it to your personal belief system. . . .The healthful effects of decreased sympathetic nervous system activity will still occur. . .The more your beliefs are integrated into the Relaxation Response, the greater your chances of making use of the Faith Factor. Furthermore, if you regularly focus your attention on a word or phrase that is tied into your basic personal beliefs, it's more likely that you'll get more deeply involved in the Relaxation-Response technique. So choosing a personally important word or phrase to focus upon can serve a dual function: (1) It can activate your belief systems and the accompanying benefits, by providing a greater calming effect on your mind than you might achieve with a neutral focus word: and (2) it increases the likelihood of your use of the technique." (Beyond the Relaxation Response, Times Books, 1984, p. 106)**

Putting this all together into a usable package is not difficult once you understand how faith must be an active psychic ingredient mobilizing the will into action. Simply take positive affirmations, like those found in Autogenic Training. Tell your body, your mind, or your soul, to do what you want it to do. (Remember in Autogenic Training, hands got warm when you said, "My hands are warm.") Then you are to repeat it in meditative style ("muttering"), and you "visualize" the effect in your body, doing all this with faith, because your body responses (biofeedback) will prove that what you are doing is helpful.

You goal is not to become "converted", "get saved", or go to heaven by this method. Your goal is to reduce stress in your life, to engage the power of the Holy Spirit by your act of faith. This synergistic combination contributes to healing. Don't forget Marilyn Ludolf, who achieved this.

Considering the power of "relaxation", "meditation", "visualization", "Autogenic training", (and possibly even self-hypnosis), there can be significant therapeutic (healing) effect in a properly written hymn. Here is a hymn which you can use.

RELAXATION HYMN

(Tune: O God Our Help in Ages Past)

(Please find a comfortable place to be seated.)
Words by Darrell Franken

1. I am relaxing in the Lord.
   I put my faith in him.
   I guide my life by God's good word,
   It quells each raving whim.

2. I put God's warmth into my heart.
   It radiates a balm
   It flows into my every part.
   And leaves me truly calm.

3. I settle back to visualize.
   The blessings I do share.
   I then look up into the skies,
   And know that one does care.

4. I meditate to be serene.
   I push my cares away.
   I focus on a radiant scene.
   It brings joy here to stay.

5. I image an embracing love,
   To melt away the strain.
   I marshal forces from above,
   To take away the pain.

6. Deep down inside there is a flame.
   My restless fever brews.
   I seek a power, my rage to tame,
   My heated heart subdue.

7. I put God's warmth into my soul.
   It calms my nervous storm.
   The flow of grace will make me whole,
   Ir – ra – di – ate the harm.

8. I claim the quiet of the night,
   To calm me in the day.
   I use the warmth of God's sun light,
   To drive my fears away.

There are a number of tunes to which these words can be sung since these words are written in Common Meter (CM). Here is the list of song tunes you can use.

"Amazing Grace"
"Am I a Soldier of the Cross?"
"O For a Thousand Tongues to Sing"
"O For a Closer Walk With God"
"The Lord's My Shepherd"
"There is a Fountain Filled With Blood"
"God Moves in a Mysterious Way"
"In Christ There Is No East or West"
"Must Jesus Bear the Cross Alone?"
"Alas, and Did My Savior Bleed"
"There Is a Green Hill Far Away
"Come, Holy Spirit, Heavenly Dove"
"Prayer Is the Soul's Sincere Desire"
"Jesus, the Very Thought of Thee"

Like Marilyn Ludolf, you need to be involved. You need to sing this hymn. You need to find a comfortable place in your home, where you can look out a window into the sky. You need to commune with God. You need to take these words and sing them to one tune, then another, and then another. Make this your relaxation, your meditation, your visualization, your spiritual commitment to doing your part in the healing process. This hymn has been recorded on a cassette tape recording, and is available.

A HYMN FOR COUNTERACTING LOW SELF WORTH

Part of the victory over low self-worth is achieved by affirming the positive, just when the negative is getting you down. When evil, pain, hurt, and the "devil" are zapping your spirits, you need to devise a mind-over-matter attitude. When the temptation is strong, to dwell on the negative, the Christian can say, **"Get thee behind me, Satan."** — **"Inferiority, get out of my life. I do not need to be pulled down the drain."** If you have attacks of low self worth, you need to "get your back up". Fight off spiraling, swirling, round-in-circles thinking.

The hymn which follows is using a meditative technique combined with a familiar tune. The repetition is like "muttering", discussed earlier. Specialists in meditative practices say that the constant repetition drives the message into the unconscious, where it can have a positive effect on future behavior.

Caution: Do not expect a few minutes of listening to bring a cure. You have to do the singing, the repeating. Mentally, muscle negativity into the ground. Remember Marilyn Ludolf. She worked at her project 10 weeks, every waking spare moment. She won. So can you.

Caution: You may also need to work on some of the life-style changes suggested in other chapters of this book to supplement this treatment. A large contributor to low self worth is suppressed anger. (See Chapter 5). If there is someone in your life, who constantly puts you down, singing this hymn may not help much at all. The Apostle Paul says, "Being angry, do not let the sun go down on your wrath, lest you give opportunity to the devil." (Galatians 5:19) Your low self worth behavior will probably continue unless you decide to speak up and defend yourself. If there are things like hypoglycemia (mood swings due to overconsumption of sugar) or allergies in your system, it may, likewise, contribute to the undermining processes. Work at eliminating stress, while silmultaneously affirming your positive attributes. Attack low self worth on many fronts, using this hymn as one tool to accomplish your task.

A HYMN FOR SELF WORTH

Tune: A Mighty Fortress Is Our God)
(Sing these self-affirming words during times of self-doubt)

(After you have learned the hymn this way, go for a brisk walk and sing these words to the rhythm of your steps.)

MEDITATION HYMN
TO CONQUER FEAR AND WORRY
(Tune: Be Not Dismayed Whate'er Betide)
(Please find a comfortable place to be seated.)

1. I am God's child; I will transcend.
      God gives me faith and peace.
    Relax in joy and fear will end.
      God gives me faith and peace.

Refrain

      God gives me faith and peace.
        I will not fear. I will not worry.
      God is in charge of my life.
        I will have faith and peace.

2. Each time I wake with some dark fear,
      God gives me faith and peace.
    There is a voice which comes through clear.
      God gives me faith and peace.

3. I tell my heart to trust in others.
      God gives me faith and peace.
    I tell my soul to bless my brothers.
      God gives me faith and peace.

4. I look today into God's will.
      God gives me faith and peace.
    He tells my fearful heart, be still.
      God gives me faith and peace.

5. From unknown fear let me be free.
      God gives me faith and peace.
    The truth of God, O let me see.
      God gives me faith and peace.

6. The Bible says, Love casts out fear.
      God gives me faith and peace.
    I love my friends, those far and near.
      God gives me faith and peace.

7. The hurts I feel, each time forgiven.
      God gives me faith and peace.
    Justice will reign when we reach heaven.
      God gives me faith and peace.
    (Words by Darrell Franken)

A HYMN FOR CHRISTIAN HEALING
JESUS CHRIST WILL HEAL TODAY
(Tune: Jesus Christ Is Risen Today)

Supplemental treatment for bringing about wellness.

1. I am on my way to wellness.   Al – le – lu – ia!
   I will triumph over illness.   Al – le – lu – ia!
   With my God I will transcend.   Al – le – lu – ia!
   Put my dreary illness on the mend.   Al – le – lu – ia!

2. I have God's word to lean on.   Al – le – lu – ia!
   It says I can be made strong.   Al – le – lu – ia!
   When my heart begins to sigh,   Al – le – lu – ia!
   Surely God will hear my cry.   Al – le – lu – ia!

3. Every moment of my day,   Al – le – lu – ia!
   I cast all my doubt away.   Al – le – lu – ia!
   I claim vic – tory in His name.   Al – le – lu – ia!
   There is nothing better I can claim.   Al – le – lu – ia!

4. I will think of nothing better.   Al – le – lu – ia!
   Than to triumph over matter.   Al – le – lu – ia!
   God has promised to defend,   Al – le – lu – ia!
   When I'm good and faithful to the end. Al – le – lu – ia!

5. I will pray until the pain,   Al – le – lu – ia!
   Is removed, or on the wane.   Al – le – lu – ia!
   God will make it go away,   pray.   Al – le – lu – ia!
   When his loving friends on earth do   Al – le – lu – ia!

6. I'm under stress, Dear Lord I pray.   Al – le – lu – ia!
   I'll resolve my strife each day.   Al – le – lu – ia!
   En–mi–ty will have to go.   Al – le – lu – ia!
   Re–con–cil–i–a–tion has to flow.   Al – le – lu – ia!

7. I stop fear before it starts.   Al – le – lu – ia!
   I block fear from my whole heart.   Al – le – lu – ia!
   Perfect love casts out all fear.   Al – le – lu – ia!
   Lov–ing–ly I live, and love life dear.   Al – le – lu – ia!

8. I choose hope for my life's chart.   Al – le – lu – ia!
   Hope guides all within my heart.   Al – le – lu – ia!
   I use faith to power my hope.   Al – le – lu – ia!
   Until I'm in wellness, I will cope.   Al – le – lu – ia!

9.   I stomp doubt and doom away.   Al – le – lu – ia!
     I tell satan; Go your way.   Al – le – lu – ia!
     I take God into my heart.   Al – le – lu – ia!
     I want all the illness to depart.   Al – le – lu – ia!

10. I will take both love and joy.   Al – le – lu – ia!
     Blend into a strong alloy.   Al – le – lu – ia!
     Send it forth to change my day.   Al – le – lu – ia!
     Taking all my pain and ill away.   Al – le – lu – ia!

11. I want a re-fa-shioned me.   Al – le – lu – ia!
     Turned around and illness free.   Al – le – lu – ia!
     I will turn away from self.   Al – le – lu – ia!
     Letting it have power to bring health. Al – le – lu – ia!

12. I rejoice in healing power.   Al – le – lu – ia!
     I have strength for every hour.   Al – le – lu – ia!
     I am filled with holy fire.   Al – le – lu – ia!
     Lif-ting me right out of all the mire. Al – le – lu – ia!
          (Words by Darrell Franken)

In this hymn there is faith, confidence, hope, assur-urance, mind-over-matter, meditation (repetitious phra-ses), visualization, self-hypnotic suggestion, Autogenic training, commitment, dedication, guts, will, character, movement forward (no regression), determination, etc. By design there is no relaxation, because the goal is healing through a combination of human and divine transcendence.

Caution: This suggested adjunctive treatment method is not to replace treatment by a licensed physician. That is true for all suggestions found in this book. It would not surprise me if persons took the exercises in this chapter and this book, and found healing for which they could give very little credit to medicine. Miracles are happening because God wants them to happen. Such "spontaneous remissions" are awe inspiring. They verify the existence of God and that inspires our faith.

CHRISTIAN TRANSCENDENTAL MEDITATION

I was asked to visit one of my clients in the hospital after his heart attack. He had just been moved out of the Intensive Care Unit. He twisted, turned, moaned, and was not in much of a mood for any religious or non-religious "talk therapy". None of my clergy skills fit the situation. Praying, reading from the Bible, quoting Psalms, chit-chat, - nothing clerical seemed appropriate. I sensed that he needed to relax. I got his attention, asked him to look at the ceiling, then close his eyes. I asked him to let his imagination float to the roof of the hospital, then to the blue sky, then to the white cloud in the sky, then to the airplane with the white trails behind it, then off into space, then to a star, then to another star. I got him to take a walk with me into infinity, using the stars as his stepping stones. As soon as he was secure on one stone, we visualized another, and moved to it.

Within 90 seconds my friend had calmed down, and within another 30 seconds he was asleep. I suddenly got worried, yet breathing was normal, color was normal. I wondered if I should call a nurse. No, everything was calm and peaceful. I let my friend sleep for about 5 minutes. Then I wakened my friend, and after a couple of stretches he said, "Hi, what happened? I'm sorry I fell asleep on you." My friend was helped through "guided imagery". Such a technique is neither eastern or western, neither religious or non-religious. God simply created mankind to spend more time mobilizing psychic processes outward, than inward. If we "think" outward, rather than inward, then we are functioning more healthily. Therefore, a converted person, thinking of others, or heaven, will find that a healthier life-style. I had simply lead my friend to participate in externalizing and transcending.

About 5000 years ago Jacob had a good sleep at Bethel, north of Jerusalem. He had fled from his brother Esau, after cheating him out of his birthright and blessing. That first night out, after fleeing in fear, he fell asleep with his head on a rock. He had a vision.

"And he dreamed that there was a ladder set

up on earth, and the top of it reached to heaven, and behold, the angels of God were ascending and descending on it! And behold, the Lord stood above it and said, I am the Lord the God of Abraham your father and the God of Isaac; the land on which you lie I will give to you and to your descendants." (Genesis 28:12-13)

Jacob felt "surely the Lord was here". That is the experience of persons who spend time relaxing, meditating, and visualizing God. In the search for communion with God, the human psyche lifts itself upward. Praying persons focus their mind, heart, soul and psyche upward like I did with my friend, or Jacob did in the dream. God is not necessarily "up there", but when Christians focus on the things of the spirit, they look up. Clergymen often look up in prayer. The cross is a lifted-up symbol. "And I, if I be lifted-up, will draw all men unto myself." said Jesus. Up and out is the psychic direction of Christian meditation and health.

Secular meditation often talks of "centering inward" on the inner person, and "getting in touch with self". Christian meditation focuses more outwardly and on a reality outside the self. I used to have a problem letting myself even think about "meditation". I had images of eastern oriental religious practices, as anti-Christian. I do not believe their religious practices are "anti" anything. They defend their benefits from meditation. Christians defend their belief in benefits accruing from Christ. Christ came to personally show how to find the good life which includes healthiness. His message is more complete, and filled with a greater element of power. The track record of Christianity (despite abuses along the way) demonstrates its life-giving power in economics, in technical development, in accumulation of knowledge, and in health, etc. Here, at health, east and west meet, coming from different directions. They have a common stress-management goal, and can use some of the skills which they have in common. Research on stress management demonstrates a power in the stress-management skills of relaxation, meditation, and visualization. Now, coupled with the Christian faith, we have even greater access to healing.

A SLEEP--INDUCING VISUALIZATION

Jacob's experience in that dream at Bethel can become a model for a thought process that can induce sleep and/or bring relaxation in general. Jacob's vision has many of the ingredients of a health-inducing relaxation, meditation, and visualization response. Let me lead you through it.

1. Find a comfortable position, either sitting in an easy chair, or lying down. Take a few moderately deep breaths, breathing in slowly, holding your breath for 3 to 4 seconds, and then breathing out slowly. Do this about 3 or 4 times, to take some of the tension out of your neck, back and chest muscles.

2, With your eyes closed, imagine the scene in which Jacob found himself. He is reclining on the knoll of a hill. There is an unobstructed view of the Jordan River valley about 15 miles away. If he looks to the left he is looking in the direction of Galilee. If he looks to the right he is looking in the direction of the Dead Sea. The sun goes down behind Jacob, in the west. Darkness and personal fatigue force Jacob to find rest. Jacob falls asleep. After an undetermined period of time, Jacob envisions a stairway inching its way from heaven and descending to touch the earth.

3. At the top, far out in space, God is standing. He is handing out assurances to his angels. These assurances are for calming anxious hearts. As each angel passes by Him, they receive a calming assurance. When the assurances have been handed out, God disappears into space.

4. The angels of God are descending. Envision with your mind, the small figures of those angels as far out in outer space as a person can see. Slowly, one by one, a long line of angels begin to make their way earthward. Step by step they descend. The whole heaven is hushed. The entire universe is awed by this spectacle.

There is a dazzling light around each angel.
They step gracefully and lovingly. They are
God's messengers of peace and glad tidings.
They bring health and healing.

5.   The background is darkness, deep black darkness.
There are star lights hanging in space. Their
twinkling beacons guide spirits in the night.
These lights beckon the mind to go off into
peaceful, silent, meditative trips, to find
calmness.

6.   The angels reach out and touch you with their
calming wands. Each in turn dispenses calm;
calm from the first one, calm from the second,
calm from the third, calm again, calm, calm,
calm, calm, calm.   Then, when each one
has allowed their calm to touch your heart,
you see the angel turn at the bottom step and
ascend the stairway.

7.   Slowly, the angels return up the stairway. One
by one, they ascend and appear further and
further away. Up they go. Upward. Upward.
Upward. Upward. Higher. Higher. Higher.
Higher. Higher. Higher. Farther and farther
into space. As they ascend they diminish in
size. They become smaller and smaller. The
lead angel, now, is almost no longer visible.

8.   Your eyes look at the steps. You imagine the
focus of your eyes going from step to step.
Rather like counting, you go from step to step,
and find your mind being pulled upward from
an invisible source.

9.   You now pass by the top step of the stairway.
Your mind leaps into the soothing silence of
space. You imagine yourself going for a walk
in space. You search with your eyes for the
nearest star. Your eyes light upon a star. You
are transported toward that star. Just about
the time that you arrive at that star, you visualize
another star, off in the distance. You allow
yourself to be transported to that star. Deep

in space you envision another magnetic star pulling you deeper and deeper into space. The process goes on into time without end.

10. You are traversing space in oneness with with God. God and universe are one. They are infinite. As you blend into the universe, you blend into God. God is the source of your peace and your healing. Be calm in His presence.

JACOB'S LADDER SLEEP-INDUCING MEDITATION

I have made a 15 minute cassette tape which I call a Jacob's Ladder Sleep-inducing Meditation. The concepts in the tape incorporate relaxation methods, meditation methods, and visualization methods. I become fascinated with imagining that Jacob experienced the first Divinely choreographed Transcendental Meditation. I hope persons will not think that I have lost touch with the realities of Divine revelation to Jacob. I do believe God spoke to Jacob in his dream, and made a promise to give that land to Jacob's descendents. In the cassette tape I only took the liberty to expand the imagery of the angels "ascending and descending", to generate a framework for Christian meditation. The tape seems to help some persons learn to relax and get to sleep. One client has said, "I haven't heard the end of the tape yet."

TRANSCENDING HUMAN MISERY

People search desparately for health and healing. The Bible is a record of people transcending human misery by faith. The record shows only a few miracles done by God. Most Improvement came through human effort which was infused with new faith, new hope, new courage, brought by inspired men of God. These prophets and apostles called forth new will, new energy, new commitment, new dedication. With that people became victorious. May I call forth the same thing from you, enabling you to become victorious in your pursuit of health?

DISCUSSION

1. A paradox is where two opposing concepts are both
    true, but logically irreconcilable. Marilyn Ludolf
    was healed by both God and her mind-over-matter
    thinking. Can you believe that? What problems
    do you have with that?

2. What happens inside your mind when you hear the
    author suggesting that prayer might not help as
    much if people carry grudges, or hold on to behaviors
    that produce illness?

3. When people attend Sunday School and memorize
    scripture, how would that be similar, in some way,
    to Autogenic Training?

4. By monitoring finger-tip temperature you should
    have some idea about the level of anxiety or arousal
    in the body. Would it be possible to warm your
    finger-tips through prayer?

5. Jesus often went into the mountains to pray. What
    is the difference between praying and meditation?
    or between prayer and Autogenic Training?

6. What kinds of illnesses are treatable with Christian
    relaxation, meditation, and visualization?

7. What songs mean the most to you? Are they thera-
    peutically helpful to your health?   How?

8. How much healing will result from singing the song
    written by the author, Jesus Christ Will Heal Today?

9. What do you think of the idea of a divine -- human
    partnership in healing?   Do you think it is a
    50--50 partnership?

10. Read Romans 12:2. Then ask, If you play a tape,
    quietly, of what you want to change in your behavior,
    while you sleep at night, will it help you learn it,
    or remember it? Can a person learn spiritual values
    through listening to subliminally recorded and played
    tapes?

Chapter 19

HEALING BY ASSERTIVENESS,

AND BY CONVERSION

"A RIGHTEOUS MAN FALLS SEVEN TIMES, AND RISES AGAIN." (Proverbs 24:16)

"I CAN DO ALL THINGS IN HIM WHO STRENGTHENS ME." (Philippians 4:13)

If you do not speak up, someone will step on you, often. If you speak up too much, people will avoid you. How to find the happy middle ground? Rule of thumb says, Speak up half the time, and keep still the other half. Anything short of that will either make you ill or will make someone else ill.

Evaluate yourself with the inventory on the following page. See if you fall in an acceptable range.

SELF WORTH AND ASSERTIVENESS

Pick out the most appropriate response. Write the number
of that response in the space provided by that statement.

0. Never   1. Rarely   2. Occasionally   3. Sometimes
4. Frequently   5. Almost always

1. _____ I am competitive.
2. _____ I like to take charge.
3. _____ I speak up for what I want.
4. _____ I have an influence on others.
5. _____ I stand up for what I believe.
6. _____ I want others to obey me.
7. _____ I try to persuade others about my views.
8. _____ I like to supervise others.
9. _____ I am reasonable in my expectations of others.
10. _____ I am a good chairman.
11. _____ I can take criticism as well as I can give it.
12. _____ I speak up against injustice and unfairness.
13. _____ I can get two arguing people to compromise.
14. _____ I get my message out without hurting feelings.
15. _____ I will complain if someone tries to take advantage of me.
16. _____ I can get my message across without yelling.
17. _____ I encourage others who may not be doing well.
18. _____ I respect the wishes of others, but I will go ahead
and do what is good for the majority.
19. _____ I negotiate or talk with others until their needs
get met as well as mine.
20. _____ I practice patience to make others happy while
also working toward an end goal.
21. _____ I ask a lot of questions so people can all have a
chance at expressing their feelings.
22. _____ If I get pushed around (verbally) by my boss I will
talk to him about it.
23. _____ If a neighbor would abuse my property, I would
talk to him about it.
24. _____ I am as good a listener as I am a talker.
25. _____ I take initiative to invite others to go places
with me.
26. _____ I claim what I want, rather than complaining
about what does not come to me.
27. _____ I stay calm and maintain self control when I am
being criticized.
_____ TOTAL (Range 0 - 185) (Enter this on Page 358)

INTERPRETATION

0 – 40
Your score on SELF WORTH and ASSERTIVENESS was in the lowest category. You do not need to stay at this low level. Something inside you is holding you back. It would be wise to see a counselor to determine what your blockage is and then spend several sessions working through the blockage.

41 – 70
Your score on SELF WORTH and ASSERTIVENESS is below average. You are probably allowing one or more persons to dominate you. Think about justice and fairness and speak up for it in your life. You can be more assertive and have a greater amount of self worth if you speak up when persons upset you, or go after what you want in this world. You deserve more self-satisfaction than you are probably getting. Therefore, get your back up a little more and (without yelling) stake a claim for your needs.

71 – 100
Your score on SELF WORTH and ASSERTIVENESS is in a mid-range. You may be speaking up adequately to get your needs met, but it is quite likely that stronger persons make you feel threatened. Many persons with problems remain silent before harsh persons and suppress their negative feelings. Enough of this suppression can produce emotional and behavioral problems. Since you are not overly assertive you could go after more of what you want without appearing to be selfish or arrogant.

101–130
Your score on SELF WORTH and ASSERTIVENESS is very good. You speak up, claim what you want, go after your needs, sense when you need to negotiate and contract or give in.

Above 130
Your score on SELF WORTH and ASSERTIVENESS shows that you are coming-on, or asserting, quite strongly. Very few actually have scores this high. Caution yourself to make sure that you do not inadvertently override others.

HEALING WITH ASSERTIVE BEHAVIOR

Healing occured instantly when a woman decided to assert herself and touch Jesus. That healing occured in a crowd walking to Jairus' house, to witness the healing of Jairus' daughter. The woman had a bleeding problem. She had suffered for years, doctoring but not finding a cure. There were illnesses which medicine could not cure then, and which medicine can not cure today.

Jesus said, "Your faith has made you whole." (Mark 5:25-34). It was not a healing through a placebo effect. It was not a healing by the laying-on-of-hands, like when Jesus touched a leper, touched the dead woman's son's bier, touched Jairus' daughter, touched a blind demoniac, touched a blind man. The healing was not a healing from the forgiveness of sins, like Jesus did with the paralytic lowered through the smashed roof. It was not a healing as a result of devils being driven out, like Jesus did to the epileptic. Nothing had to precede this healing except assertiveness.

How about you? Are you suffering mental deterioration, physical deterioration (illness), or spiritual deterioration because of your lack of assertiveness?

SELF WORTH AND ASSERTIVENESS

Assertiveness starts in self-worth. That is its home operating base. Self-worth generates the power and the rationality of the assertiveness. Sometimes self worth never had a chance to grow in a person's childhood. It was not fed with positive experiences and feelings. Stunted self-worth comes out of a variety of hereditary and environmental factors. Heredity factors that stunt self-worth are fatness - skinniness - shortness - tallness - freckles - warts - moles - birth marks - birth defects - intelligence quotient - race - nationality - skin color - attractiveness - muscle size - sex organ size - hair color - scars - genetic defects. Environmental factors that stunt the growth of self-worth are yelling mothers or fathers - hostile mothers or fathers - overstressed mothers or fathers - indifferent mothers or fathers - low self-worth mothers or fathers - teasing of brothers, sisters, or school mates - economic deprivation - feeling socially outcast – tragedy – abuse – cruelty – divorce or alcohol in the family. ———— There is something in this list for everyone. No one in the world escapes some form of negative input, or lack of positive input. All persons experience some retardation of growth in self-worth. So everyone has some obstacle to overcome to have a maximum amount of assertiveness.

FEAR KILLS SELF WORTH AND ASSERTIVENESS

If your score on the Assertiveness Inventory was low, will you do something about it? What are you afraid of? Are you afraid of what people will think if speak up and go after what you want? Are you afraid of more responsibility put on you if you begin to show some assertiveness? Are you afraid someone will humiliate you if you are more assertive? You say, "None of these.", Ahhhhh. You like to feel put down? You like to feel those low self worth feelings? No, that is not it either.

Gideon was faced with invading Midianites and Amalekites, a generation or two after the Israelites entered Canaan. Gideon trumpeted a call to arms. Thousands of Israelites came to do battle. The Word of the Lord came to Gideon, saying that the army was too large "lest Israel vaunt themselves against me, saying my own hand has delivered me." (Judges 7:2) To cut the army down in size Gideon was commanded to say

"Whoever is fearful and trembling, let him return home." (Judges 7:3)

If fear paralyzes a soldier, that soldier is not worth very much. Is fear paralyzing you, so you cannot conquor your low self worth and poor assertiveness? God needs the committed ones, the ones with back bone, the ones with conquering in their bones, to do battle against invading sin and corrupting influences in this world. Does God need more assertiveness from you?

Peter almost lost his life from drowning, when fear crept in as he walked on the waters of Galilee with Jesus (Matthew 14:31). Fear comes when trust and faith slip. You only sink worse and worse unless you can get hold of the faith which will make you stable in your walk of life.

FAITH IS NEEDED TO RISE

Moses saw the Israelites suffering from low self worth. They were oppressed by the Egyptians. Moses felt the call of God to lead those people out from their lowly estate. He saw no reason for them to live being oppressed. Moses took the leadership role.

> **"By faith he left Egypt, not being afraid of the anger of the king; for he endured as seeing him who is invisible (He did it by believing in the invisible God.)" (Hebrews 11:27)**

Moses transcended fear with faith. This rising up against national suppression was unprecedented. It was a rebellion against man's inhumanity to man. Moses helped them throw off the chains of bondage to low self worth. It took faith to make this possible. You will probably never find a stronger argument for the urgency of faith in God, to rise out of a position of low self worth.

LOVE IS NEEDED TO RISE

You can buy a book on assertiveness, but you need love to enable you to rise out of low self worth and poor assertiveness. Joining a class on self worth and assertiveness will give you some of the support you need. The better classes and workshops on the subject will spend as much time facilitating the group relationships as they will filling your head with techniques.

Historically, you do not find people rising out of bondage without someone's love and compassion. For the Israelites, it came from Moses and Aaron and God. For black people in America it took a President Lincoln to begin the emancipation, and marching by blacks and white supporters in Selma and Birmingham to promote justice and freedom. For Africa, it took Christian missions to bring education to the Africans, and once they felt they could handle their own affairs, the French, Belgians, English, and other nations had to leave. On the local front, it takes Women in Transition organizations to crusade for a wife's freedom from her husband's beatings. It takes someone's love to make a change.

But deeper yet, it takes a special kind of love for persons to rise. There are three Greek words for love. The word "eros" is the word for a sexual or object love. The word "philos" is the word for friendship. The Greek word "agape" is another word for love. "Agape" is a sacrificial, a giving, an outgoing kind of love, which expects nothing (or less) in return. This "agape" love is the kind of love we see in Jesus Christ. When a person has that kind of love, he has access to something that can build self-worth. When you experience "agape" coming into your life, it will give you energy to rise up. This is why group support is so important.

More than group support is needed. The inner psyche needs to be granted the freedom to visualize a new life-style. This envisioned life-style is a key ingredient. It is a life-style free from fear, because "Perfect love (agape) casts out fear." (I John 4:18) The new life-style includes a sense of freedom, tied to moderation and responsibility. This new life-style will include an inner sense of compassion for others. It will include a sense of service to others. This "agape" love, which becomes the basis for living, rejoices in what is right.

CONVERSION IS NEEDED TO RISE

For some persons an assertive style of life, built on self-worth, will require a 180° turn-around. Some persons will never know what self-worth and assertiveness are until they are literally converted. They have lived such a self-oriented, narcissistic, withdrawn, retrogressive, fearful life-style, that any change in behavior, short of a radical conversion will be relatively useless. If that conversion does not succeed in creating a forward, faith-living, hoping, loving, serving, caring, helping, self-denouncing life-style, then it will be meaningless.

Some persons seem to have this outgoing life-style, even though they are not converted or faithful Christians. I see them too. I do not know where they got their self-worth and assertiveness. Perhaps their parents or grand parents were people who secured ample self-worth through faith, and passed it on to their children. Perhaps God doled out some special grace. But do not get entangled in "why".   Rise up to see that you can have this life-style of self-worth and assertiveness, by believing, then loving, then hoping, and finally proving. We call it conversion.

The kind of conversion I am talking about is a complete one. It is a conversion which converts more than just the dress style, the attitude toward Sunday, or any superficial behavior.   The conversion which is needed for self-worth and assertiveness is a conversion of the deepest regions of the psyche.   The very "ego" structure of the psyche has to change.   The action of the extensors of the psyche must start exceeding the action of the retensors.

Jesus describes it best in Matthew 20:20ff.   James and John ask for special favors to sit at Jesus left hand and at his right hand in the kingdom.   Jesus told them that those places were reserved by "my father in heaven".

"And when the ten heard it, they were indignant at the two brothers. But Jesus called them to him and said, . . . Whoever would be great among you must be your servant, and whoever would be first among you must be your slave; even as the Son of man came not to be served, but to serve."   (Matthew 20:20-28)

"Serving" represents the clearest picture of the life of a Christian.   The psyche is not turned inward toward the self, but outward toward others in service. "Service" is therefore, a direction of the psyche.   The direction is not a "poor me" direction, spiraling downward into deeper panic, and producing greater stress on the body. You cannot "serve" laying on your back from a traumatic illness, but there are many smaller illnesses, and some major degenerative diseases, that leave a person half way between illness and health.   If you can keep your psyche in "serve" mode, your chances of healing are better.

Isaiah really was on the same frequency when he preached to his congregation of renegades and saints. At one point he articulated in preacherly fashion regarding Israel's hypocricy.   He promises them "healing" for their charitable service.

> "Is it not to share your bread with the hungry,
> and bring the homeless poor into your house;
> when you see the naked, to cover him, and not
> to hide yourself from your own flesh? Then
> shall your light break forth like the dawn, and
> __your healing__ shall spring up speedily."
>
> (Isaiah 58:7-8)

Conversion, which ultimately is a straightening out of the narcisistic processes of preoccupation with self, should issue forth in service. That sensitive service to others, says Isaiah, brings healing. Whatever way you want to cut it, secularly, religiously, practically, the persons who maintain their love for others, even when they are ill, have a greater chance of healing.

HEALING WITH AN ACTIVATED WILL

Assertiveness is impossible without some sort of engagement or mobilization of the will. Norman Cousins, author of Anatomy of an Illness, employed "laughter therapy" along with intravenous Vitamin C, to conquer a degenerative illness twenty years ago. Yet, it was more than laughter and Vitamin C which brought the cure. There was a "will to live", which he and others believe has a biochemical effect on the body.

> "What we are talking about essentially, I suppose,
> is the chemistry of the will to live. In Bucharest
> in 1972, I visited the clinic of Ana Aslan,
> described to me as one of Romania's leading
> endocrinologists. She spoke of her belief that
> there is a direct connection between a robust
> will to live and the chemical balances in the
> brain. She is convinced that creativity — one
> aspect of the will to live — produces the vital
> brain impulses that stimulate the pituitary
> gland, triggering effects on the pineal gland
> and the whole of the endocrine system. . . .
> I have learned never to understimate the capacity
> of the human mind and body to regenerate —
> even when the prospects seem most wretched.....

At any rate, long before my own serious illness, I became convinced that creativity, the will to live, hope, faith, and love have biochemical significance and contribute strongly to healing and to well-being." (p.47, 48, 86)

Norman Cousins checked out of the hospital, secured a hotel room, viewed Candid Camera and Marx Brothers to make himself laugh. Laughter was his "internal jogging", and after sessions of laughter his sedimentation rate (a measure of inflamation) dropped point by point. All this was done under medical supervision. He subjected his "incurable disease" to his will to live. He transcended the normal encroachments of "panic" which he believes to be a major contributor to the downward spiral of degenerative disease. He won with assertiveness, invigorated in the presence of faith, hope and love.

CHANGE A BEHAVIOR OR CHANGE A LIFE STYLE

Assertiveness Training books and workshops currently abound and prolifereate. Most of them are excellent sources of information on a variety of skills and techniques people can use. Yet, if the person coming into a life-style of more assertiveness, is not prepared to make a mind-set change, nothing beneficial may happen.

What the Assertiveness Training courses do is help people see how they can become assertive without letting the pendulum swing into aggressiveness. Aggressiveness is the opposite of passiveness. The aggressive person speaks out bluntly, acts selfishlessly, behaves indecently, verbalizes cruelly, and alienates people.

The "assertive" person believes in justice, fair play, decency, and probably lives out of the fruits of the spirit; love, joy, peace, patience, kindness, goodness, faithfulness, gentleness, self-control (Galatians 5:23) The assertive person is taught to avoid attacking-"you" sentences, and use more confessional "I" sentences, sharing feelings and not making accusations. Assertiveness Training classes teach a lot of "Active Listening" to replace some of the harsh demanding. We should probably all learn and practice more of these skills in our daily lives.

Assertiveness Training classes for the Israelites living under the Egyptians, is not something I believe would have helped. The Israelites simply had to get out from the life-style that shackled them. There are times when one should probably be content with the life-style one experiences. The Apostle Paul once recommended this. In the case of the Israelites under the Egyptians, there is a larger issue at stake. God, being a just God, does not honor one people making slaves of another people. That is a basic injustice which violates divine character. Why God allowed the bondage to take place, other than to make a lesson-in-history for us, is still a mystery. It becomes a lesson in transcendence, or conquering low self worth. The Israelite's story is one of salvation, emancipation from fear and hopelessness and bondage. You need faith for that kind of salvation.

To change low self-worth, the Israelites had to change a life-style. To change that life-style required a change from suppression of negative feelings, to expression, from self-degradation to self-exhonoration. They changed from a "passive" style to an "assertive" style, without using "aggressiveness" like fighting and retaliation. It took faith and and commitment to secure those life-style changes, which eventually brought health and happiness.

CASE STUDY —

Sandy split, left her husband, left her children, rented an apartment 30 miles from home, near her job. The man she worked with had become her friend, companion, confidant, and lover. He made it easier for her to leave, but he was not the real reason for her leaving. Sandy (not her real name) grew up with a slight handicap. She felt people looked at her. Psychologically, she turned inward when people stared. She married, more for security than for love. She missed not being in love with a man who made her "flip". Sandy was not assertive in her marriage. Her husband had some jealousy feelings which made him control her, though not overpoweringly. That combination spawned an enormous amount of unrest in Sandy. Then, add to this two pre-school children, which made her feel tied down, more than she could stand. The job was a nice relief. It became almost too much of a relief. It was such a good thing that it made her avoid the issue of suppressed hostile feelings. She "let the sun go down on her wrath" so often that she was now out of control. The wrath had become overwelming, over-consuming, demonic. "She gave opportunity to the devil." She blew out of her marriage, as the Apostle Paul predicted in Ephesians 4:26.

Scores of people felt sorry for this fine young person and her husband. People prayed for a miracle to change the hearts of Sandy and her husband. Too little, too late. Not denying that "all things are possible with God", we conclude that when a person lives with a life-style of non-assertive behavior, they will pay a price.

The Sandys of this world are not trained as children to transcend their handicaps. They were not instilled with the triumphant model of positive Christian living. Under stress their psychic systems turn inward, narcissisticly, rather than outward, in faith, in hope, in love.

GUIDEPOSTS INSPIRATION

There is a small, but powerful magazine called Guideposts, edited by Norman Vincent Peale. Every month, for 40 years, that magazine has been promoting the gospel of triumph over sin, pain, evil, and handicap. The magazine has its critics, but its power lies in inspiring persons to triumph over difficulty. Guideposts depicts persons who have both cried out and challenged God in a desperate moment. They have encountered God in some very significant way. No whimps in Guideposts; just persons with divinely infused strength and inspiration. Oh, the agony, seeing so many "Sandy"s who do not have this transcending mentality. Such persons need to learn to follow Jesus' four problem-solving steps in Matthew 18:15-17. They need to know that the love of God is an empowering love, not a decelerating and decompensating behavior. Norman Cousins had some of that Guideposts-type inspiration. For Christians, Jesus becomes the model. Jesus encountered (was) God. Jesus broke the power of sin. Jesus rose from the dead, and broke open the grave. He ascended into heaven. He triumphed. He lead the way. You and I can now triumph.

SELF WORTH — A DIRECTION OF THE MIND

The woman with the bleeding problem, who came to Jesus for healing, finally reached out in faith. The Israelites, under Moses' leadership, marched out of Egypt in faith. Jesus called on his disciples to "serve" others instead of being self-seeking. Isaiah promised "healing" to those who would be sensitive to others. Norman Cousins engaged his "will to live" in a battle against illness and its self-defeating panic. Sandy found out too late, what assertiveness could do to lift her out of her miserable condition. ——— People conquer giant problems when they become mobilized outwardly. Being mobilized outwardly, takes the kinks out of the cord of life. The invisible goal magnetizes the person, and as the person concentrates on the goal, he will not walk in circles of self-defeat. Directionless, a person wanders until despondent or dead. Jesus said it this way.

> **"No one who puts his hand to the plow
> and looks back is fit for the kingdom
> of God." (Luke 9:62)**

The direction is always forward for Jesus. There is no time for self-pity or self-doubt. There is time for reflection, relaxation, meditation, but it is geared to surmounting, transcending, curing, and living victoriously. This mind-over-matter principle has roots going back into the Wisdom Literature of the Bible.

> **"All day the wicked covets, but the
> righteous gives and does not hold back."
> (Proverbs 21:26)**

The direction is always toward others, and away from self. Obviously, a life so set on others, and never giving oneself time to nurse a wound, is pushing the point too far. Yet, due to our tendency to drift back to substandard behavior, we are urged in the healthy direction.

GETTING IT ALL TOGETHER

I hope you have understood all along that healing comes from managing out the bad stress and managing in the coping skills. I doubt that anyone finds healing through management of one single stress factor. Problems that make people sick come in bunches.

The "will" is the integrative factor that identifies the multiple stress factors and marshals energy against all of them simultaneously. Attacking a health problem will, ideally, include dealing with every factor in this book and more.

The Christian faith puts it all together for us in about the simplest formula. From the beginning God has given mankind a choice. Mankind may choose a health-enhancing behavior or a sickness-enhancing behavior.

> **"See, I have set before you this day,**
> **life and good, death and evil .....**
> **therefore, choose life, that you may**
> **live, you and your descendents."**
> **(Deuteronomy 30:15,19)**

A mind-over-matter mentality makes it work. Choice involves commitment, and commitment sets the will in motion. With that combination, not only will health be better, but one's entire religious, political, social, and professional outlook will be operating according to the finest of divinely ordained principles.

One of the finest leaders America ever had, never gave up. His faith, hope, and love shined with the sun, and twinkled at defeat.

1832	Lost his job
1832	Defeated for the legislature
1833	Failed in private business
1834	Elected to the legislature
1835	His sweetheart died
1836	He had a nervous breakdown
1836	He was defeated for house speaker
1843	Was defeated for nomination to congress
1846	He was elected to congress
1848	He lost his renomination
1849	He ran for land office and lost
1854	He was defeated for senate
1856	Defeated for vice president nomination
1858	Defeated for the senate again.
1860	Elected president of the United States

This man was Abraham Lincoln. His perseverence is second only to his faith. You cannot believe that he was naturally gifted with a gigantic self-worth system. Often, he must have picked his self-worth up off the floor, dusted it with more faith, hope, and love, and put it back on again. Often, he must have visualized, meditated, prayed and muttered his goals about "serving" both God and man. Abraham Lincoln had enough of it together to win the hearts of the world. If we, you and me, could get our act together, we would be happier and healthier.

CASE STUDY — HELENE

Helene told her story of sickness and recovery through stress management skills in Third Reformed Church, in Holland, Michigan. Her story gives glory to God, to her Christian psychologist, but also to herself for all the assertiveness which was needed to become well.

Helene lost her mother at age 17. There was no time, opportunity or permission to grieve. She stepped into a substitute mother role for a time, and then became an R.N. Upon graduation she took a position as a mission nurse on an Indian reservation.

While home on a vacation visit she was water skiing. She took a bad spill and was badly hurt. The family took her to a nearby hospital where pulse and blood pressure were not measurable. Body temperature was 93 degrees. Her body was becoming bluish in color, and from the voices of the people around she believed she was dying.

At that moment she had a near-death experience of walking down a road with a friend, whom she knew was Jesus. She was filled with peace and calm. They were walking, in the picture of her mind, on a road to heaven, when suddenly they both turned around and began walking back to earth. Helene revived and the medical staff went on with innumerable tests to determine the cause of the problem. Finally, an immunologist discoverd a very weakened immune defense system. There is no medicine known to cure such a problem. She was allergic to many things. Her body would react with inflamation.

She remained at home for months of pain and confinement to bed, she read, wrote her angry questions and praise in her journal, received guests, and fought pain with pills. All the stress of unresolved grief, and overwork getting her R.N. degree, had so weakened the immune system, that, like Selye's experimental animals, she suffered from the General Adaptation Syndrome. She had gone through Stage 1 which is Arousal to the challenge of the stress. Stage 2. Resistance or fixation in the stress adaptation mode. Now Helene was in Stage 3. Exhaustion.

She was referred to a Christian psychologist who had been trained in pain-control methods of relaxation and visualization. Using those skills, coupled with her faith in Jesus Christ, and promises from the Bible, Helene spent the next weeks practicing, going over and over the exercises. These were mind-over-matter skills she was employing. Some of them have their origin in eastern cultures, but are, in fact, not antithetical to Christian practices. She used the Christian psychologists techniques, and planted healing thoughts in her mind in a self-instructing (self-hypnotic) way. She did what God told the Israelites to do with the "law" four thousand years ago. God wanted the Israelites to drill the law into their minds and hearts so that it would affect their behavior. Helene drove the relaxing and healing promises of God into her heart, mind, and soul, down to the subconscious level, so healing would take place.

Never, along the way, did she abandon medical treatment. She, the psychologist, and the medical people kept in communication. Psychotherapeutic processes over many weeks enabled her to ventilate feelings, and see connections between some inner negative feelings and the stress they produced. The pain of the loss of her mother had to be dealt with in many ways, including "journaling", and finally making a trip to the hometown cemetery.

Helene is well now. She maintains her well-being through many stress management practices, such as relaxation, meditation, exercise, proper food, adequate socializing, serving others, prayer, and other good health practices.

Helene bobbed up and down with her "will to live" in the early stages, but with the help of friends, a Christian psychologist, and an unmeasureable amount of divine grace, she has recovered.

THE GOSPEL AND ASSERTIVENESS

Major psychological tests find the **assertive** person far more healthy. Passiveness invites put-downs, insults, sarcasm and a host of hurts.

Helene had learned to be a nice passive girl, who wasn't supposed to hurt others, cry when suffering loss, or ventilate anger to God over letting a mother die. Jesus advocated a gutsy style of Step 1, "tell him his fault"; Step 2, "take a witness along"; Step 3, "tell the elders"; Step 4, "let him be to thee as a heathen and a publican (i.e. go to hell)." This is not the gospel of passiveness which some persons preach.

The Apostle Paul was not so sure about this notion of passiveness either. He said, "Do not let the sun go down on your wrath (i.e. ventilate if you must)." (Ephesians 4:26)

There is room in the gospel for the passive element, the passive moment, the passive approach. The Israelites waited around in the desert, passively, for 40 years, before they became quite assertive, even aggressive, and took over the land of Canaan. We need to learn to use passiveness and assertiveness at the right time and in the right balance.

THE GREATEST OF THESE IS ASSERTIVENESS

If I speak with the tongue of ordinary people,
    And have not self worth,
        I can be mentally ill and easily sick.
If I look pretty, and have a good brain and physique,
    And my father owns a thousand chain stores,
    But I do not have self worth; I am nothing.
If I give away all my money to make friends,
    And deliver a new car to every neighbor,
    But if I do not have self worth, I gain nothing.
Self worth is patient and kind to others.
    Self worth is not jealous or boastful.
      It is not arrogant or rude.
        Self worth does not insist on its own way.
        It is not irritated or resentful.
It does not rejoice in personal success.
    It rejoices in the achievement of others.
    Self worth bears all things.
      Self worth believes all things.
        Self worth hopes all things.
        Self worth endures all things.
Self worth never runs out of sunshine.
    As for passiveness, it brings on depression.
    As for aggressiveness, it hurts others.
    As for assertiveness, it comes out of self worth.
For passiveness is a problem,
    And aggressiveness is a problem..
So when assertiveness comes out of self worth,
    then passiveness and aggressiveness will go
    away.
When I was a child I was more passive.
    I spoke non-assertively.
    I acted non-assertively.
    I thought non-assertively.
When I grew up I found out I had a right to be
    assertive.
Now I practice assertiveness carefully,
    And if I practice it in the future, I will gain
      even more self worth.
So,
PASSIVENESS, AGGRESSIVENESS, ASSERTIVENESS,
    these three,
But the greatest of these is ASSERTIVENESS.

340   Darrell Franken

DISCUSSION

1. Does lack of spirituality affect assertiveness? Does lack of assertiveness affect spirituality? Can you be spiritual and not assertive?

2. What would you say is lacking if a person claims to be a very spiritual person, and yet is very passive, suppressing lots of hurt feelings?

3. What is the main sin and/or difficulty which contributes to passiveness? (Ans. Suppression, Eph 4:26)

4. How would you explain the difference between being passive, aggressive, and assertive?

5. What are the ingredients that make up assertiveness?

6. Healing, according to Isaiah, comes out of loving service. If you have cancer, lupus, multiple sclerosis, arthritis, asthma, digestive disorders, neruological disorders, emotional disorders, or any other ailment which can be classified under "degenerative disease", how could you "serve", so that you increase your chances of healing?

7. Prayer, meditation, relaxation, and visualization all promote externalizing the psyche. How do you pray a prayer that is not an internalizing, "poor me", prayer?

8. Is your church a healing church? How can church people promote healing in the church?

9. If every time you felt low self-worth feelings, you told them to go away with a "Get thee behind me, satan." attitude, would your low self-worth feelings go away?

10. If you played a tape recording before you went to sleep of your own voice repeating over and over, saying, "Inferiority, Go away. Self-worth is here to stay." or "I will think positively about the self-worth I have.", would your feelings of self-worth grow?

Chapter 20

HEALING WITH FAITH

LAYING-ON-OF-HANDS, PRAYER

"Is any one among you suffering? Let him pray. Is any cheerful? Let him sing praise. Is any among you sick? Let him call for the elders of the church, and let them pray over him, anointing him with oil in the name of the Lord; and the prayer of faith will save the sick man, and the Lord will raise him up; and if he has committed sins, he will be forgiven." James 5:13-15

DIVINE HEALING

Stress management treatments need, finally, to be combined with Divine healing. If you only looks for Divine healing, without cleaning up your life-style, you might be wasting your time.   No doubt God has brought miraculous healings even though people did not quit their indulgences, or get out from under their stresses.   Yet, Stress Management research hits hard, with information that people set themselves up for some of their illnesses by a life-style that is devoid of mind-over-matter or moderation.   God probably does rescue more people from their self-destructive life-styles than we can imagine. On the other hand, there are probably more people dying, who could live, if they would change some life-style behaviors, as well as seek divine healing.

SEEK DIVINE HEALING — (1) WITH ASSERTIVE FAITH

Jesus brought healing in several ways. Jesus responded primarily to persons who had positively assertive faith and commitment to him.   Some persons were so assertive they came from Syria (Matthew 4:24) which is a 3 - 15 day trip away from Galilee.   Without their assertive behavior, or that of their friends, they would not have found healing from Jesus

The woman with the bleeding problem (Mark 5:25) called forth all her faith and her nerve to reach out in a crowd and touch Jesus.   Her assertiveness paid off. Jesus told her it was her "faith" that made her well again.

Jesus healed a blind beggar who was sitting outside of Jericho, along the road which leads to Jerusalem. The beggar heard the crowd walking with Jesus, and when the beggar learned it was Jesus of Nazareth, he cried out, Jesus, Thou son of David, have mercy on me. When he did not get heard, the beggar got more assertive and belted it out again.   Then Jesus heard, and healed.

How assertive are you in securing healing for your illness?   Like the woman with the bleeding problem, have you spent a lot of money on doctoring, but are no better?   How about being assertive with your pastor and the elders of the church as you have been assertive with going to doctors? Do you have the courage to seek out men and women of God for healing? How about insisting that your clergyman bring the elders of the church, daily, weekly, monthly, perpetually if necessary, until you have found healing at an appropriate level.

Most sick people unwittingly play a game with God, their clergymen, the elders, and their friends. The game is, "If they think I can be healed by prayer, they will come and do that?" Let us stop this non-assertive, this whimpish faith. How about megaphoning a message that you want prayer! that you insist on healing!

> **"Is any among you sick, let him call**
> **for the elders of the church, and let**
> **them pray for him (her)."**
> **(James 5:13)**

Pastors are doing fairly well in their ministry to the sick. They meet the expectations of most persons. But what could happen if the expectations of the people increased? Can you see more miracles happening if sick persons would simply be more assertive. Sick persons can blame the church for not caring if they want. Yet, in Jesus' day, the people came to Jesus. They believed in his healing. James said, **Let the sick one call.** You just get on the phone, and call some of your friends in for prayer, then the elders and the pastor. Tell them to come back next week, and the next. It might take a few more sessions than with Jesus. Jesus' healing connection was a bit stronger!

SEEK SPIRITUAL HEALING — (2) FOR SOMEONE ELSE

When you evaluate the 25 individual healings recorded in the gospels, the second category of healings centers around persons who came to Jesus for healing someone else. The most famous of these is the healing of the paralytic (Mark 2:1-12), who was carried to the roof of Peter's house, and lowered through a hole made in the roof. Jesus saw the faith of the palet bearers, forgave the sick man's sins, and cured his palsy. There may have been "faith" in the palsied man, but Jesus acknowledges the faith of the beloved friends.

You did not have to be present to be healed. Jesus could heal with remote control. You just had to have a friend who has faith, even perhaps, a persistent faith. A nobleman's son was ill at home, and the nobleman came for healing. Jesus teased him a bit about looking for a "sign" like so many. The nobleman was upset and persistent, so Jesus healed the son. (John 4:46-54) The nobleman compared the hour of the son's healing and it was identical with his encounter with Jesus. He was delighted that Jesus had such power of remote command.

Jesus did the same with the Centurion's servant at Capernaum (Luke 7:1-10). He also used his remote-control healing power and healed the Syro-Phoenician (Greek) woman's daughter (Mark 7:24-30). That a parent would become that assertive is understandable, but not so, with the Centurion, except that the Centurion had great faith. All these are instances of healings wherein someone claimed healing for someone else, even though the sick person was not present.

That presents a unique picture of spiritual healing. People pray for others. If there was a healing service in your town, would you bring a sick friend for healing? That takes faith. Would you ever go to a healing service and ask the healer to heal your friend without the friend being there? That may sound somewhat presumptious or improper. Yet some of the known healers of our time have apparently produced some results.

Prayer meetings are our contemporary way of asking Jesus to use his remote-control healing power. Every Christian saint has probably known of answers to prayer, which are indelibly written into their hearts. The Great Physician continues to heal, apart from, and in addition to medical treatments.

SEEK SPIRITUAL HEALING — (3) BY EXORCISM

In 6 of the 25 recorded healings in the gospels, Jesus exorcises demons. He commanded the demons to leave. 1. A mentally disturbed person disrupted Jesus' speech at Capernaum. Jesus "rebuked" the "devil" in the man, and he was healed. (Mark 1:21-28) It is not uncommon for emotionally disturbed persons to become exceptionally religious themselves, and challenge established religious practices.   2. Jesus healed a blind and dumb person "one possessed with a devil". (Matthew 12:22-37) In the psychiatric world, such blindness and dumbness are hysterical reactions.   They occur in some persons whose mental condition is deteriorating.   Paul once said, "Being angry, do not sin; do not let the sun go down on your wrath, (lest) you give opportunity to the devil." (Ephesians 4:26) Repressed hostility has been known to create emotional disturbance.   Jesus healed the blindness and dumbness by driving out all the past stored-up anger. Health came when anger was removed. 3.   Then Jesus healed two mentally disturbed persons in the territory of Gadara. They had lived among the tombs of a cemetery.   Jesus transferred the devils to a herd of 2000 swine which immediately committed suicide by running headlong into the sea. (Mark 5:1-20) What were these "devils"? They were what Paul talked about in Ephesians 4:26. "Devils" are what can happen to you if you bottle too many hostile feelings. So when you resolve hostile feelings, the "devils" have to leave, and you will have regained your health. 4. Matthew records a healing of a dumb (non-speaking) person, by exorcism of the "devil". (Matthew 9:32-34) Here is another case of psychiatric hysteria, probably from repressed anger, bad nutrition, genetic predisposition, or some unknown factors.   5.   Jesus   healed   the   daughter   of   a Syro-Phoenician   woman   by   remote-control   exorcism of an unclean spirit, a "devil". We do not know what symptoms the daughter suffered from. We only know that she was made whole. (Mark 7:24-30)   6.   Jesus healed an epileptic boy, with symptoms of deafness, dumbness,   seizures,   foaming-mouth,   grinding-teeth, and falling. (Mark 9:14-29) All but the last healing, are exorcisms of demonic processes which resemble mental illness from suppressed anger.

Since anger is such a destructive instrument, both to oneself as well as to others, a person's healing may not be possible until the person's internal anger is resolved. Counselors help people work through their past resentments, and current tendencies to be angry. They spend hours with persons exhuming and burning off the loads from the past. Christian counselors teach persons how to resolve their anger through the four steps found in Matthew 18:15-17.

If you have been mentally, physically ill for some time, it might be good for you to examine your spiritual health. Too much suppressed negativity in life can drain a person. Bitterness can deteriorate every metabolic, hormonal, neurological, (etc.) action in your system, and prevent healing.

Deal with your feelings of anger, injustice, and guilt. Talk to the people who hurt you. Speak up about the injustice. Ventilate the hurts. Shout, scream, pound a pillow. Confess it to a friend or counselor. Pray if you wish, but the Bible says,

> **"Confess your faults one to another,**
> **and pray for one another, that ye may**
> **be healed." (James 5:16)**

Seek spiritual healing by exorcism, your own exorcism. Deal with your anger, wrath, strife, enmity, (Galatians 5:19). Drive that "devil" out of your life; the one that is setting you up for your own chronic illness.

Many years ago I spent almost one year helping a couple and their family work through some problems. I made house calls to see the entire family. When I first worked with them, there were times when some of their sentences simply did not make sense. They functioned as human beings but at a very animal-like existence. Week after week I listened and intervened, taught and prayed. After months they were really functioning significantly better, but I knew mental processes were still not normal. One day the father told me that I was no longer needed. They were extremely appreciative, but hesitant to explain more. Finally, they told me that some people had come to visit them. They came in and talked with them briefly, whereupon, they started denouncing the devils in the house, and rebuked the presence of these devils with loud voices. I was slightly startled by the description. I looked at the father and it was true. He was clean-shaven, spoke in decent language, was open and receptive. I saw with my own eyes that a major change had taken place, above and beyond what I thought I had accomplished. They explained in detail what the visiting church people had believed and had taught. I was invited back later, and have seen the people while shopping. I am convinced that an exorcism took place. They put away all the hate, fear, and hurts from injustice they were harboring. The father changed jobs and was trained in this type of work. The facts of the case establish a validity for exorcism. There is an exorcism which we can all do by ourselves when we resolve conflicts, but there is an exorcism available to us from above. Let us not fail to avail ourselves of both.

SEEK SPIRITUAL HEALING — (4) BY THE—LAYING—ON—OF—HANDS

In 9 of the 25 recorded individual healings by Jesus, there is some body contact such as touch or laying-on-of-hands.

1. **Peter's mother in law (Matt 8:14-17) —Jesus touched her hand.**
2. **A Leper (Matthew 8:2-4) —Jesus touched him.**
3. **The woman with the issue of blood (Matthew 9:18-26) —The woman touched Jesus.**
4. **Jairus' daughter (Matthew 9:16-26) —Jesus took her by the hand.**
5. **Two blind men (Matthew 9:27-34) —Jesus touched their eyes.**
6. **Deaf and dumb person (Mark 7:31-8:9) —Jesus "put his finger into his eyes, and spat and touched his tongue".**
7. **The blind man of Bethsaida (Mark 8:13-26) —Jesus "spit on his eyes" and "laid his hands upon him".**
8. **The man born blind (John 9:1-41) —Jesus "spat on the ground, and made clay of the spittle, and anointed his eyes with the clay and said, Go wash in Siloam."**

9. The hunchback woman of 18 years (Luke 13:10-21) —Jesus "laid his hands upon her".

Sometimes Jesus touched the ailing body organ, and sometimes he touched some other part of the body than the head. He touched Peter's mother-in-law's hand, and the fever left. Since we cannot exactly compare ourselves with Jesus, it may be difficult to determine from him just how the "laying-on-of-hands" is best administered.

When does a person seek out the laying-on-of-hands, or ask for a rebuke? Or, when does a pastor, and elders, decide to administer the laying-on-of-hands? Jesus never touched persons who were emotionally ill. Jesus "rebuked" the devil, the cause of hysterical conversion reactions like blindness, deafness, dumbness, or whatever. It was apparently more of a verbal process. Since we live 2000 years away from those events, we can only tentatively see a connection between the verbal processes we use in psychology, and the verbal processes Jesus used to heal the emotionally disturbed. Healers today seem not to make a distinction between the emotional or biological causes for illness. Healers touch or lay-on-hands, and disregard the nature of the source. This fits with stress theories, which generally suggest that "overload" in a variety of physical, mental, and spiritual ways can produce either emotional or physical illness.

There is healing power, not in a touch, but in the love and care which flows through the touch. If healing came through a touch, you would find all sick persons in massage parlors. There is no healing in the laying-on-of-hands, but in the capacity of the "healer" to identify and empathize with the "healee". This explains why "faith healing" is practiced in all the religious cultures of the world. People practice and become powerfully able to be empathetic to persons, regardless of their religious orientation.

The fact that persons other than Christians practice laying-on-of-hands and "faith healing" may startle some, and even anger others. Mostly, it is an embarrassment to the Christian church. Christians, who claim to have so much love, ought to be the strongest "faith healers" in existence. All the reputable, scientific, and religiously credible books or articles I have, say that its the "love" and the "care" in the healer which are focused on the healee, that become the main ingredients in this kind of healing. Thus, Christians who fail to integrate healing into their ministry, bring some shame on themselves.

Olga Worrall allowed herself to be evaluated by Dr. Beverly Rubik, of San Francisco State University, and Dr. Elizabeth Rauscher, of the University of California's Richmond field station. Olga Worrall clasped sealed test tubes of bacteria while allowing her healing self to work. The bacteria in these test tubes fared better than the control test tubes of bacteria. Olga Worrall also put her hands on slides of bacteria doused with phenol, an antiseptic. The bacteria lasted 12 minutes with Olga's loving healing,instead of the usual 2 minutes without it. A third experiment reported in Science Digest, May, 1982, indicated that when Olga Worrall put her loving-healing to work on bacteria flooded with chloramphenicol and tetracycline, the bacteria survived longer.

Dr. Bernard Grad, McGill University biologist, set up an experiment for Hungarian emigre, Oskar Estebany, a healer. Mice were deprived of iodine and developed a goiter condition. Under Estebany's healing the goiters in the mice grew slower than the untouched, but electrically warmed mice. Also mice were given a surgical removal of a patch of skin. Estebany treated one group by touching their cage. Another group was treated by students. A third group was left untreated. Estebany's mice healed the fastest. "Love is the essence of healing" says Dean Kraft, a healer, who strives for "oneness" with the healee. (See Science Digest, May, 1982)

Healing happens when someone shows love and care. Franz Anton Mesmer (1734-1815), Austrian physician, hypothesized that an energy can pass from one person to another. It is not electrical. It is not yet measurable, though persons involved with "faith healing" and laying-on-of-hands, all agree that some energy with physical properties is transmitted. (Other good reading is, Biological Effects of Laying on of Hands, by Bernard Grad, Chapter 12, in Dimensions in Wholistic Healing, (Ed: Herbert Otto and James Knight)

You can understand "faith healing" and the "laying-on-of-hands" as an imparting of love to someone else. Early psychoanalytic theory describes the "ego" as having a "libido" , an arm which could reach out and "cathect" (connect) with reality outside the self. In emotionally disturbed persons the "libido" only "cathected" back on the self. It was functioning in this way like a short circuit. There was no flow outward. Freud, inadvertently made it clear what conversion was by this description. Conversion was a complete turning around of the "libido" so that it could "cathect" with people and things outside of the self. When that "libido" is disconnected from self, it can impart "agape", pure love, which expects nothing in return. In healing there has to be a great amount of "agape" flowing outward toward the healee from the healer. If the healor is narcissistic, healing cannot take place through this means.

I have put our younger son to sleep this way. As I lay beside him, I would think of something flowing from my body, mind, and spirit, into his being. I would think of love, God's love, my human love, our family love, all of it filling every miniature sized component of him. I did not do it for healing. I did it for love, and to give some love which I had failed to give, perhaps, in the day.

When you approach your spouse, to embrace, you can do it with enthusiasm, or with indifference. Your spouse will know. The body generates messages, which come from the inner depths. Narcissistic persons never give much love away. Mostly, they drink in what others have to offer. Some do not know what giving love is all about. Do not seek out such a person for healing.

Reach out for the superior kind of care people can and are willing to give. Not even the best therapists are able to radiate peek caring all the time. Thus, finding multiple persons and groups where this deep caring is going on, is part of the healing treatament you may need. Go look for it.

Touch gets at the will. Perhaps not completely, but more thoroughly than anything else. If you have lost your will to live, fight, or struggle against odds, you need touching.   Dr. Dolores Krieger, professor at the New York University School of Nursing, urges "touching" for people in the medical profession.   Above and beyond diagnostic and medical treatment, sick people need some deeper personal contact.   They are afraid, lonely, and sometimes in despair.   The touch is simply one part of her view of good nursing care.   Can the Christian church do less for its hurting, lonely, and sometimes disillusioned flock?

Ask people who come to visit you to touch you, or hold you.   This is appropriate when the visitor is a relative, or of the same sex. It is also appropriate when a group touches, lays on hands, and prays.   A 5 to 15 second laying-on-of-hands is hardly appropriate. It might be adequate if we were more spiritual, like Jesus.   We may have to make up in numbers and time, what Jesus had in power.   We may have to touch with more people and pray longer.

There is a lot of visualization going on in healers when the healee is being sent healing power. The healer is visualizing the energy flowing and doing what it is supposed to do.   There is something like a psychological thruster behind every charged and sent prayer.   Rather than the person thinking up picturesque and pleasing words, the healer is concentrating, focussing, generating, radiating, zapping, transmitting whatever Franz Anton Mesmer believed would be communicated from one person to another. If you do not have persons who know how to pray like this for you, call your friends and get a book on this subject to study together.   Then include this in your life-style changes for your own healing.

HEALING RETREATS

Overly stressed persons have found refuge and healing in the monastic system for centuries. Obviously, it was not a place for persons ill with contagious diseases. Rather, it was a place where hurting people found healing. They found healing from irrational pressures of the society in which they lived. For some, the stressful winds of social interaction had blown them into deviant life-styles which nearly destroyed them. They found forgiveness in the monastic system. They found acceptance. They found love. They found healing. Always a few remained on for years to pay back the debt for their rescue.

The life style of the monastic orders is highly conducive to healing. I have visited three monasteries, and recall them as making a positive contribution to the lives of those living there. I have visited the monastery near Dubuque, Iowa., the monastery northwest of Jerusalem, and one on the island of Cyprus. All of these were islands of mercy in a merciless world. The people of the monasteries lived very structured lives, ordered by the person in charge, but agreed upon by the persons choosing to live there. They all worked in fields or vineyards. The exercise was good for them. They ate food which was close to nature. There were almost no refined foods, just what could be grown by themselves and stored in a way that preserved all the natural nutrients. Whole grains were used instead of refined grains. Fresh fruit was a part of the diet. Meats were used sparsely. It was macrobiotic. Their devotional life dominated a large part of the day. You heard reading, singing, praying, chanting, meditating, muttering, mumbling Biblical phrases. Each person lived half way in between expectations and acceptance.

We can learn a lesson by reflecting on the common ingredients in the monastic system, and in the current stress management movement. **We need more group processes to facilitate a healthy life-style and mediate Divine healing love.** This could be a Health and Healing Ministry in the church. This could be the focus for some time set aside in a Retreat Center. Sick persons need a place where they can go to find the kind of healing which incorporates all the components of the healing process. 354

PUTTING IT ALL TOGETHER

By now you know that wholistic thinking simply must replace singular cause-effect thinking. We fall into cause-effect thinking when we see Vitamin C as the solution for scurvy. We fall into cause-effect thinking when we get a prescription to combat an illness. Logic wants us to trace sequences in singular cause-effect terms. Wholistic thinking transcends cause-effect thinking. Existentialism, in philosophy, opened up the world of multiple interrelations producing complex and varied results. "Systems" theories in psychology attempted to account for multiple causal factors. "Relativity" concepts practically made simple sylogistic thinking obsolete, and opened up the complex world of relational thinking. The computer made it possible for people to abandon some singular cause-effect diagnoses, and open up flexible and fluid wholistic understanding.

Now it is easier for persons to think about healing from a wider number of sources. Any person who simply sits and waits for a pill to work, is cheating himself or herself out of some health and healing.

DISCUSSION

1. Why do we need "faith healing" in this day of excellent medicine?

2. If people do not ask for prayer, is that a sign of their weak faith? or the elder's weak faith? or the pastor's weak faith?

3. What do you think of "faith healers" as you see them on television?

4. Jesus told many people that it was their "faith" that made them whole. Is faith a requirement for every healing? (See John 5:1-47 and Mark 3:1-16)

5. Why has "faith healing" been ignored, or even avoided by the church?

6. While many healers are Christians, how do you explain where non-Christian healers get their power?

7. Exorcism is the rebuking of devils. In Ephesians 4:26 demon possession can come from the suppression of "anger". Is a pastoral counselor an exorcist if he gets people to resolve their "anger".

8. Jesus could touch and instantly heal. How much do we need to touch, or how long do we need to lay-on-hands to create the same results as Jesus created?

9. The disciples could not heal the demon-filled boy described in Mark 9:14-29. Jesus told them it was due to their lack of faith, and more prayer and fasting was needed. Must fasting accompany prayer to be more effective?

10. Jesus said to the paralytic lowered through Peter's rooftop, "Thy sins be forgiven thee." The paralytic was healed. Does the forgiveness of sin contribute to healing? Is it necessary for healing to occur?

SCORING

AND

INTREPRETATION

SCORING

1. Changes in Life Style .... __________

2. Symptoms of Stress Related Illnesses .... __________

3a. Anxiety .... __________

3b. Depression .... __________

4. Stress in Marriage .... __________

5. Suppression of Negative Feelings .... __________

6. Job Stress – Burnout .... __________

7. Financial Stress .... __________

8. Stress from Excess Alcohol Consumption .. __________

9. Stress from Smoking .... __________

10. Overweight Stress Factor .... __________

11. Nutrition Deficiency .... __________

12. Excess Sugar Consumption .... __________

13. Allergic Reactions .... __________

14. Stress from Caring .... __________

LIFE STRESS TOTAL ______________

____

15. Socialization Skills .... __________

16. Health Giving Values .... __________

17. Physical Fitness .... __________

18. Relaxation (Biofeedback) Skills .... __________

19. Self Worth – Assertiveness .... __________

COPING STRENGTH TOTAL ______________

INTERPRETATION

LIFE STRESS TOTAL

IF YOUR SCORE WAS BETWEEN

000 – 400 Your stress level score is IDEAL. You appear to have a very good life style which helps you fight illness. Such a score is quite exceptional. You seem to live a life of moderation in most, if not all, things. Congratulations!

401 – 650 Your stress level score is ADMIRABLE. The score indicates that you have a below average stress load. Apparently, you resolve problems quickly enough to prevent stress overload. Your health should be better than average due to the low level of stress factors in your life.

651 – 700 Your stress level is in the MID RANGE as measured by this inventory. Consider yourself fortunate that your behavior is proper enough to keep stress and illness down to a minimum. You could work on lowering some stress factors, and, thereby, increase wellness.

701 – 1000 Your stress level is SERIOUS. Mental and physical illness occurs in persons who experience overload of stress. You may be safe from stress overload, if your Coping Strength scores are high (above 500, see next page), but if Coping Strength scores fall below 400 your overload factor is getting higher.

Above 1000 Your stress level is CRITICAL. You need to identify the specific areas of your life which have high stress scores. Make some changes to relieve the stress. If the stress factors cannot be changed, switch to using the coping skills of increased socialization, setting your mind on the higher values of life, exercise, relaxation with meditation, and assertiveness.

INTERPRETATION
COPING STRENGTH TOTAL

IF YOUR SCORE WAS BETWEEN

000 – 400 — Your coping strength score is POOR. You do not appear to have an adequate mind-over-matter attitude or skills to beat stress. Such a deficiency in the area of socialization, higher values, exercise, relaxation, meditation, and assertiveness, undermines one's mental and physical health.

401 – 475 — Your coping strength score is BELOW AVERAGE. Resolution of interpersonal problems, good nutrition, good sleep and the elimination of stress factors like cholesterol, weight, alcohol, smoking, etc., are all good for us. Yet, coping strength also comes from socialization, higher values, exercise, relaxation, assertiveness, etc.

476 – 500 — Your coping strength score is ABOVE AVERAGE. You are, apparently, involved with enough friends and enough exercise, along with knowing how to relax, to keep you healthier than you might be without these skills. You probably also hold fast to values like love, service, honesty, fairness, etc. Even your capacity to speak up is helping you maintain your mental, physical, and spiritual health.

Above 500 — Your coping strength score is EXCELLENT to SUPERIOR. It appears that you have been programming yourself to behaviors which are going to help you maintain your health. There may be times when "stress" runs high in your life, but the behaviors you have adopted will sustain your health to a greater measure than if your score would be lower. Congratulations for living by a mind-over-matter style of life.

A

PROGRAM

for

STRESS REDUCTION

A PROGRAM FOR STRESS REDUCTION

The counselor, pastor or wellness professional who is administering the program of stress reduction will contract with the client to undertake certain stress reduction measures. This can be the counselor's and the client's worksheet.

This worksheet is especially appropriate for dealing with a group of persons all of whom undertake to reduce the stress in their lives and thereby reduce the risk-of-illness level. Persons may chose an area in which they plan to undertake stress reduction measures. Or they may do a variety of things in combination.

YOUR GOAL IS TO GAIN POINTS IN THE FIGHT AGAINST STRESS. LOOK AT YOUR HIGHEST AREAS OF STRESS AND YOUR LOWEST AREAS OF COPING STRENGTH. DECIDE WHAT YOU WILL DO FROM THE FOLLOWING ITEMS. CHART THE POINTS YOU GET FROM EACH OF THE LISTED ITEMS.

DISCUSS THE FOLLOWING WITH YOUR COUNSELOR OR WITH YOUR GROUP.

1. MULTIPLE STRESS FACTORS

These are factors which are almost inevitable in the course of living. They are factors over which we have very little control. No points are offered for you to eliminate this stress.

2. STRESS RELATED ILLNESS

Persons living under stress develop pains. Medical assessment is urged, but after that develop your coping skills; socialization, adopting higher values, physical exercise, relaxation and assertiveness.

3. ANXIETY AND DEPRESSION (Inner conflict stress)

Talk to a friend about your feelings.
You get 25 points for each time you do.............
Talk to professional counselor.
You get 100 points a week if you do.................
Exercise 15 minutes a day, bringing up
heartbeat rate to your aerobic level.
You get 25 points a day if you do.....................
Relax with Jacobson Relaxation exercises.
You get 25 points a day if you do.....................

4. MARITAL STRESS

Use one of the marriage stress-reduction or
problem-solving techniques in this book.
You get 100 points a week for doing this
with your spouse...

5. SUPPRESSED ANGER AND GUILT

Decide to speak up about something that
bothered you. Do so kindly and with an
approach that is non-attacking.
You get 100 points for doing this.....................

6. JOB STRESS — Burnout

Share your feelings with your boss.
You get 100 points for this..............................
Do something kind and helpful to a fellow worker.
You get 25 points for each thing done..............
Do something after work that is fun.
You get 25 points for each things done.............

7. FINANCIAL STRESS

Work out a budget.
You get 100 points for doing this.....................
You get 100 points each week for sticking
with the budget..................................
Keep a record of every item purchased.
You get 100 points a week for this.....

RECORD FOR 12 WEEKS

1	2	3	4	5	6	7	8	9	10	11	12

8. STRESS FROM EXCESS ALCOHOL CONSUMPTION

Drink milk, diet pop or juice instead of alcohol.
    You get 25 points for each time you do............
Eat fruit or vegetables instead of alcohol.
    You get 25 points for each time you do............

9. STRESS FROM EXCESS SMOING

Stop smoking.
    You get 100 points for stopping smoking...........
    You get 100 points each week for stopping........
Cut back to 10 cigarettes a day.
    You get 10 points a day for cutting back..........

10. OVERWEIGHT

Eliminate all sugar-containing foods.
    You get 50 points per week for this.................
Eliminate all flour containing foods.
    You get 50 points per week for this................
Eliminate fatty foods.
    You get 50 points per week for this.................

11. STRESS FROM POOR NUTRITION

Eat 2 servings from the Milk group.
    (3 servings for children, 4 for teens)
Eat 2 servings from the Meat and Nut group.
Eat 4 servings from the Fruit and Vegetable group.
Eat 4 servings from the Whole Grain cereal group.
    You get 25 points each day you do this.............

12. STRESS FROM EXCESS SUGAR CONSUMPTION

Cut back consumption of sugar-laden foods
so that your consumption is less than 100 tea-
spoons a week.
    You get 50 points per week if you
    previously ate more sugar than that
    and you are cutting back...

RECORD FOR 12 WEEKS

1	2	3	4	5	6	7	8	9	10	11	12

Refrain from adding sugar to the things you eat
so that your consumption of sugar added to cereal,
coffee, tea, etc., is cut down to zero.
> You get 50 points per week if you
> previously added sugar and are now
> not doing so...
If you cooked or baked, using sugar, find recipes
which reduce sugar by half the amount, or find
recipes which are higher in the use of whole grains.
> You get 50 points per week if you cooked
> or baked with such recipes, or cut back on
> the sugar content by more than 50%...................
(See the information in Chapter 12 on sugar in food)

13. STRESS FROM ALLERGIC REACTIONS

Check for an increased pulse rate of from 10-20
beats after eating foods or sniffing fumes you suspect
for allergic reactions. (Go without that food 4 days
before you try.)
> You get 25 points for each food you try and
> also 25 points for each re-try ("challenge")
> of that food...

14. THE STRESS OF CARING

Find someone to do your work and go away
for at least 4 hours.
> You get 50 points for doing that ....
Find a professional counselor and unburden yourself.
> You get 100 points each time you do.....................

15. SOCIALIZATION SKILLS

Visit a neighbor, relative, friend,——just drop in.
> You get 50 points for doing that........................
Invite a person to a movie, play, musical or other.
> You get 50 points for doing that........................
Take someone fishing, hunting, cycling, boating, etc.
> You get 50 points for doing that........................
Invite a friend out for coffee, dinner, etc.
> You get 50 points for doing that........................

1	2	3	4	5	6	7	8	9	10	11	12

16. STRESS REDUCTION THROUGH VALUE ELEVATION

Go to church, synagogue or temple.
    You get 50 points each time you do that...................
Meditate on such values as love, service, honesty,
self-control, peace, humbleness, friendliness, justice, etc.
    You get 10 points each time you read the list of 31
    higher values found in Chapter 16.............................

17. STRESS REDUCTION THROUGH PHYSICAL FITNESS

Exercise 3 times a week for 15 minutes at a heart beat
rate that is "aerobic" for you. (See Chapter 17 for
rules.) You get 25 points for each time you do this...........

18. RELAXATION—MEDITATION COPING STRENGTH
Do either the Jacobson relaxation exercises, the
Autogenic training or the Deep Breathing
    exercises found in Chapter 18.
    You get 25 points for each completed session...........
Do some type of meditation for 15–20 minutes.
    You get 25 points for each completed session...........

19. SELF WORTH AND ASSERTIVENESS COPING SKILLS

Decide not to think of yourself so much.
Do a deed of kindness for someone else.
    You get 25 points for each one...........................
Learn one new name, or refresh your memory on a name.
    You get 25 points for each one...........................
Speak up when you feel you have been treated badly.
    You get 50 points for each time you do...................
Volunteer your services.
    You get 50 points for each time you do...................
Set a new goal and go after it.
    You get 100 points if you reach that goal ....

YOU ARE NOT ELIGIBLE TO COLLECT POINTS IN THOSE
AREAS WHERE YOU ARE WITHIN NORMAL LIMITS.

1	2	3	4	5	6	7	8	9	10	11	12

TOTAL POINTS FOR EACH WEEK OF STRESS REDUCTION

1	2	3	4	5	6	7	8	9	10	11	12

Work at behavior changes which will give you at least 100 points per week. Persons with multiple stress areas will need to accumulate more points per week, or use a longer time than 12 weeks.

"Heal Me, O Lord"

Jeremiah 17:14

by Marilyn Ludolf, Winston-Salem, North Carolina

I woke up with the same tormenting headache I'd gone to bed with, and struggled to the bathroom. I grasped the sink with both hands and reluctantly raised my pounding head to stare in the mirror. The face reflected in the glass was a fiery red mask of tiny bumps and large acnelike sores. Hundreds of them. The horrible rash covered my face like the Egyptian plague of boils in the Bible. The unending headache and rash comprised the mysterious condition I'd lived with for 12 long, unbearable years. A plague that had appeared out of nowhere when I was 32 years old. It had grown steadily in intensity, until here I was a middle-aged woman with two teenaged sons and a husband who served on a church staff . . . and I could hardly bear to raise my head and look in the mirror.

Tears blurred my eyes as I tried to remember the smooth, milk-white complexion I used to have. My fingers twitched, longing to claw at the fiercely itching skin on my face.

I'd tried everything I knew—diets, oatmeal soap, baby oil, vitamins and enough creams and ointments to fill a small drugstore. And the long line of doctors I'd seen had passed by like a dwindling parade of hope. The rash had only grown worse, and my face swelled, itched and turned deep tomato-red at the slightest stimulus.

Suddenly the pain behind my eyes tightened as if someone were packing cotton into my sinuses. I reached for a bottle of pain medication and quickly swallowed a couple of pills. I took the maximum of eight pills a day. But they only forestalled the worst of it—when the pain crept down my neck, making clear thinking difficult.

I felt swallowed up by despair, by the long years of this strange affliction. I'd prayed so many times for it to go away. "Oh, God, why don't You help me?"

I dabbed at my eyes and, leaving my secret misery in the bathroom, dressed for work. My head was so sore from the headache, I could hardly pull a comb through my hair. I thought about crawling back into bed. But of course, I couldn't. Actually I liked my work as a third grade schoolteacher. And I had to keep going. I pushed myself into church and community activities.

As I entered school that morning, a little girl peered up at me, her eyes wide with surprise and dismay.

"How come your face looks like *that?*" she asked. (Oh, the blunt honesty of children!)

I raised my hands over my cheeks and tried to explain. But I fell silent. I had no answer.

Not long after that someone told me about a dermatologist at the hospital. I'd seen half a dozen specialists already, but I made an appointment, ready to grasp at anything.

I sat slumped on his examining table after a long series of allergy tests.

Even the children in my classroom stared at my face— and wondered.

"Well, maybe we have an answer," the doctor said. "It appears you are allergic to yourself."

I gazed at him incredulously. "Allergic to myself? You must be kidding!"

"I know it sounds strange, but these allergy tests show you are allergic to your own bacteria."

Hope blew away like the last autumn leaf. Allergic to my own self. How could I escape that?

"We'll make a special serum, using your own saliva," said the doctor, "and teach you how to inject yourself."

And so began the next three years of giving myself shots. The headaches were not quite as severe, nor the rash quite as red—partial relief. The doctor did everything he could, prescribing medicines, creams and consultations. Still, the ever-present plague was agonizing, embarrassing.

So I followed my old, exhausted pattern and found yet another doctor. This time an outstanding allergist. More tests. More money. He decided I was allergic to a long list of foods, and put me on a diet. For another year I existed on nothing but peas, potatoes, carrots, lettuce and meat. My weight plummeted to 102 pounds.

"You're wasting away, Mama," said my son one morning, as I dropped my lunch of canned peas in my purse. He was right. Something dreadful was happening to me. And despite it all, the daily headaches persisted and the humiliating rash and acne were splashed across my face big and red as ever. I could no longer even open a box of detergent to do the laundry without my eyes swelling and my skin itching till I was in torment.

This is no way to live, I thought dismally as I draped a scarf across my head and left for work. And worse, there seemed to be no answer at all.

Then one Sunday as I struggled to teach my Sunday school class with a riveting headache, I heard myself saying, "God is the answer." I paused, the echo of my words thundering in my head. As the class continued, the words burrowed inside me like a small, uncomfortable splinter.

After church, I lay on the sofa with a warm cloth across my forehead. I gazed out the broad windows at the tall, silent woods across the road, as the words I'd spoken that morning nudged at me like an unseen elbow. *I am a Christian*, I thought. *I tell other people that God is the answer, that they can find wholeness through Him. Yet I've been a prisoner of this condition for nearly sixteen years.*

Suddenly the familiar old story of the woman in Mark 5:25-34 focused in my mind. The woman who touched the hem of Jesus' robe and was healed. I was so much like her. I, too, had suffered a condition for many years, gone to many physicians, spent nearly all I had to spend and was not better, but worse. The difference was, the woman in Mark had finally gone to Jesus with faith—and was healed.

Did such healings still happen today, I wondered. If so, could healing really happen to me? There on the sofa, the idea of real healing from God spun in my head. It almost seemed too ancient to be real. If only I could be sure.

The weeks passed and winter melted away. The incredible idea of healing lingered in my mind like a held-over

BUSINESS OFFICE: Guideposts Associates, Inc., Carmel, N.Y. 10512. EDITORIAL OFFICE: 747 Third Avenue, New York, N.Y. 10017. 60¢ per copy; $4.95 a year. Add $1.00 per year for Canadian and foreign. Entered as 2nd class matter, October, 1953, at the post office at Carmel, N.Y. and additional entry offices, under the Act of March 3, 1879. Accepted for mailing at special rates of postage provided for in Section 538, Act of February 28, 1925, authorized April 16, 1948. Copyright ⁺ 1981 by Guideposts Associates, Inc., Carmel, N.Y. Printed in U.S.A. Volume 36, No. 5. Nonprofit. Guideposts (USPS 231-460) is published monthly. Postmaster: Send notice of undeliverable copies and change of address form 3579 to Guideposts, Carmel, N.Y. 10512. Guideposts invites but cannot be responsible for unsolicited manuscripts. To be returned, manuscripts must be accompanied by a self-addressed, stamped envelope.

Christmas present. I toyed with the ribbons, afraid to open it, afraid it might turn out empty . . . but strangely, unable to turn away from it.

Then one Sunday, as forsythia framed the world with spring, something happened. I lay in bed trying to find diversion from my headache by watching television. On the screen stood a beautiful young woman — Cheryl Prewitt, Miss America 1980.

"God healed me," she said. "I prepared myself to be healed, and God healed me."

My heart began to pound with a strange excitement. She was speaking to me! No, *God* was speaking to me! He *did* still heal people today.

"Come quick!" I called to my husband and boys. As they hurried to the bedroom, I pointed to the TV where the radiant young woman still spoke. Tears poured down my face. "If God can heal her, then He can heal me," I said.

Finally . . . finally after 16 desperate years of trying everything else, I was ready to turn to Jesus — as the woman in Mark had done. Again I relived that Biblical story in my mind. What was it Jesus had said to her after she had brushed her fingertips across His robe . . . "Your *faith* has made you whole." And what had Cheryl Prewitt said . . . "I prepared to be healed by strengthening my *faith*."

Faith. There was the key. There was what was missing before. My faith had grown flabby, like out of shape muscles. I knew intellectually that God is powerful and can heal. But somehow I had to get that knowledge from my mind down into my heart. I had to believe it as fervently as I believed the sun would rise tomorrow.

On May 1, I began to prepare myself for healing like an athlete training for the Olympics. I sat down in the kitchen rocker with a lap full of clean paper and my Bible. I flipped to the concordance in the back — to the headings of healing, health and faith. I picked out verses, then looked them up, writing each one down word for word on paper. It took a couple of days, but I finally compiled a list of 36 Scriptures — sort of a training manual for my faith.

The next day I tucked the papers in my purse. Driving to work, I pulled them out and laid them on the car seat. At the first stoplight I focused on a Scripture, Psalm 103:2-3. "Bless the Lord, O my soul, and forget not all His benefits . . . Who healeth all thy diseases," I whispered. I closed my eyes, saying it over and over, letting it sink down inside me. At a stop sign, my eyes fell on another. "Heal me, O Lord, and I shall be healed. . . ." (Jeremiah 17:14) I said over and over.

All day I kept it up. Before getting out of the car, walking along the school corridors, sitting on the playground at recess. Even in the classroom.

"Children, turn to page two hundred in your math books," I said. As the pages rustled, I looked down at my papers . . . "And He said unto her . . . go in peace, and be whole of thy plague." (Mark 5:34) I repeated it with a prayer for it to sink into my subconscious.

Not a spare moment was lost. By the end of the schoolday my Scripture papers were dog-eared from wear.

I continued my faith exercises throughout the evening. Between stirring a pot and chopping vegetables, I read the verses and meditated on them. At last I put my dog-eared papers on the bedside table and fell asleep, whispering the verse, "If thou canst believe, all things are possible. . . ." (Mark 9:23)

In the weeks that followed this became my constant routine. The papers became attached to me — as inseparable as my own shadow. And by some inexplicable process, the 36 Scriptures

5

were slowly sinking into the very core of my being with roots of belief. I was actually beginning to believe—really believe—that I could be healed. I could almost feel my faith stretching and rippling with new strength.

I circled July 12 on the kitchen calendar. "Lord, this is the day I'm asking for complete healing," I said.

Then I added another exercise. I began to visualize my complexion as pink and clear as a newborn baby's and my sinus passages free and well. I imprinted it on my mind day and night. This exercise became rather a strenuous one, because the mirror was such a contrast from my image. The red rash and acne, the throbbing headaches continued. But after a while the image, like the Scriptures, began to sink into the deep believing places of my life. The mirror is wrong, I told myself. Soon it will reflect my inner image.

Late that spring I hurried past a mirror at school. Suddenly I stopped, backed up and peered into it. I ran my fingers across my face. Was it my imagination or did the fiery red rash seem a bit faded? And my headache. Didn't it seem better today? "Oh, thank You, Lord!" I cried. "You're healing me."

Still I clung to my dog-eared papers, moving through the now well-memorized verses. As my faith deepened and gradually grew stronger, the headaches lessened, and almost imperceptibly my face improved.

July 12 dawned warm and shiny through the bedroom window. I tiptoed to the bathroom mirror, took a deep breath and peered in. The rash *still* lingered on the lower part of my face and a faint sinus headache tugged behind my eyes. *I will not give up*, I thought. *The day is not over.*

With a sudden burst of faith, I said, "Well, Lord, this is the day! I know it will happen."

As the sun set in an orange glow, I crept to a mirror. As I stared at my reflection, tears sparkled on my face. A face completely smooth and clear. It was the face in my image. The headache of the morning had drifted away as well. Like the woman in Mark, God and faith had made me whole.

For almost a year now I have not experienced another single headache, and my skin remains free and clear. I've gotten rid of all the old ointments, medicines, allergy shots and diets. The only thing I've kept are my precious dog-eared papers—those powerful Scripture-exercises that brought my faith to life. For there's one thing I've learned. While it's important to keep physical muscles strong and well-toned, it's even more important to keep "faith muscles" strong. For they are the ones that churn the spiritual energy, that move the mountains in our lives. Even a mountain like mine, that had towered over me for 16 years.

A few weeks ago at a meeting, a stranger tapped my shoulder. "Your complexion is so beautiful," she said.

"Oh, thank you," I gasped, my face bursting into an unusually big smile. A smile, I'm sure, no one there really understood ... except me and God.　◄

Here are the	Matthew 9:29,35	Mark 9:23	Hebrews 13:8	I Peter 2:24
36 Scriptures	Matthew 14:14	Mark 11:22-24	Malachi 4:2	Psalm 42:11
Marilyn used:	Matthew 15:30	Luke 6:19	Matthew 4:23,24	Psalm 6:2
	Matthew 17:20,21	John 14:13,14	Psalm 30:2	Psalm 41:4
Proverbs 4:20-22	Matthew 19:2	Acts 10:38	Psalm 91:9,10	Psalm 103:2,3
Romans 10:17	Mark 1:34	Galatians 3:13	Proverbs 3:7,8	Isaiah 53:4,5
Matthew 7:7,11	Mark 5:34	John 10:10	Exodus 15:26	Jeremiah 17:14
Matthew 8:7,13,17	Mark 10:52	III John 2	James 5:15	I John 4:4

GUIDEPOSTS, JULY 1981

HEALING SCRIPTURE

Collected by Marilyn Ludolf

"My son, be attentive to my words; incline your ear to my sayings. Let them not escape from your sight; keep them within your heart. For they are life to him who finds them, and healing to all his flesh."
(Proverbs 4:20–22)

"So faith comes from what is heard, and what is heard comes by the preaching of Christ." (Romans 10:17)

"Ask, and it will be given you, seek, and you will find; knock, and it will be opened to you." (Matthew 7:7)

"If you then, who are evil, know how to give good gifts to your children, how much more will your father who is in heaven give good things to those who ask him."
(Matthew 7:11)

"And he said to him, I will come and heal him. . .And to the Centurion Jesus said, Go, be it done for you as you have believed. And the servant was healed at that very moment. . . This was to fulfil what was spoken by the prophet Isaiah, He took our infirmities and bore our diseases." (Matthew 8:7,13,17)

"Then he touched their eyes saying, According to your faith be it done to you." (Matthew 9:29)

"And Jesus went about all the cities and villages, teaching in their synagogues and preaching the gospel of the kingdom, and healing every disease and every infirmity."
(Matthew 9:35)

"As he went ashore he saw a great throng; and he had compassion on them, and healed their sick." (Matt 14:14)

"And great crowds came to him, bringing with them the lame, the maimed, the blind, the dumb, and many others, and they put them at his feet, and he healed them." (Matthew 15:30)

"He said to them, Because of your little faith. For truly I say to you, if you have faith as a grain of mustard seed, you will say to this mountain, Move, hence to yonder place, and it will move, and nothing will be impossible to you."   (Matthew 17:20,21)

"And large crowds followed him, and he healed them there."   (Matthew 19:2)

"And he healed many who were sick with various diseases, and cast out many demons, and he would not permit the demons to speak, because they knew him."
(Mark 1:34)

"And he said to her, Daughter, your faith has made you well; go in peace, and be healed of your disease."
(Mark 5:34)

"And Jesus said to him, Go your way, your faith has made you well.   And immediately he received his sight and followed him on the way."   (Mark 10:52)

"And Jesus said to him, If you can! All things are possible to him who believes."   (Mark 9:23)

"And Jesus answered them, Have faith in God. Truly, I say to you, whoever says to this mountain, Be taken up and cast into the sea, and does not doubt in his heart, but believes that what he says will come to pass, it will be done for him.   Therefore, I tell you, Whatever you ask in prayer, believe that you will receive it, and you will."   (Mark 11:22-24)

"And all the crowd sought to touch him, for power came forth from him and healed them all." (Luke 6:19)

"Whatever you ask in my name, I will do it, that the Father may be glorified in the Son; if you ask anything in my name, I will do it."   (John 14:13-14)

"How God annointed Jesus of Nazareth with the Holy Spirit and with power, how he went about doing good and healing all that were oppressed by the devil, for God was with him."   (Acts 10:38)

"Christ redeemed us from the curse of the law, having become a curse for us, - for it is written, cursed be every one who hangs on a tree." (Galatians 3:13)

"The thief comes only to steal and kill and destroy; I came that they may have life, and have it abundantly."
(John 10:10)

"Beloved, I pray that all may go well with you and that you may be in health: I know that it is well with your soul."   (III John 2)

"Jesus Christ is the same yesterday, and today and forever.
(Hebrews 13:8)

"But for you who fear my name the sun of righteousnes shall rise, with healing in its wings. You shall go forth leaping like calves from the stall."   (Malachi 4:2)

"And he went about all Galilee, teaching in their synagogues and preaching the gospel of the kingdom and healing every disease and every infirmity among the people. So his fame spread throughout all Syria, and they brought him all the sick, those afflicted with various diseases and pains, demoniacs, epileptics, and paralytics, and he healed them."   (Matthew 4:23-24)

"O Lord my God, I cried to thee for help, and thou has healed me."   (Psalm 30:2)

"Because you have made the Lord your refuge, the Most High your habitation, no evil shall befall you, no scourge come near your tent."   (Psalm 91:9,10)

"Be not wise in your own eyes, fear the Lord, and turn away from evil. It will be healing to your flesh and refreshment to your bones."   (Proverbs 3:3,8)

"Saying, If you will diligently hearken to the voice of the Lord your God, and do that which is right in his eyes, and give heed to his commandments and keep all his statutes, I will put none of the diseases upon you which I put upon the Egyptians: for I am the Lord, your healer."
(Exodus 15:26)

"And the prayer of faith will save the sick man, and the Lord will raise him up, and if he has committed sins, he will be forgiven." (James 5:15)

"He himself bore our sins in his body on the tree, that we might die to sin and live to righteousness. By his wounds you have been healed." (I Peter 2:24)

"Why are you cast down, O my soul, and why are you disquieted within me? Hope in God; for I shall again praise him, my help and my God." (Psalm 42:11)

"Be gracious to me, O Lord, for I am languishing: O Lord, heal me, for my bones are troubled." (Psalm 6:2)

"As for me, I said, O Lord be gracious to me: heal me, for I have sinned against thee." (Psalm 41:4)

"Bless the Lord, O my soul, and forget not all his benefits, who forgives all your iniquity, who heals all your diseases."
(Psalm 103:2,3)

"Surely he has born our griefs and carried our sorrows; yet we esteemed him stricken, smitten by God, and afflicted. But he was wounded for our transgressions, he was bruised for our iniquities; upon him was the chastisement that made us whole, and with his stripes we are healed." (Isaiah 53:4,5)

"Heal me, O Lord, and I shall be healed; save me, and I shall be saved; for thou art my praise."
(Jeremiah 17:14)

"Little children, you are of God, and have overcome them; for he who is in you is greater than he who is in the world." (I John 4:4)

APPENDIX B

JACOBSON PROGRESSIVE RELAXATION

Dr. Edmond Jacobson developed exercises of tensing and relaxing muscles to produce the relaxation response. Jacobson used the discoveries of Luigi Galvani who first discovered the role of electrical energy in muscle movement. Jacobson became the first person to make electromyography (EMG) (measuring the electrical signals coming to the muscle) useful to psychologists. The series of tensing and relaxing steps that he used could lower the intensity of the electrical messages arriving at the muscle. The effect of his exercises could be measured in microvolts. As the person relaxed the microvoltage dropped. Almost 50 years have gone by since Jacobson developed his tensing and relaxing exercises. Now there is a wide variety of instrumentation, as well as numerous numerous variations of his original exercises. one form of his exercises which you may use. Find a tape recorder and read the following script into the recorder. Read slowly and pause enough to allow time for the activity suggested..

Jacobson Relaxation Script

Let's begin. I am sitting in a comfortable position or lying on the floor. My goal is not to go to sleep but to get into a deep state of relaxation. I am dressed in comfortable clothing and I have taken precautions not to be distracted. I am ready to begin.

Make a tight fist with both of your hands by clenching your fingers together. Hold it to the count of three. ——— Again, make a tight fist with both hands....tighter.... Hold it....one.... two....three....Relax....one....two....three.... Finally, make a tight fist with both hands.... Hold them tight......one...two...three...Relax...

Clench both fists and bring them up to your shoulders to tense your bicepts....Tense your bicepts tightly.... Hold them... Relax... Again, clench your fists tightly and bring them up to your shoulders... Make them tight... Hold it.... Relax........... Finally, clench both fists and bring them up to your shoulders and tense your bicepts...Hold them... Relax.........

This time, tighten the muscles in your forehead and scalp by wrinkling up your forehead and raising your eyebrows at the same time..... Hold it to a count of three.... Relax... to the count of three...... Again, tighten the muscles in your forehead and scalp by wrinkling up your forehead and raising your eyebrows at the same time....Hold it...Relax.... Finally, tighten the muscles in your forehead and scalp by wrinkling up your forehead and raising your eyebrows at the same time..... Hold it... Relax....
Pucker up your lips, wrinkle your nose and squint... Hold it to the count of three....Relax....
Again.......(Repeat above phrase)...
Finally...(Repeat above phrase)...

Push your head as far back as it will go....
Hold it to the count of three......Relax.........
Again...(Repeat above phrase)...
Finally...(Repeat above phrase)...

Bend your head forward touching your chin on your chest......Hold it to the count of three...
Again...(Repeat above phrase)...

Take a deep breath and fill your lungs to capacity.
Hold it to the count of three... Relax.....
Again...(Repeat above phrase)...
Finally...(Repeat above phrase)...

Tighten your stomach muscles and make the stomach rigid..... Hold it to the count of three....
Relax...
Again...(Repeat above phrase)...
Finally...(Repeat above phrase)...

Lift your shoulders as high as you can up toward
your ears....Hold it to the count of three...Relax...
Again...(Repeat above phrase)...
Finally...(Repeat above phrase)...

Tighten your thigh muscles by lifting your feet
a few inches off the floor....Hold it...Relax...
Again...(Repeat above phrase)...
Finally...(Repeat above phrase)....

Tighten your shin muscles by pointing your toes
toward your chin....Hold it...Relax...
Again...(Repeat above phrase)...
Finally...(Repeat above phrase)...

Tighten your calf muscles by pointing your toes
toward the wall...Hold it...Relax...
Again...(Repeat above phrase)...Hold it...
Finally...(Repeat above phrase)..

Arch your back by making your stomach stick
out... Hold it to the count of three... Relax...
Again...(Repeat above phrase)...
Finally...(Repeat above phrase)...

Take a deep breath and fill your lungs to capacity.
Hold it to the count of three... Relax...
Again...(Repeat above phrase)...
Finally...(Repeat above phrase)...

Enjoy the silence for a bit and then get up.

If you do the Jacobson Progressive Relaxation exercises but do not experience any effect, you may need
to practice a few times until you become comfortable
with them.   Not experiencing any results may also be
an indicator that this is not the correct treatment for
your problem.

HEALTH THROUGH STRESS REDUCTION

This book examines 20 stress factors. Each chapter begins with an inventory. The stress factors are analyzed from a scientific and research point of view. The contents of each chapter motivate persons to change life–style behavior for illness–prevention and healing. The book is ideal for counselors, counseling clients, persons interested in wellness in industry, social workers, general public.

HEALING THROUGH STRESS MANAGEMENT

This is book is a religious counterpart to Health through Stress Reduction. It deals with the same 20 stress factors, and the same tests precede each chapter. The Biblical material would make it ideal for a person teaching a class in a church on Health and Healing. It is very helpful to use in regaining the Healing Ministry of the Church. Both of these books are written to motivate persons to make life–style changes which promote health and healing.

LIFE STRESS AND COPING STRENGTH INVENTORY

This is the inventory found in the books above. There are 519 questions in 20 categories. It takes 45 minutes to take, and 15 minutes to score. Teachers can give this to students who attend a Health and Healing class. Profile score sheets are included with each self-administered test. Minimum order of 10 copies. Non–returnable when opened.

CHRISTIAN STRESS MANAGEMENT FOR HEALTH AND HEALING

These cassette tapes help to promote the theories and practices which are described in the books. There are 6 tapes.

1. The Christian Use of Relaxation, Meditation, and Visualization for Healing,   Side 2 Jacob's Ladder Sleep–Inducing Meditation
2. Christian Meditation for Wellness Using Church Hymns, Side 2 "I Am On My Way To Wellness"
3. Christian Meditation for Wellness Using Church Hymns, Side 2 "I am O.K., I Have Strong Faith, I Claim God's Healing."
4. Christian Meditation and Exercise; A Healing Treatment Combination, Side 2 Guided Exercise and Meditation (Walking at 105 paces per minute while reciting God's promises for healing.)
5. Christian Meditation and Exercise: A Healing Treatment Combination, Side 2 Guided Exercise and Meditation (Walking, Trampoline Jogging, Indoor Bicycling at 120 beats/paces per minute.)
6. Jacobson Relaxation Exercises, Side 2 Autogenic Training (Mind–over–matter stress–management techniques developed over 50 years ago.

COMPUTER PROGRAM for Life Stress and Coping Strength Inventory

Counseling clients can take this Inventory sitting at the computer, or use the test booklet, and feed the results into the computer for a printout of the person's results. The four–page printout requires a printer. Available in TRS–80 Color (one disk), TRS–80 Model 3 (Useable in Model 4), IBMpc or MS–DOS compatible operating systems.

DAILY DEVOTIONS FOR HEALTH AND HEALING

366 Daily Devotions using Biblical and scientific guidelines to facilitate Health and Healing. (Available after July 1986)

WELLNESS PUBLICATIONS
P.O. Box 3021
Holland, Michigan 49423

Please send me the following materials by Darrell Franken

_____ copies of HEALTH THROUGH STRESS
            REDUCTION - - - - - - - - - - @ $12.95 _________

_____ copies of HEALING THROUGH STRESS
            MANAGEMENT _ _ _ _ _ _ _ @ $14.95 _________

_____ copies of LIFE STRESS AND COPING
            STRENGTH INVENTORY–@ $2.00 each
            (Minimum order of 10 - - - - -@ $20.00 _________

_____ copies of CHRISTIAN STRESS MANAGE-
            MENT FOR HEALTH AND HEALING
            (6 cassettes described on reverse side.)
            - - - - - - - - - - - - - - - - - - @ $49.95 _________

_____ copies of COMPUTER PROGRAM for
            LIFE STRESS AND COPING STRENGTH
            INVENTORY - - - - - - - - -
            —— TRS – 80 Color - - - - - - @ $89.95 _________
            —— TRS – 80 Model 3 and 4 - @ $89.95 _________
            --MS–DOS compatible systems @$89.95 _________

_____ copies of DAILY DEVOTIONS FOR YOUR
            HEALTH AND HAPPINESS – @ $14.95 _________
            (Available after July, 1986)

TOTAL AMOUNT OF ITEMS - - - - - - - - - - -
SHIPPING AND POSTAGE ($1.25 per item)- -   _________
TAX on Michigan residents only, 6% - - - - - -   _________
                  TOTAL FOR ORDER   _________
(20% discount on direct mail orders for 10 or
more copies of one title. — 10% discount if
the first four items are ordered together.   _________
            TOTAL AMOUNT ENCLOSED   _________

NAME: ____
ADDRESS: ______________________________________
CITY: _____________________ State ______ Zip ______
Charge to my credit card: VISA _____, Mastercard ______
Card Number _____________________________ Expires ______
Signature: ______________________________________
(All sales, check, money order, credit card. Satisfaction is
  guaranteed or your money will be refunded upon receipt of
  resaleable items.)

HEALTH THROUGH STRESS REDUCTION

This book examines 20 stress factors. Each chapter begins with an inventory. The stress factors are analyzed from a scientific and research point of view. The contents of each chapter motivate persons to change life-style behavior for illness-prevention and healing. The book is ideal for counselors, counseling clients, persons interested in wellness in industry, social workers, general public.

HEALING THROUGH STRESS MANAGEMENT

This is book is a religious counterpart to Health through Stress Reduction. It deals with the same 20 stress factors, and the same tests precede each chapter. The Biblical material would make it ideal for a person teaching a class in a church on Health and Healing. It is very helpful to use in regaining the Healing Ministry of the Church. Both of these books are written to motivate persons to make life-style changes which promote health and healing.

LIFE STRESS AND COPING STRENGTH INVENTORY

This is the inventory found in the books above. There are 519 questions in 20 categories. It takes 45 minutes to take, and 15 minutes to score. Teachers can give this to students who attend a Health and Healing class. Profile score sheets are included with each self-administered test. Minimum order of 10 copies. Non-returnable when opened.

CHRISTIAN STRESS MANAGEMENT FOR HEALTH AND HEALING

These cassette tapes help to promote the theories and practices which are described in the books. There are 6 tapes.

1. The Christian Use of Relaxation, Meditation, and Visualization for Healing,   Side 2 Jacob's Ladder Sleep-Inducing Meditation
2. Christian Meditation for Wellness Using Church Hymns, Side 2 "I Am On My Way To Wellness"
3. Christian Meditation for Wellness Using Church Hymns, Side 2 "I am O.K., I Have Strong Faith, I Claim God's Healing."
4. Christian Meditation and Exercise; A Healing Treatment Combination,   Side 2 Guided Exercise and Meditation (Walking at 105 paces per minute while reciting God's promises for healing.)
5. Christian Meditation and Exercise: A Healing Treatment Combination,   Side 2 Guided Exercise and Meditation (Walking, Trampoline Jogging, Indoor Bicycling at 120 beats/paces per minute.)
6. Jacobson Relaxation Exercises,   Side 2 Autogenic Training (Mind-over-matter stress-management techniques developed over 50 years ago.

COMPUTER PROGRAM for Life Stress and Coping Strength Inventory

Counseling clients can take this Inventory sitting at the computer, or use the test booklet, and feed the results into the computer for a printout of the person's results. The four-page printout requires a printer. Available in TRS-80 Color (one disk), TRS-80 Model 3 (Useable in Model 4), IBMpc or MS-DOS compatible operating systems.

DAILY DEVOTIONS FOR HEALTH AND HEALING

366 Daily Devotions using Biblical and scientific guidelines to facilitate Health and Healing. (Available after July 1986)

WELLNESS PUBLICATIONS
P.O. Box 3021
Holland, Michigan 49423

Please send me the following materials by Darrell Franken

_____ copies of HEALTH THROUGH STRESS
       REDUCTION - - - - - - - - - - @ $12.95 _________

_____ copies of HEALING THROUGH STRESS
       MANAGEMENT _ _ _ _ _ _ _ @ $14.95 _________

_____ copies of LIFE STRESS AND COPING
       STRENGTH INVENTORY-@ $2.00 each
       (Minimum order of 10 - - - - -@ $20.00 _________

_____ copies of CHRISTIAN STRESS MANAGE-
       MENT FOR HEALTH AND HEALING
       (6 cassettes described on reverse side.)
       - - - - - - - - - - - - - - - - - - @ $49.95 _________

_____ copies of COMPUTER PROGRAM for
       LIFE STRESS AND COPING STRENGTH
       INVENTORY - - - - - - - - -—
       —— TRS - 80 Color - - - - - - @ $89.95 _________
       —— TRS - 80 Model 3 and 4 - @ $89.95 _________
       —MS-DOS compatible systems @$89.95 _________

_____ copies of DAILY DEVOTIONS FOR YOUR
       HEALTH AND HAPPINESS - @ $14.95 _________
       (Available after July, 1986)

TOTAL AMOUNT OF ITEMS - - - - - - - - - - - _________
SHIPPING AND POSTAGE ($1.25 per item)- - _________
TAX on Michigan residents only, 6% - - - - - - _________
          TOTAL FOR ORDER _________

(20% discount on direct mail orders for 10 or
more copies of one title. — 10% discount if
the first four items are ordered together. _________
        TOTAL AMOUNT ENCLOSED _________

NAME: _______________________________________
ADDRESS: ____________________________________
CITY: ___________________ State _____ Zip _______
Charge to my credit card: VISA _____, Mastercard _______
Card Number _______________________ Expires _______
Signature: ___________________________________
(All sales, check, money order, credit card. Satisfaction is
  guaranteed or your money will be refunded upon receipt of
  resaleable items.)